POSTCARD HISTORY SERIES

South Carolina Postcards

VOLUME IV

LEXINGTON COUNTY AND LAKE MURRAY

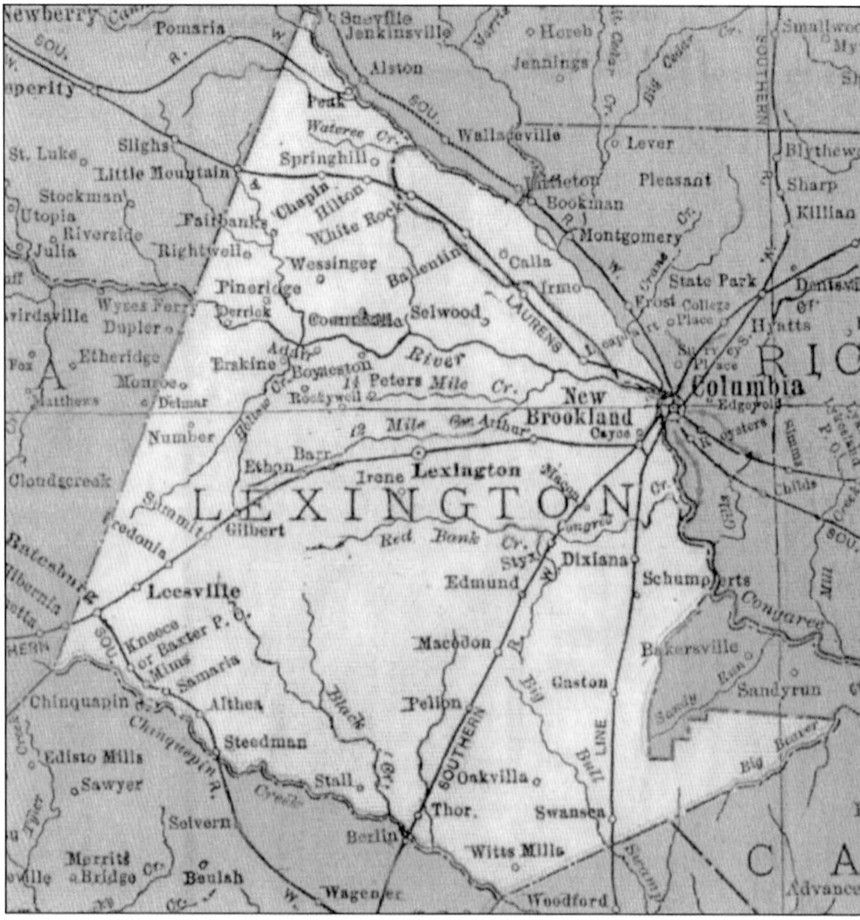

[MAP OF LEXINGTON COUNTY, 1910.] This 1910 map shows the Broad River as the turn-of-the-century northeastern border of Lexington County, the four major rail lines that crossed it, and the small towns that developed around the depots along these routes. The map also indicates the path of the Saluda River and the location of its adjacent communities that were flooded by the creation of the Dreher Shoals Dam and Lake Murray. Regional sections of a 1940 map are included at the beginning of each chapter in order to provide more focused views of the various areas covered by this book: east central, page 8; southeastern, page 24; western, page 52; and northern, page 80.

ON THE FRONT COVER: [TWO MEN IN A HORSE-DRAWN BUGGY IN FRONT OF THE SCOTT HENDRIX STORE, LEXINGTON.] Subjects in a horse-drawn buggy would have been a frequent and typical sight in the rural Lexington County of the early 1900s. Distances were relatively short and familiar, and inexpensive automobiles had not yet generally begun to be attainable. Even the sheriff traveled on horseback.

ON THE BACK COVER: [PORTRAIT OF TEACHERS IN SUMMER SCHOOL, LEXINGTON COUNTY.] The schoolteachers portrayed here in summer session include Bertha Kleckley (second row, first chair), who graduated with a ninth-grade education from Lexington's Palmetto Collegiate Institute in 1904. The summer programs for these rural teachers were usually taught by college professors who, as in this 1904 session, would have offered upgrading in everything from algebra and geography to history, literature, rhetoric, and pedagogy.

POSTCARD HISTORY SERIES

South Carolina Postcards

VOLUME IV

LEXINGTON COUNTY AND LAKE MURRAY

Howard Woody and Thomas L. Johnson

ARCADIA
PUBLISHING

ISBN 978-0-7385-0609-8

Published by Arcadia Publishing
Charleston, South Carolina

Printed in the United States of America

Library of Congress Catalog Card Number: 98-87877

For all general information contact Arcadia Publishing at:
Telephone 843-853-2070
Fax 843-853-0044
E-mail sales@arcadiapublishing.com
For customer service and orders:
Toll-Free 1-888-313-2665

Visit us on the Internet at www.arcadiapublishing.com

In memory of my mother, Mildred Howard Alford—H.W.

For Carolyn and William Carson, and Suzy and Wilson Farrell—T.L.J.

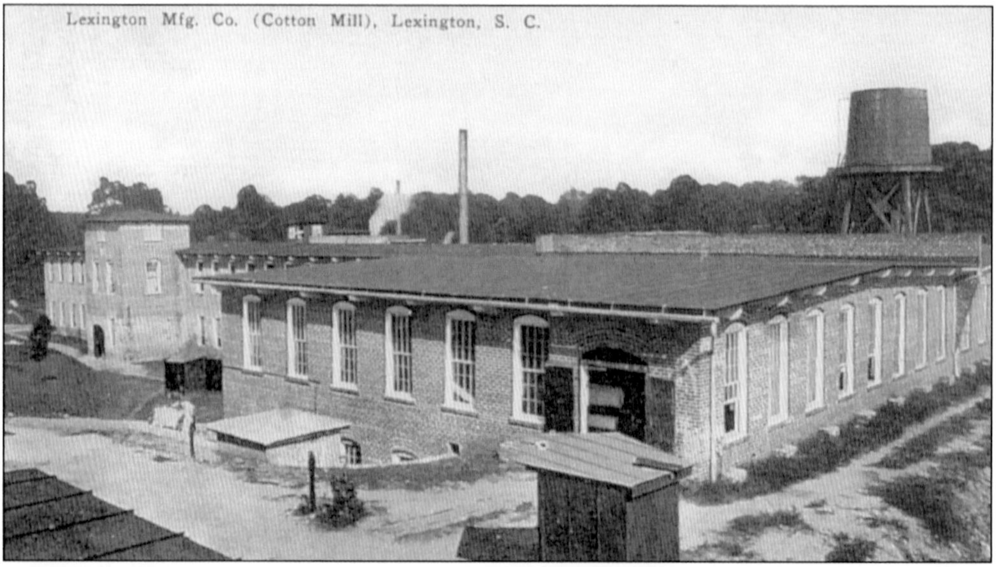

LEXINGTON MANUFACTURING COMPANY, LEXINGTON, SC, 1923. The Lexington Manufacturing Company was established in 1894 with a capital stock of $150,000. The cotton mill made 6-ounce bed ticking using 7,100 spindles and 204 looms, which consumed 3,120 bales of cotton annually. The salaries of the 150 workers ranged from $1 to $2 for adults and 50¢ to $1 per day for children (some as young as five years old). The standard work schedules for mill operatives were from 6:00 a.m. to 6:00 p.m. on weekdays and 6:00 a.m. to 4:00 p.m. on Saturdays. At that time these working conditions seemed more desirable than the uncertainty of tenant farming.

Contents

Introduction

For this fourth volume in Arcadia's special series on South Carolina postcards we step from Saluda, the county presented at the end of Volume III (*South Carolina Postcards: West Central Carolina—Aiken to Saluda,* 2000), eastward into the special world of its neighbor—Lexington.

This is the first book in the series to be devoted exclusively to one county. So many postcards turned up on Lexington, from so many sources and exhibiting such unusual thematic strength, geographical variety, and striking photographic imagery, that there was no other choice than to devote an entire volume to it.

The county's unique situation, furthermore, warrants separate treatment. For as W.T. Walker states in the Lexington *Dispatch-News* of September 18, 1929, it is an important link in connecting four major sections of South Carolina—the Piedmont, the Coastal Plain, the Pee Dee, and the Savannah River Valley. "Stretching from Newberry, in the foothills of the Piedmont, on the north, to Orangeburg, in the coastal plain on the south, and from the Congaree river on the east to Aiken and Saluda on the west," he writes, it partakes "in some measure of the characteristics of most of these sections."

Lexington, of course, has traditionally been an agricultural county. As J.E. Stockman summarized in the 1923 monograph *Lexington County: Economic and Social,* "From the early days of the county to the present time, her chief industry has been raising cotton" (cotton-related images will be found here from Batesburg to Swansea). "The population of the county," Stockman observed, "has always been mostly of the agricultural class . . . and made up largely of descendants of German-Swiss colonists, along with some English and Scotch." "The greater percent of Lexington's population," he concludes, "were born within her borders, and stay pretty close to the farm on which they were reared."

Not far from the farms, and critical to their existence, were the towns. The 12 county towns which had become incorporated by 1920 owed their existence, growth, or flourishing condition during the two generations from 1870 to 1930 to the phenomenon of the railroad, whose significance to the county's economy and way of life cannot be overestimated. Most of the postcards in this book focus upon the architecture and life of these towns, simply because they constituted the centers of population, however small, and thus provided numbers of places and persons to be photographed.

The town of Lexington, of course, with its courthouse, architecture, and activity as the county's seat of government, was a key "postcard town." The west central area had its Ridge towns of Batesburg, Leesville, Summit, and Gilbert; the northern sector, the towns of Irmo, Chapin, and Peak (which in 1920 became part of Newberry County); the southern region, Gaston, Pelion, and Swansea; and the east central corridor, New Brookland (now West Columbia) and Cayce. The value of so many of the views of these towns is that they provide a record, in some cases extremely rare, of the way some of the early landmark buildings and sections looked before they were destroyed by fire, purposely demolished to make room for new structures, or naturally changed with the passage of time.

For the most part, the images here, as in the previous three books, would probably have been made chiefly by itinerant photographers. Many others were produced by amateurs who took the pictures and then processed and marketed them as best they could.

A local case in point is that of Lexington photographer William P. Steele, 11 of whose pictures are reproduced here. Evidence has turned up among the papers of the Harmon Drug Company indicating that a series of 12 views taken by him was published in 1919 by the E.C. Kropp Company of Milwaukee. Among other area photographers whose work has shown up on Lexington County–related cards are Walter L. Blanchard, whose Columbia studio apparently received the commission to take pictures at the National Guard encampment at Styx, west of Cayce, in 1916; and Grover C. Goodwin, 11 of whose images document the picture-taking career of this Gaston farmer. The range of subject matter on these cards is significant, revealing some unknown or long-forgotten dimensions of the county's history and of it places, projects, and people. We see, for instance, pictures of downtown Lexington the way it looked prior to the calamitous fire of 1916, and there are many other pictures throughout that show structures—municipal, commercial, residential, and church—which no longer exist.

Several groups of pictures are especially valuable for their revelation of the details of certain projects and developments. Five views at the beginning of chapter four illustrate the massive operations that went into the landmark construction of the Saluda River dam and the creation of Lake Murray between 1927 and 1930. Another five are witness to the reality of the legendary Camp Moore at Styx, which for several months brought a concentrated army presence to the county as the site of South Carolina's National Guard encampment—a staging and drilling area for the State's troops being readied for possible duty in Texas at the time of the border dispute with Mexico and the attacks against United States citizens by the troops of Pancho Villa.

Perhaps the rarest single unit of pictures that Lexington yielded, collected from various public and private sources, is that depicting the old one- and two-teacher rural schoolhouses and their students. Here we have a photographic record of many of the old county school buildings, which began disappearing from the scene with the push towards school consolidation from the 1920s to the 1950s. Today only a few of these structures survive.

Of course, among the highlights of the book are the many pictures of Lexington County folk of all ages. There are images of schoolchildren and their teachers, farmers, other workers of all types, mourners, a congregation gathered for a pond baptism, a milliner with colleagues in her shop, an integrated team of auto garage workers, and onlookers at the scene after the explosion of a boiler.

The object of the previous books in this series has been the two-fold one of edification and enjoyment, and we hope that these experiences may be found in this one too.

Acknowledgments

Many persons and institutions have contributed to the preparation of this book. We wish to express our gratitude, as always, to Allen H. Stokes, Henry Fulmer, Beth Bilderback, Robin Copp, and Thelma Hayes of the South Caroliniana Library, University of South Carolina.

Essential contributions were further made by Davie Beard, Paul Jeter, and Sylvia Whitney (S.C. Postcard Collectors Club); and by the following individuals who, by offering repeated assistance from their respective sections, became critical to the successful completion of the project: (Lexington area) Horace Harmon (Lexington County Museum), Mark Mancuso (Lexington County Library), Steven D. Tuttle (S.C. Department of Archives and History), and Blondelle Harmon; (Gaston-Swansea-Pelion area) Davie E. Craft, Melva Hoover, Annette S. Lucas, and Terry Pound; (Batesburg-Leesville-Gilbert area) Carolyn and William Carson, Joyce Ricard, Louise Riley, Harva Ray Sease, and Nancy Taylor; (Lake Murray-Irmo-Chapin area) Ed Fetner, Judy Galloway (Dunbar Funeral Home), Richard Lee (S.C.E. & G.), Robert Lorick, Randal Shealy, Stanley Shealy, and Mrs. Furman Younginer; (Styx-Cayce-West Columbia area) Lauriston Blythe, Robert L. Busbee, Cayce Museum, Ruth Hoover, W. Harold Jones, Anne R. Rikard (Lexington School District #2), and Richard Sawyer.

For their generous loan of postcards or provision of information we also wish to thank these persons and institutions: Carole Allen, Jennette Bergeran (Lutheran Theological Southern Seminary), William Black, Pat Blackwell, Brookland United Methodist Church, Jimmy Bundrick, Douglas Comalander, Carolyn Crick, Dutch Fork High School, Mary J. Dyches, the Reverend Andrew Eargle, Louise Farmer, First Baptist Church of West Columbia, Constance Caractor Flemming, Beth Giles, Clara Haigler, L.C. "Sonny" Hall, Princetta Harris, David Herron, Jane S. Holman, Dick Holstein, Gwen Huckeriede, Frank Kelley (Lexington Baptist Church), Ralph Kennedy, Linda Matthews, Trisha Mauldin, Loretta Price, Nancy Reamer, the Reverend Fletcher Rice, Benjie Rikard, Jack Roof, Austin Sheheen Jr., the Reverend Lonnie Shull, Rosalie Shull, Melanie Stamper, Virginia Waites, and Bill West.

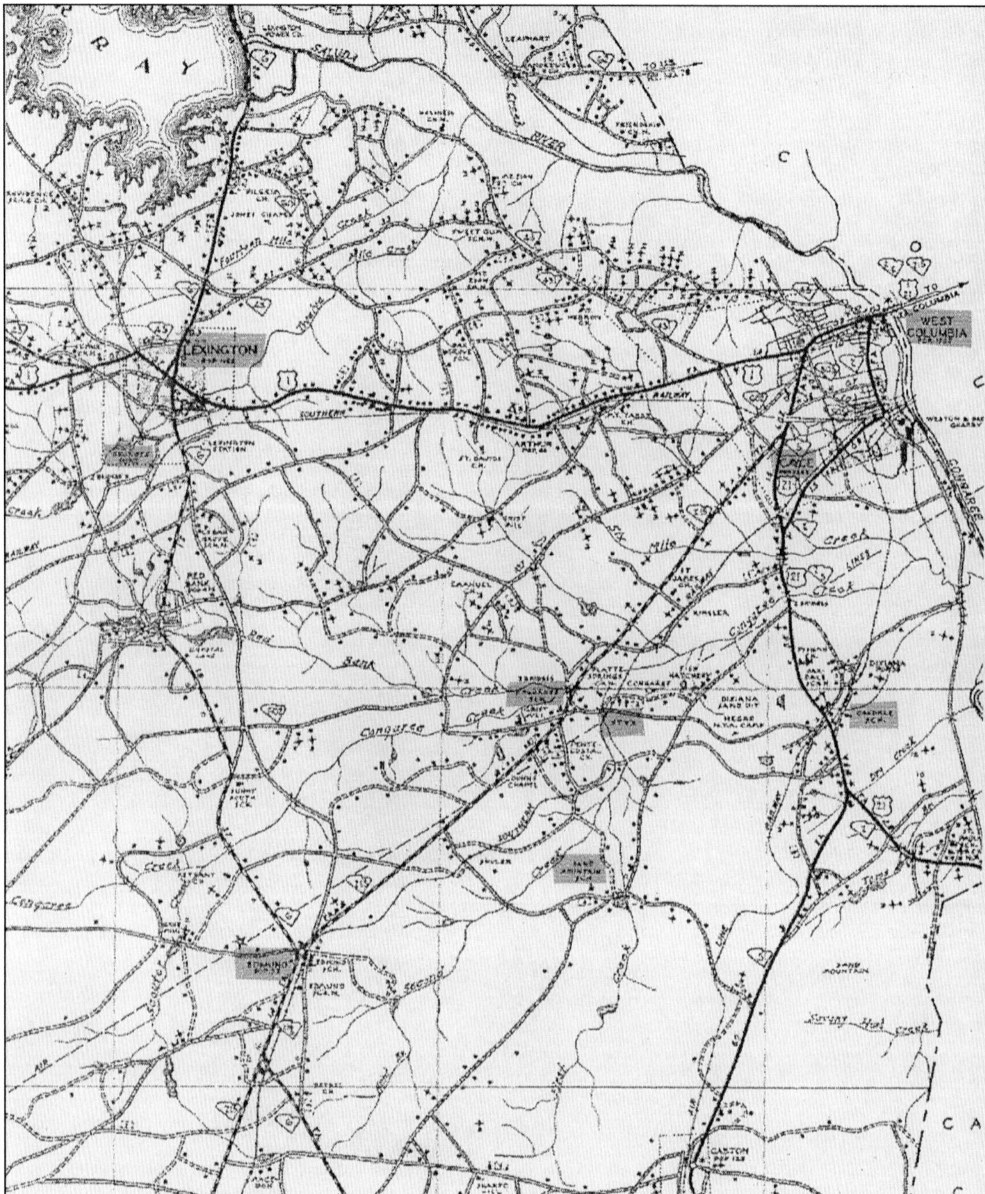

[Map of Central and East Central Lexington County, 1940.] This enlarged regional section of a 1940 highway map of Lexington County provides bearings for the town of Lexington and its environs and of the east central section of the county, which are the subject of the first and fifth chapters, respectively. The small dark strips indicate the location of school sites. Highway jurisdictional abbreviations used in the captions are as follows: LC (Lexington County), SC (South Carolina), and US (United States). Other map sections are found on pages 11, 52, and 80.

One

Central Region

Like the capital city 12 miles east, the town of Lexington had its beginnings as a planned city for governmental purposes (see Clayton B. Kleckley, "Lexington: A Planned Town," in Sandlapper, *November 1968), taking its name from that of its district (which honored the first battle of the American Revolution). With the decline of Granby, the small but important commercial center on the west bank of the Congaree (just south of present-day Cayce), which had also served as the district's court of justice, a healthier and more central site was sought for the court house. Thus in 1820 the village of Lexington Court House was established on property purchased from Anna Barbara Drafts Corley on a hill near Twelve Mile Creek on the Augusta Stage Coach Road. The community consisted of some ten families—about 80 individuals—living in a 4-by-16-block area.*

This initial chapter—principally on the county's courthouse town, which in 1895 officially became known as Lexington—establishes the pattern for much of what follows in this volume: a period look at the place and its rural surroundings, with glances at the early commercial, residential, and institutional architecture; and glimpses of some of the people who owned, maintained, and operated the farms, stores, schools, and light manufactories portrayed here.

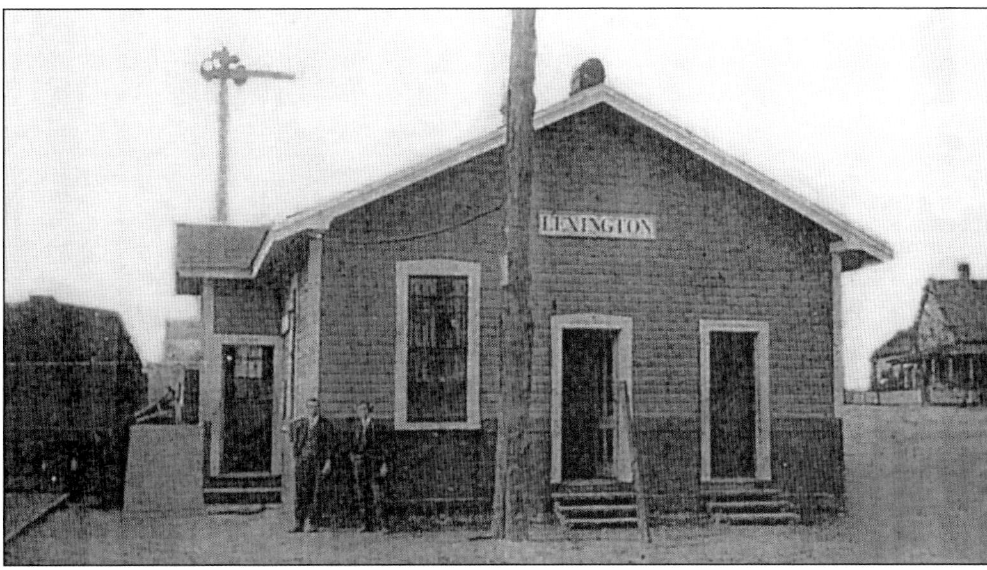

[Depot, Lexington, c. 1910.] In 1869–1870, the Charlotte, Columbia & Augusta Railroad was established, passing through Lexington, Gilbert, Summit, Leesville, and Batesburg on its path to Augusta. In 1894, it became a part of the Southern Railway System. The early steam locomotives needed a level terrain with frequent stops for fuel and water. Many stops became towns that developed around the depots. Because Lexington township was situated on higher ground, its track and depot were located about a mile south of the court house and business district at a site on S. Lake Drive. The business leaders decided not to relocate their town at the depot. The depot above no longer exists.

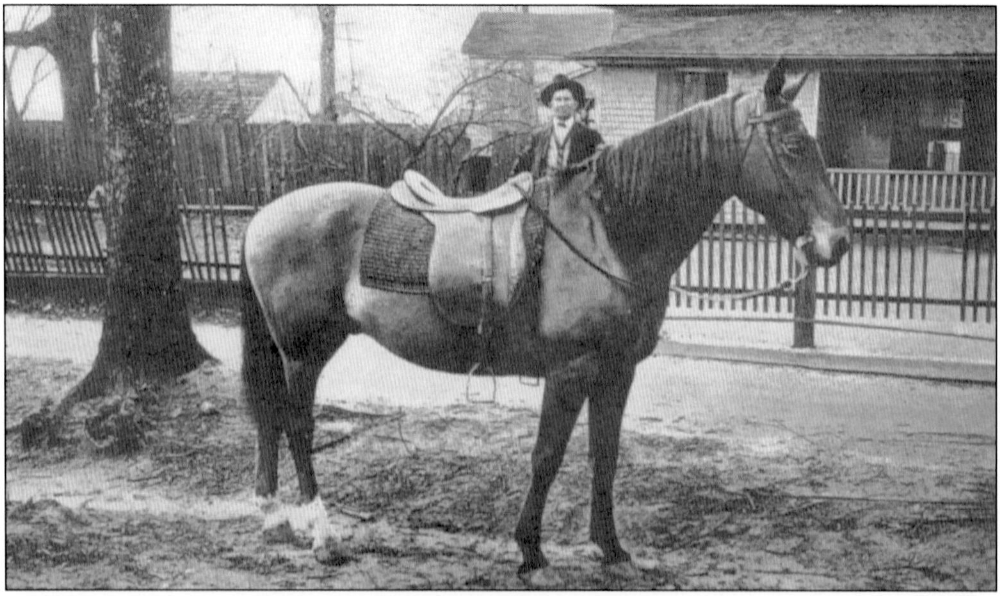

SHERIFF CORLEY AND HIS FAITHFUL HORSE BILLY, LEXINGTON, SC [*c.* 1908]. Patrick Henry Corley (1864–1948) served Lexington as sheriff from 1904 to 1911, when the town had a population of 1,000. This postcard was published by Corley for use in his bid for re-election.

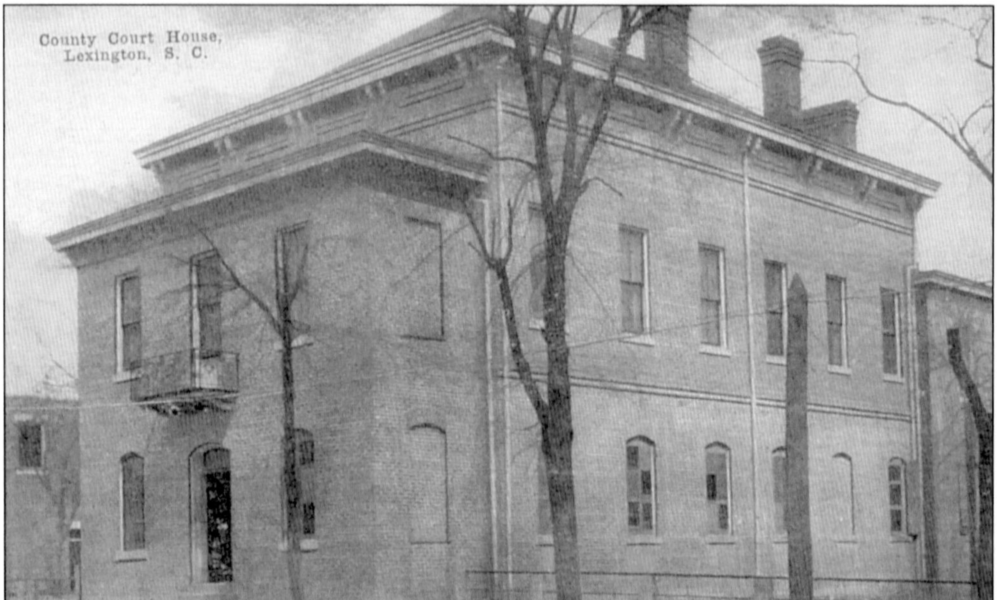

COUNTY COURT HOUSE, LEXINGTON, SC [*c.* 1919]. In 1820, Barbara Anne Corley deeded land in the present town of Lexington for a centrally located court house. The edifice above is the fourth court house to have been located on the north side of E. Main Street and N. Lake Drive. Built in 1881 and razed in 1957, it succeeded a poorly constructed frame building erected in 1866. The one before that, an 1839 granite-block structure, had been burned by Sherman's army on February 17, 1865. The next court house (the fifth) would eventually be built across E. Main on the site of the old county jail.

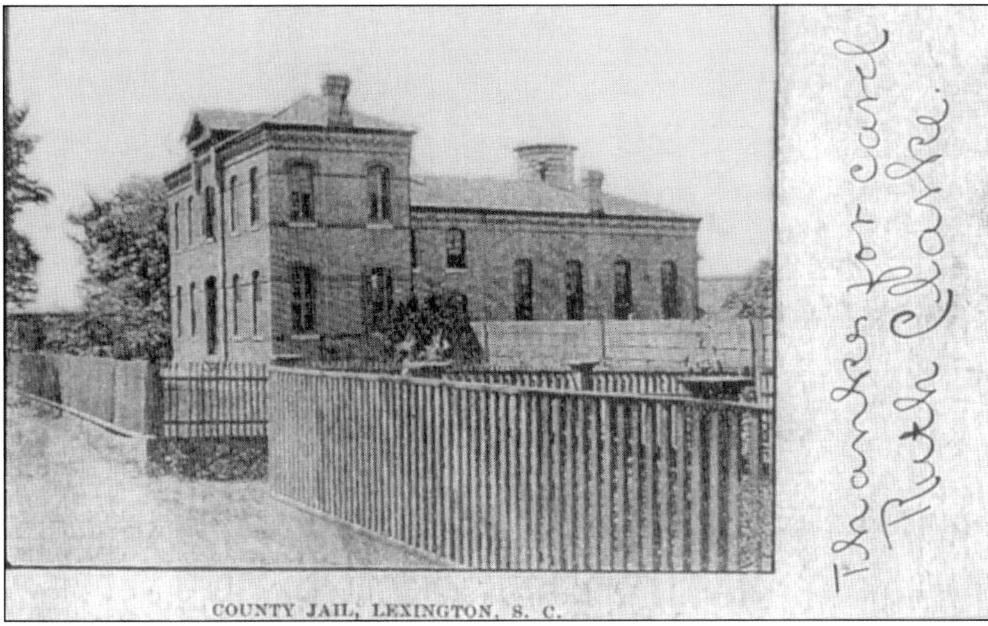

COUNTY JAIL, LEXINGTON, SC [1906]. The picture above was taken before the fire of 1916 and shows the west side of the square granite jail viewed from Harman Alley on the corner where the Godfrey Harman residence once stood. "Uncle Josh" in his newspaper articles reveals that at the rear of the building in the jail yard stood a public whipping post where convicts received from 10 to 40 lashes for horse stealing or house breaking, until the law was deemed cruel and was discontinued. This edifice was razed and replaced with the current Lexington County Court House, which was dedicated on January 15, 1940.

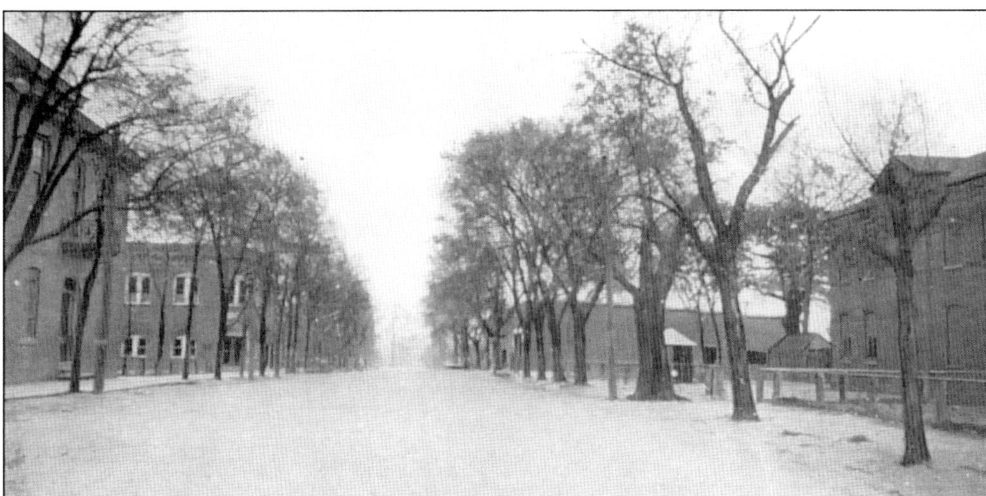

MAIN STREET LOOKING EAST, LEXINGTON, SC [C. 1919]. Looking east, this view of the 100 block of E. Main Street shows, at left, the court house with a balcony above its entrance and, in the distance, the Home National Bank building at the corner of N. Lake Drive. Beyond Harman Alley, at right, is the county jail that faces the court house. The electrical poles and wires that at the time ran up the middle of the street have been removed from the photo-negative in order to present a less cluttered image.

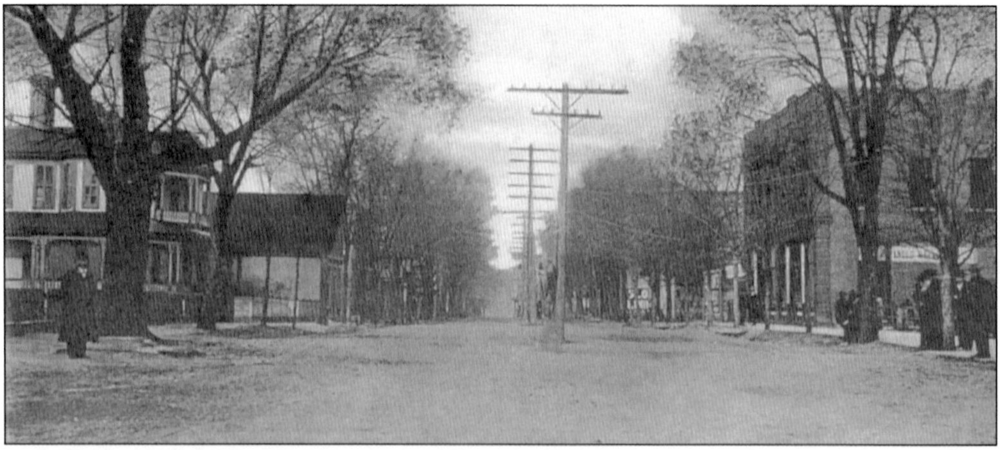

Main Street Looking North, Lexington, SC [c. 1910]. This view reveals how the south side of the 100 block of E. Main Street appeared before it was destroyed by fire in 1916. Looking north from Harman Alley, one sees at left the residence of Godfrey Harman and his building, which housed the Harman Bazaar (front) and the offices of the *Dispatch-News* (back). One of the businesses that for many years occupied a site in the new four-unit block erected in 1917 was the Harmon Drug Company, which was eventually transformed into the law offices at 135 Main. A hardware store went in at 133; the *Dispatch-News* offices at 131; and a new Bazaar at 129. Across Main was the brick Kaufmann Drug Company (first floor) and the telephone company and law offices (second floor).

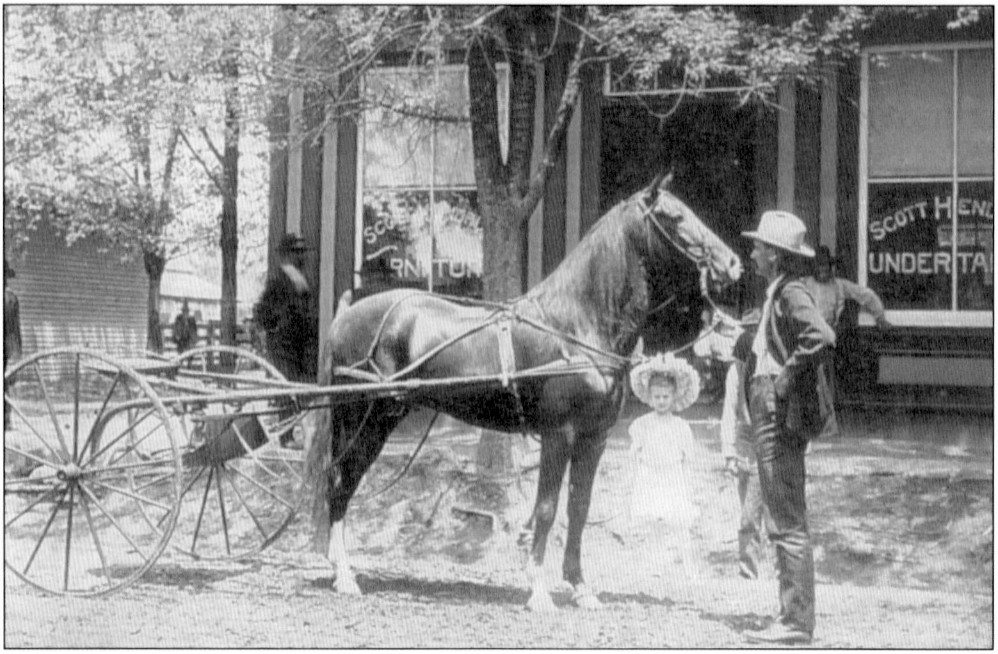

[Scott Hendrix Furniture and Undertaking Company, Lexington, c. 1912.] The frame building of Scott Hendrix's enterprises at the corner of N. Church and 102 W. Main Street was destroyed in the 1916 fire and replaced by a brick structure. Sam George, shown here standing by his horse, was the Clerk of Court for Lexington County. His family owned the flour and gristmill on the south side of Twelve Mile Creek at George's Pond.

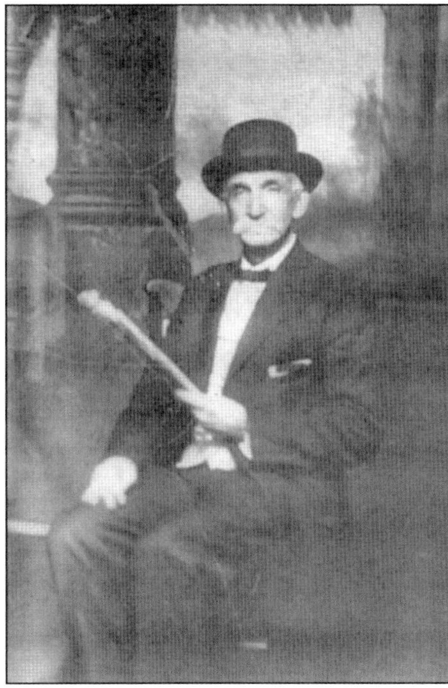

[PORTRAIT OF GODFREY MICHAEL HARMAN, LEXINGTON, C. 1920.] Godfrey Michael ("Uncle Josh") Harman (1845–1931) was born in the Harman Hotel across from the court house. He was educated in the "village academy" and later served in the Confederate Army. In 1870 he founded the weekly *Lexington Dispatch*, which in 1909 merged with the *News*. In 1919 the paper was sold to Messrs. Sligh & Walker. Harman always lived "within sight of the county courthouse," heard the county's stories, and witnessed the events of his day. In 1922 he wrote a series of articles reflecting the turn-of-the-century life of the county as he remembered it and signed them "Uncle Josh."

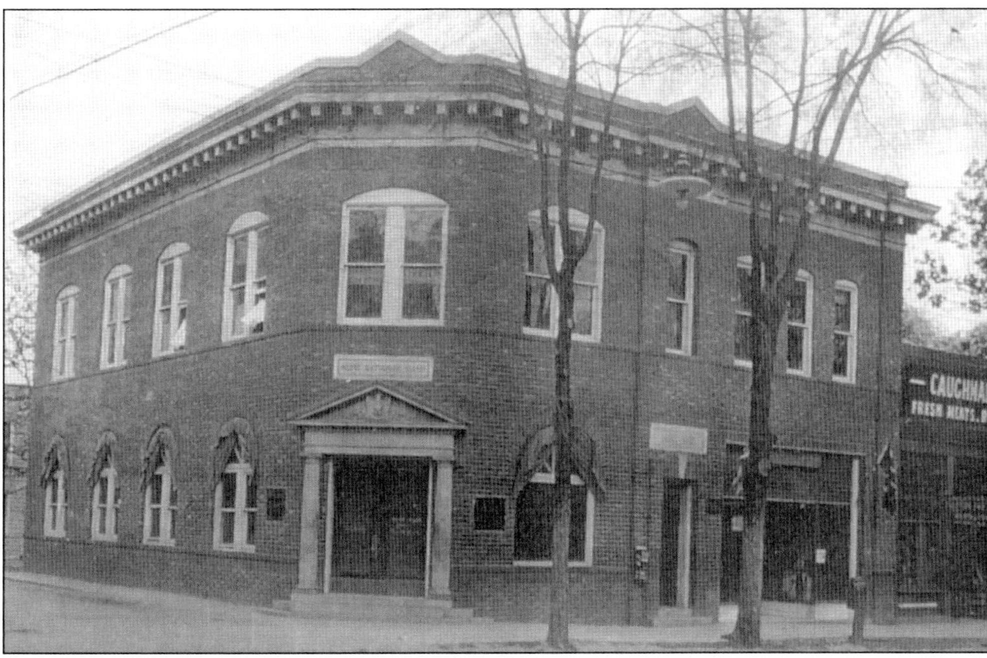

HOME NATIONAL BANK, LEXINGTON, SC [C. 1912]. The brick Home National Bank was built in 1912 at the corner of E. Main Street and N. Lake Drive and across from the court house. The bank was on the left (N. Lake) side of the ground floor, and the post office, on the right (Main Street) side. The stairway in the center of the right side led to various offices (including that of Dr. P.H. Shealey, dentist) and the town's library upstairs. The bank went bankrupt in 1932. The 200 E. Main building still stood in 2000.

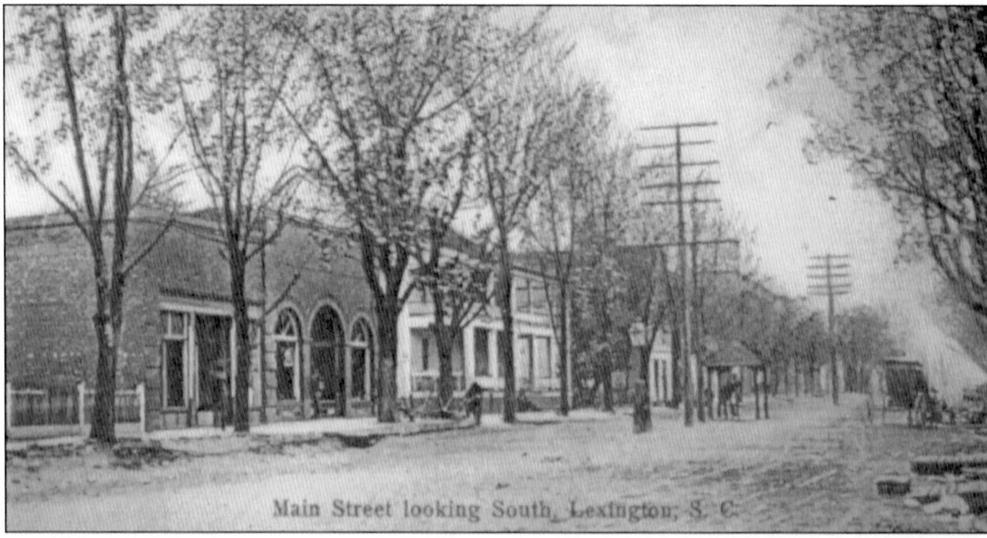

MAIN STREET LOOKING SOUTH [*SIC* (EAST)], LEXINGTON, SC [*C.* 1910]. This view shows the north side of the 100 block of E. Main Street, starting on the east side of the Scott Hendrix Store at N. Church and Main Streets. The two brick buildings survived the 1916 fire and exist today, but in altered condition, as 102 and 104; the Meetze Hotel at 106 was lost. The structures and trees obscure the view of the court house at the end of the block. Electrical poles were positioned down the middle of Main Street along with the covered well that was located almost in front of the hotel.

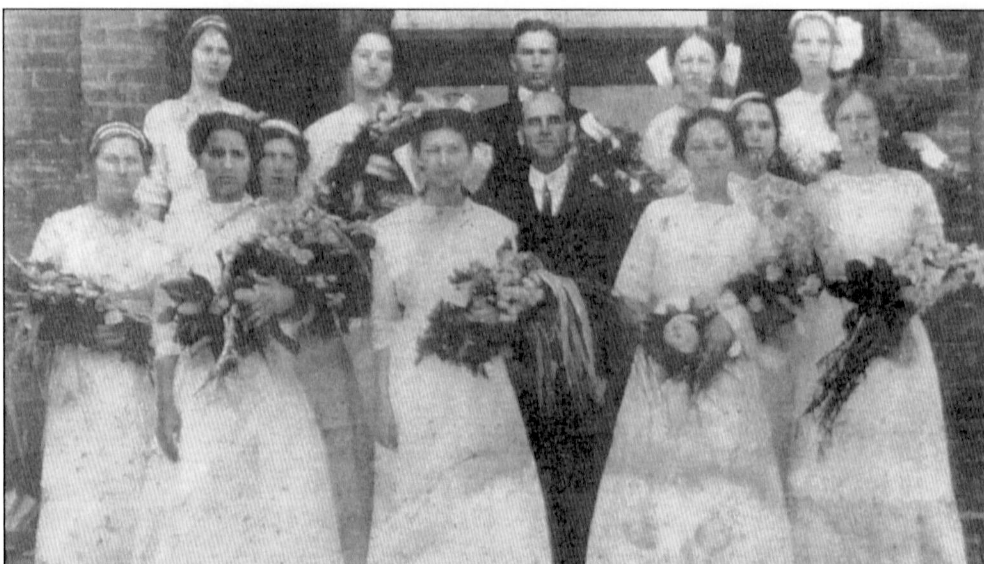

[CLASS OF 1912, LEXINGTON HIGH SCHOOL.] The Class of 1912, the first to graduate (at the tenth grade level) from Lexington High School, posed for this outdoor portrait in front of the school's main entrance. The students and their teacher have been identified, from left to right, as follows: (front row) Mary Ballentine, Zula Meetze, Aline Harman, Mary Belle Corley, Professor W.E. Black, Cecile Barre, Josephine Brown, and Lily Butler; (back row) Gladys Dent, Julie Shealy, Homer Long, Annie Caughman, and Vera Corley.

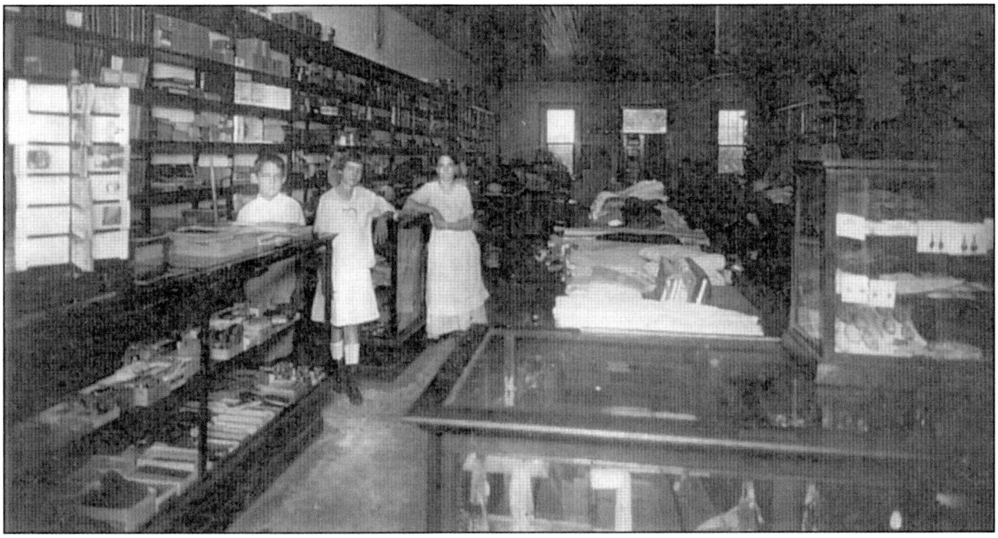

[**Sarratt's Bazaar, Lexington,** *c.* **1918.**] Sarratt's Bazaar, built after the 1916 fire, was located at 129 E. Main Street (on the south side next to the alley). Initially Harman's Bazaar, this general store was managed by Icoline Harman Sarratt and was one of four buildings owned and operated by the Harman family. Shown here amid their inexpensive merchandise are Christopher Kaufmann (later president of Newberry College), Blondelle Harmon, and Icoline Sarratt. On the display cabinet at left stands a rack of postcards published by the Harmon Drug Company.

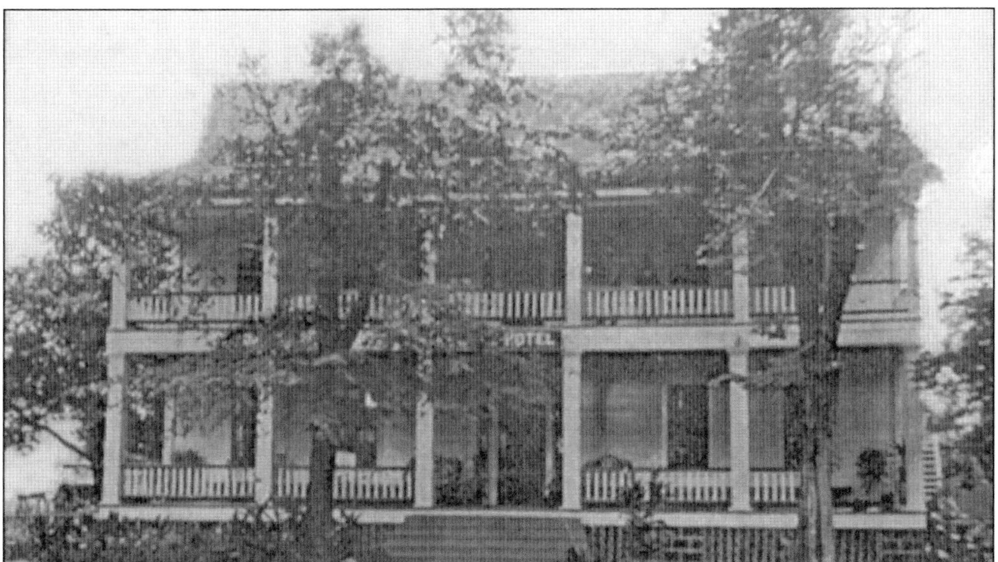

Meetze Hotel, Lexington, SC [*c.* **1906**]. Built in 1830, the frame Meetze Hotel, at 106 E. Main Street (north side), continued to operate until 1916 when, along with the Roof block across the street and every other frame building downtown, it was destroyed by fire. A covered well with pump, which during this time was a source of water for the town, was located almost directly in front of the hotel. The old hotel site is near Sessions Department Store, which in 2000 stood vacant.

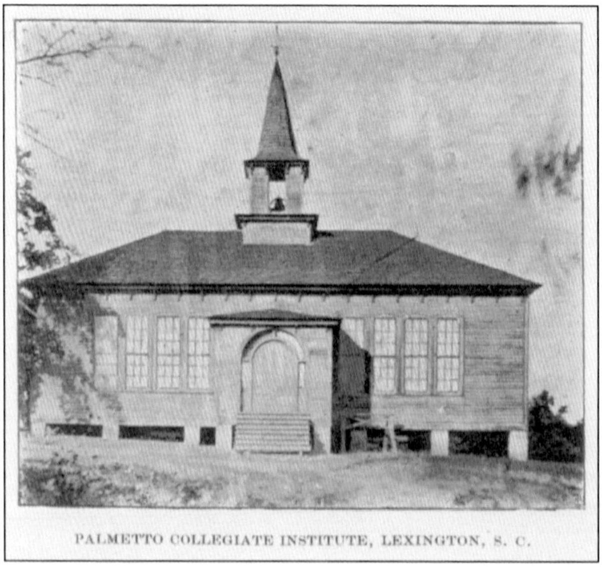

PALMETTO COLLEGIATE INSTITUTE, LEXINGTON, SC [1907]. Built in 1881, the private white Palmetto Collegiate Institute, which once stood on Hendrix Street, consisted of seven grades. In 1900, eighth and ninth grades were added, and its 153 students were taught by three teachers in a 13-week session. By 1906, when C.M. Efird was president and W.E. Black was principal, the school had an enrollment of 223 students in its three departments: Primary (1–3), Intermediate (4–6), and Collegiate (7–9). Parents paid between $1.10 and $2.90 for each child per month, and the teachers were paid 5¢ a day for each pupil. The old wooden schoolhouse still survived in 2000.

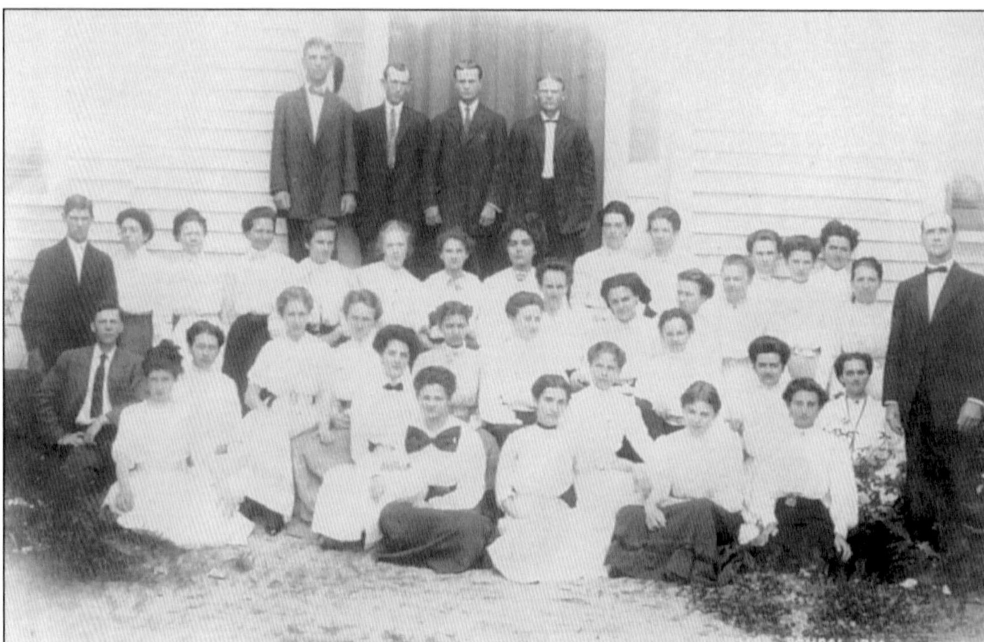

[PORTRAIT OF TEACHERS IN SUMMER SCHOOL, LEXINGTON, 1910.] The public school teachers gathered for this group portrait in front of the Palmetto Collegiate Institute were attending summer school where they could improve their teaching skills and upgrade their subject knowledge. In 1919, there were 141 white teachers in the county (86 women and 55 men) and 62 African-American teachers (36 women, 26 men). The average salary paid the white teachers was $333 and the average for African-American teachers was $57.

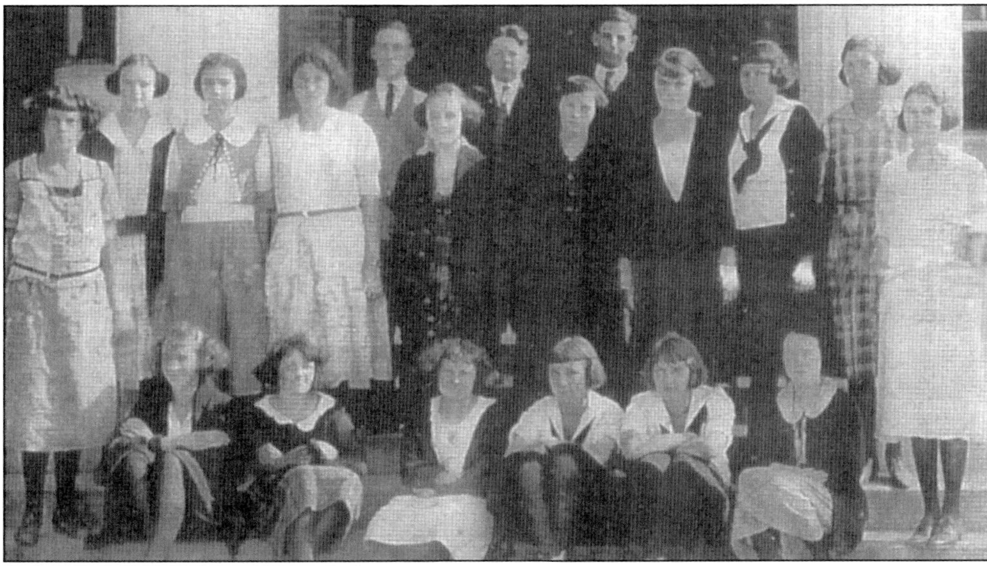

[Lexington High School, Class of 1923.] Students of the Class of 1923 were the first class to begin and finish Lexington High School through the 11th grade. Class members, from left to right, are as follows: (seated) B. Harmon, V. Evans, C. Whitten, C. Roof, M. Kyzer, and J. Feibrich; (standing) A. Franklow, M. Redd, L. Griffith, V. Meetze, E. Harmon, L. Roberts, C. Harmon, A.M. Sharpe, B. Goodwin, L. Caughman, O. Corley, and R. Hallman. Of the 19 pupils in the class 15 graduated.

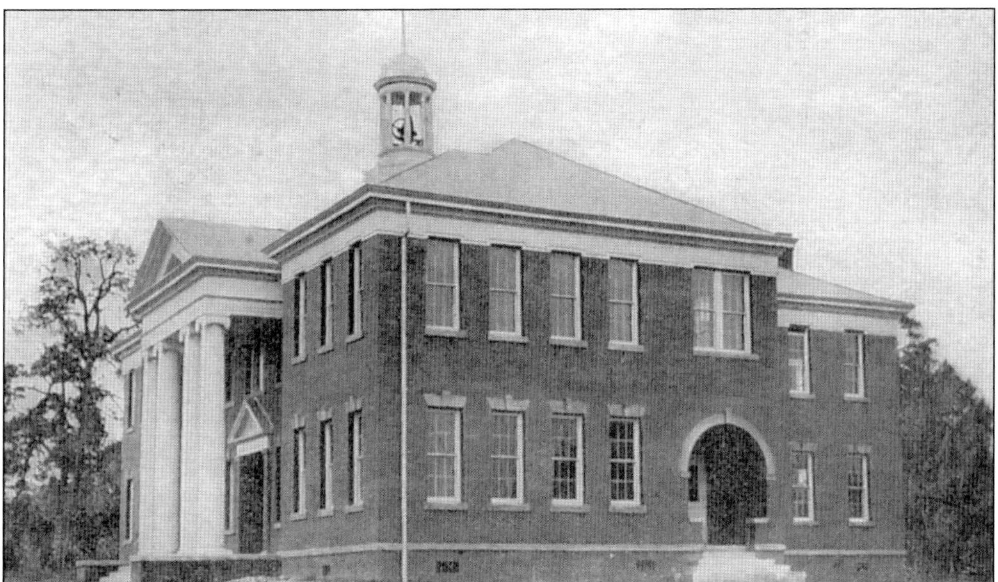

Lexington High School, Lexington, SC [*c.* 1913]. The two-story brick neoclassic Lexington High School was built on N. Lake Drive in 1912 to house grades one through ten. In 1919, W.E. Black was principal and the school was described as a second-class high school (a four-year curriculum and two to three full-time teachers). In 1922 it had 124 students and offered the only music course in the county. The school at the time it was demolished in 1985 was believed to have been the county's oldest surviving structure of its style.

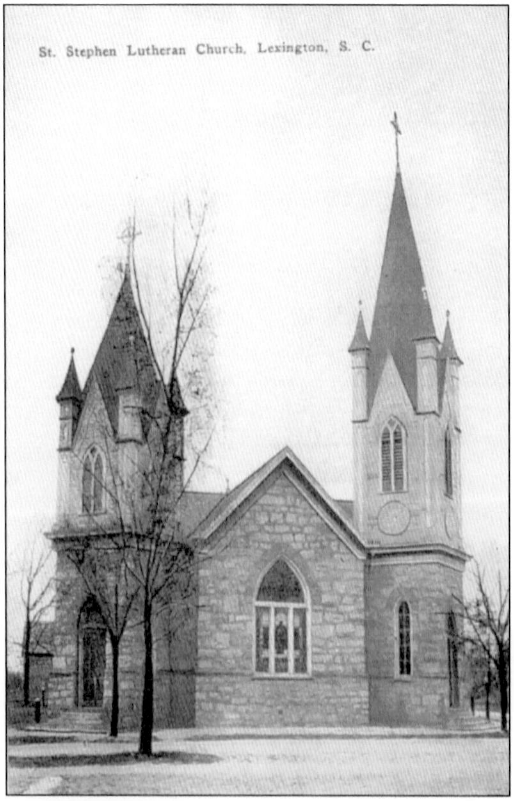

St. Stephen Lutheran Church, Lexington, SC [1923]. The first sanctuary of St. Stephen's Lutheran Church, which was organized in 1830, was burned by vandals during Sherman's raid in 1865; a second one, built in 1870, burned in 1897. The third one, seen here, built of stone across the street from the first site, was completed in 1900 and served the congregation until 1957, when it was torn down to make room for the present sanctuary.

Main Street Scene, Lexington, SC [*c.* 1906]. The frame W.P. Roof block was built in 1904. Located on the corner of S. Church and E. Main (from 101 to 113 at the alley), it faced the Meetze Hotel. Roof's mercantile store utilized the first two units on the street level, while the second floor contained offices and an auditorium. The Savings Bank occupied the third unit; the post office, the fourth. It was destroyed in the 1916 fire.

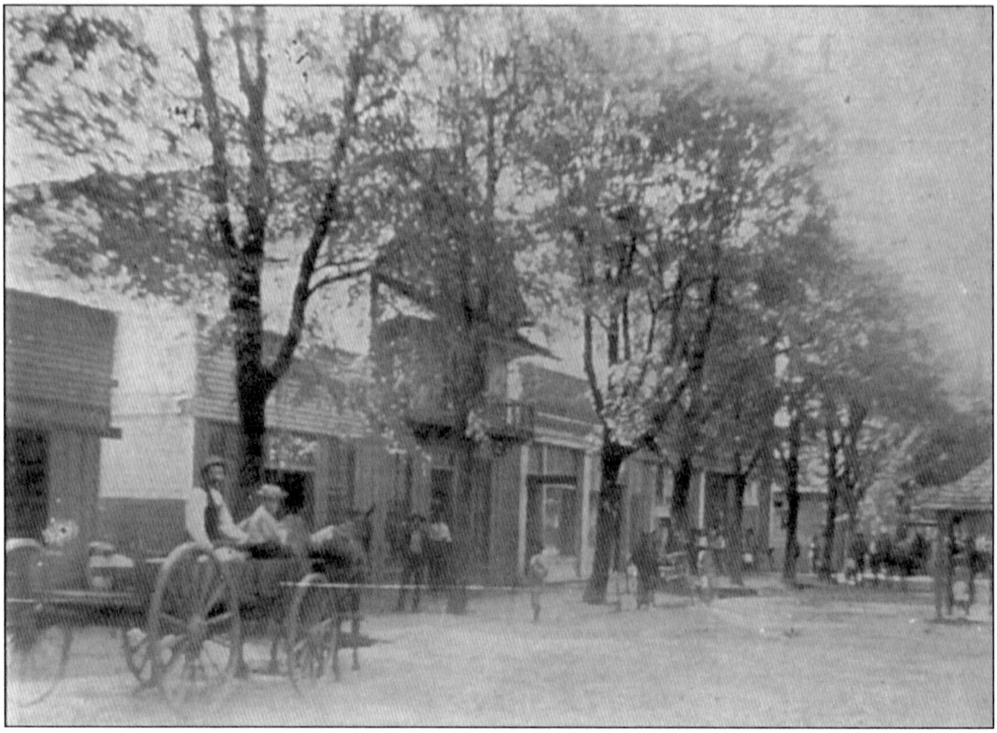

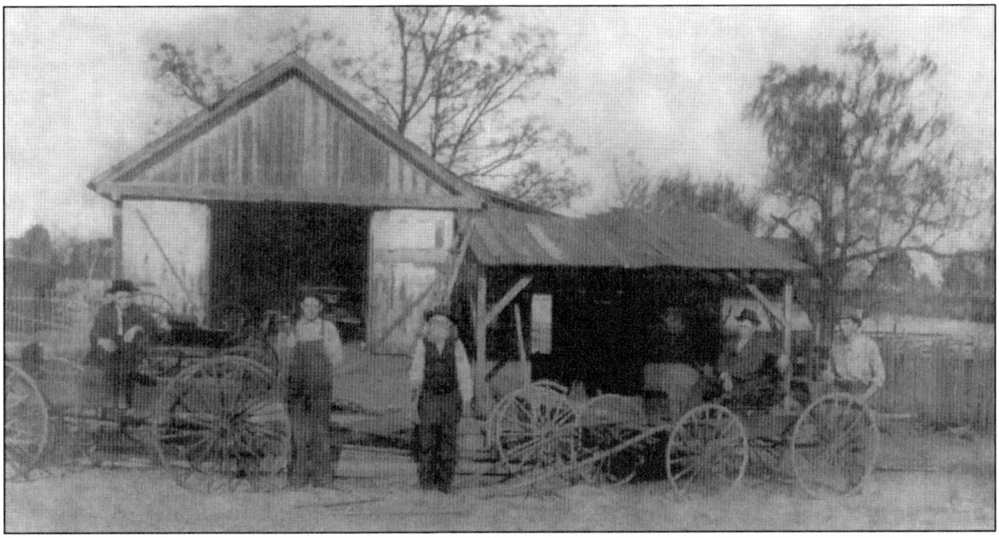

[Rawl's Carriage Factory, Lexington, c. 1920.] According to Godfrey Harman, David Rawl's carriage factory, established in the 200 block of W. Main Street in the 1850s, grew to become "an immense business" with a substantial payroll that employed a large number of men who made and repaired buggies and wagons. Although all but one of the factory's buildings were destroyed when Sherman's troops swept through Lexington, James E. Rawl (David's son, seen here in the center of the picture) continued in the declining buggy trade until his death in the 1920s.

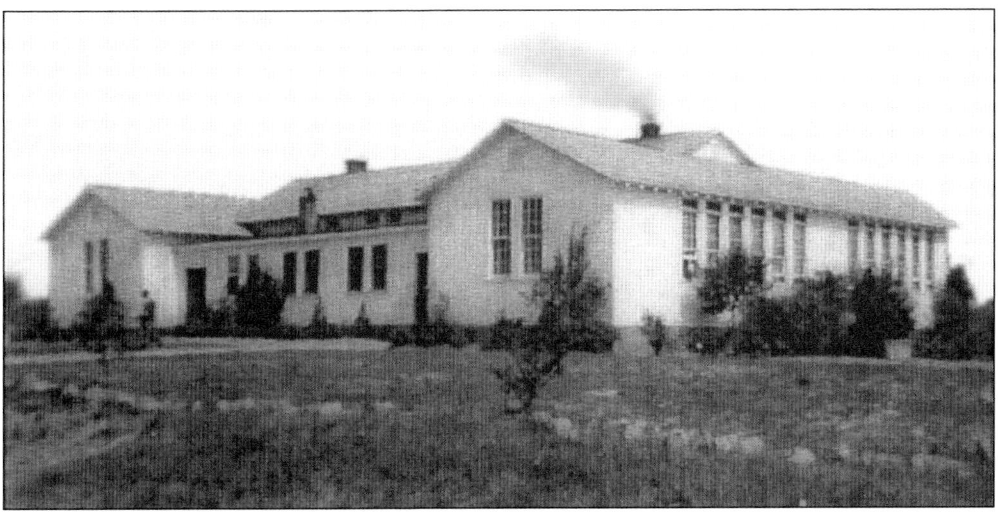

[Rosenwald School, Lexington, c. 1930s.] In 1868, Judge Lemuel Boozer created and funded the private Boozer School for all children, and by 1900 it had 76 black students. After the establishment in 1917 of the Julius Rosenwald Fund, whose purpose was to erect and equip modern black schools, Lexington received a grant and purchased a lot on Hendrix Street. In order to receive the $500 grant from Rosenwald, the county and the state each had to contribute $400. This school was built during the 1919–1920 school term. The picture above shows the school in the 1930s, when it was probably the largest school for black children in the county. Some rural African-American families sent their children to this school so that they could obtain a better education. The building no longer stands.

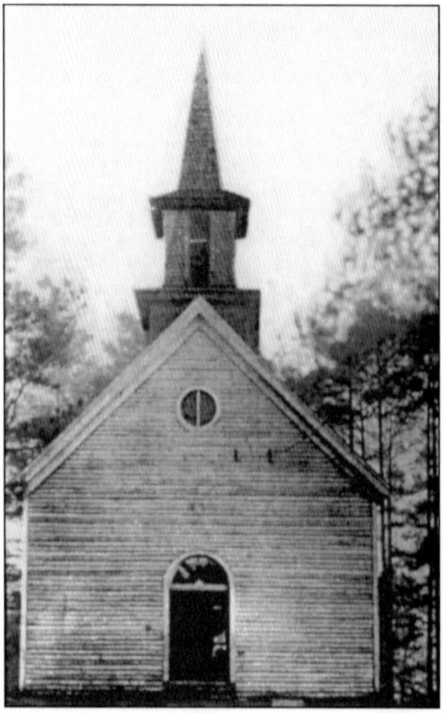

[Lexington Baptist Church.] A Baptist Mission was started in Lexington in 1892 with the support of the local church convention and with the Reverend N.G. Kooner from Batesburg as mission pastor. On May 21, 1893, the Lexington Baptist Church was constituted in its new one-room frame building with the Reverend J.J. Myers as its first regular minister. In 1896, a 30-inch church bell was purchased. Most of the growing congregation, 10 to 58 members in the first ten years, came from the mill families who moved to town. This wooden church was dismantled in 1924 and materials from it were used in the building of the new chapel across the street at 308 East Main.

[Baptism at the Mill Pond, Lexington, *c.* 1924.] Baptismal services of the Lexington Baptist Church were held in the pond belonging to the Lexington Manufacturing Company during the time when the sanctuary was located near the mill. Shown here standing in the mill pond are members of the Corley, Gibbs, Harmon, Keisler, Shealy, Sons, Sox, Steele, and other families while the sacrament is being administered by the Reverend W.C. Wallace, who was minister of the church from 1921 to 1928.

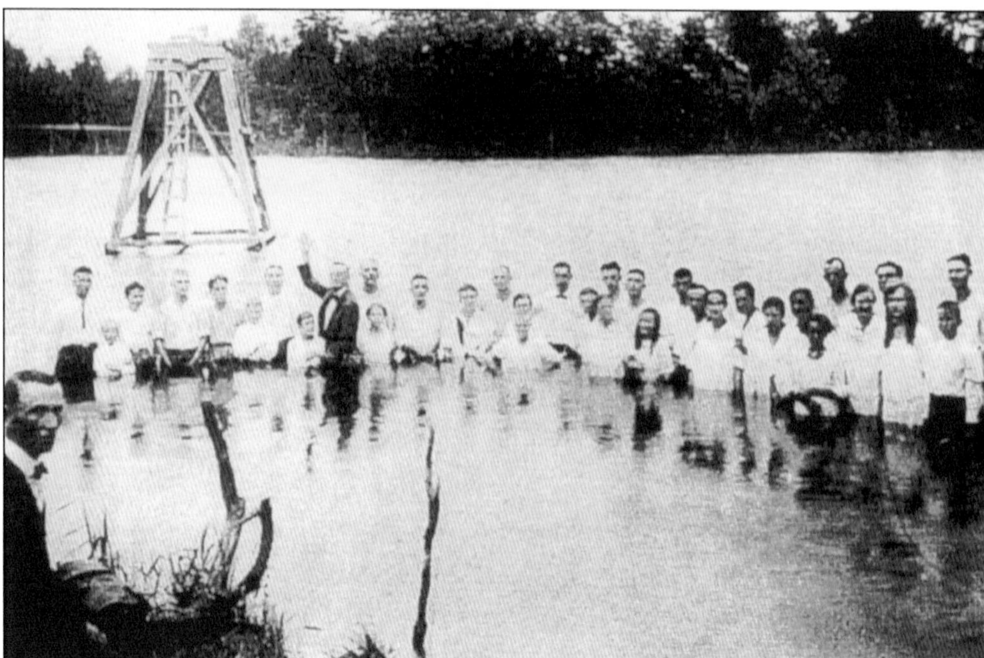

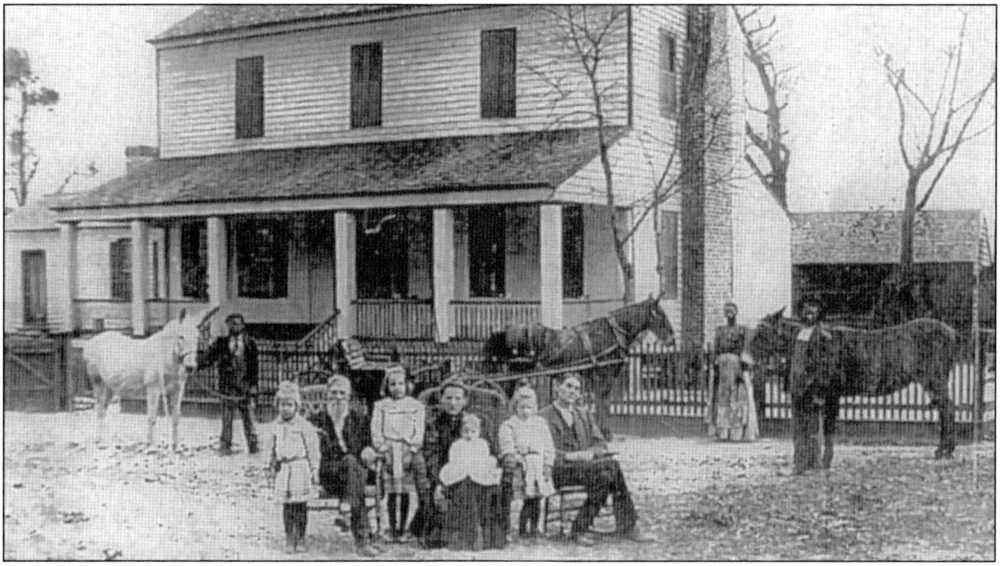

[Berly House, Lexington, c. 1900.] The Berly House, at 121 Berly Street, built in 1825, was purchased in 1860 from the Lutheran Seminary by the Reverend William Berly (1810–1873), a preacher and teacher who was a professor of theology in the seminary and the principal of its Literary and Classical Institute. When the seminary moved to Newberry, he established a female academy in Lexington, where he remained as principal until shortly before his death. He also served many churches in the synod and was its president for two terms (1849 to 1851 and 1863 to 1865). Grandson William Berly and his family are shown above in a picture taken about 1905 in front of his grandfather's house.

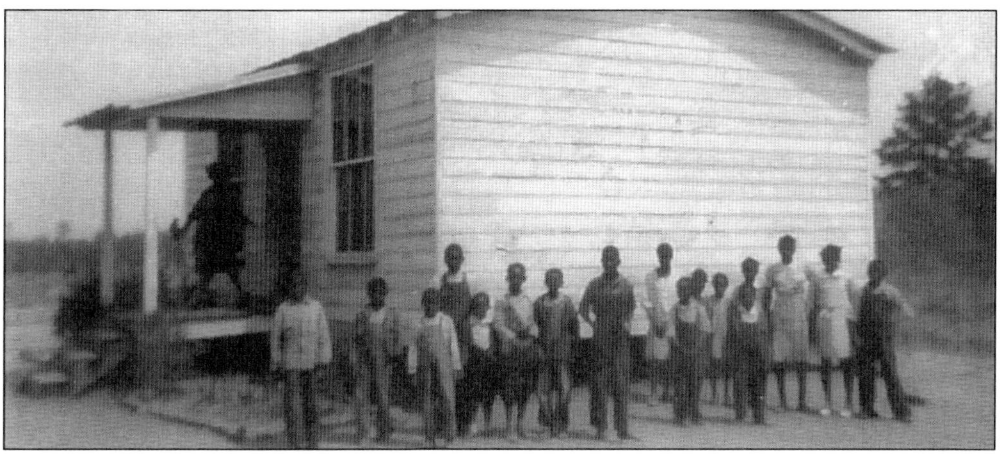

[Midway School, c. 1930s.] Midway School, one of the county's schools for African-American children in the days before integration, once stood on Midway Road, which branches off Andrew Corley Road near the south side of the Lake Murray Dam. In his 1916 monograph *Public Schools of Lexington County,* Lueco Gunter says little about the black schools but does reveal that there were 57 of them, of which 52 were one-teacher units, and that the county's black student enrollment was 3,027 with an average school session of 69 days. Lexington's black teachers, 26 men and 36 women, were often former students or graduates from the black colleges in Columbia or Orangeburg. The county's total black expenditure for schools was $3,665.35, of which $3,549.35 went for teachers' salaries that averaged $57.85. Average expenditure per pupil was $1.27.

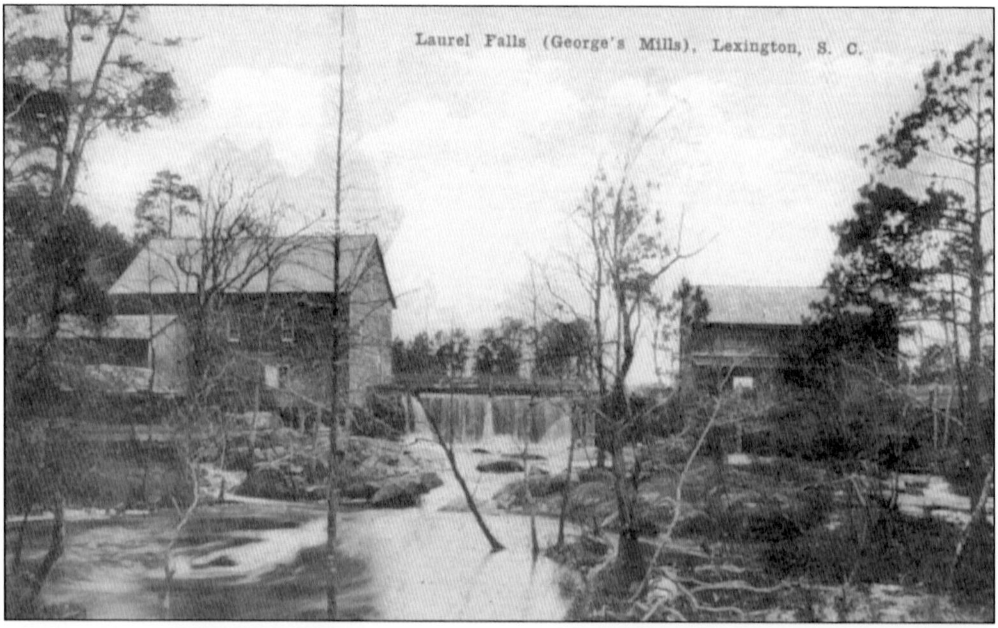

LAUREL FALLS (GEORGE'S MILL), LEXINGTON, SC [C. 1923]. Laurel Falls at George's Pond, now called Gibson's Pond, about 2 miles southwest of the court house on Twelve Mile Creek was once a site for gristmills and sawmills and even a small six-spindle cotton mill that burned about 1850. The boys enjoyed the pond for swimming and fishing for its red-breasted sun-perch and mollies. Young and old found the site popular for parties, picnics, barbecues, and fish fries. The pavilion was considered the best dance hall in the county. In 2000, the pond was a major source for the town's water.

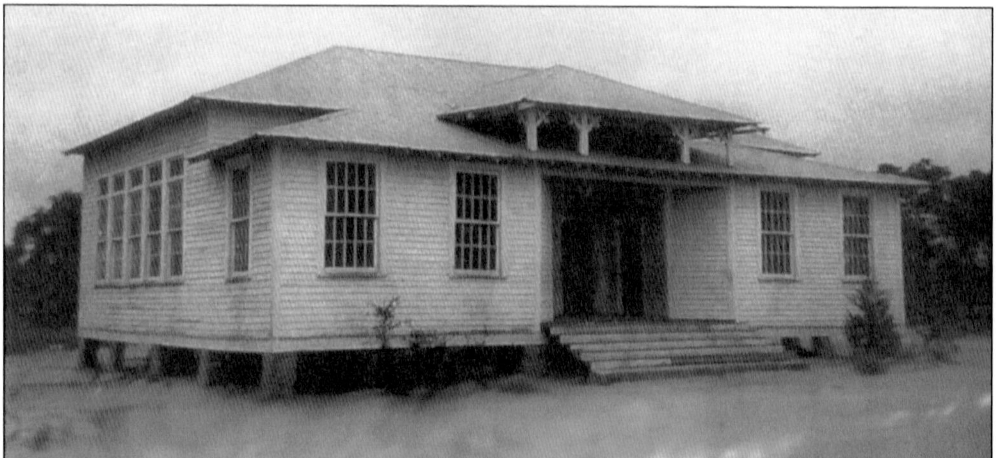

[ROUND HILL SCHOOL.] The Round Hill schoolhouse was built some time after 1916 to replace an earlier one-teacher structure, which Gunter in his study described as an unpainted building with homemade desks and blackboards and practically no other teaching equipment. Located on Two Notch Road about 7-miles southwest of Lexington and 4.5 miles east of Gilbert, Round Hill was one of the county's longer-lived rural schools. It is listed for the last time in the 1952–1953 issue of the annual *School Directory of South Carolina*. In 2000, a community center occupied the site, with a fire station next to it.

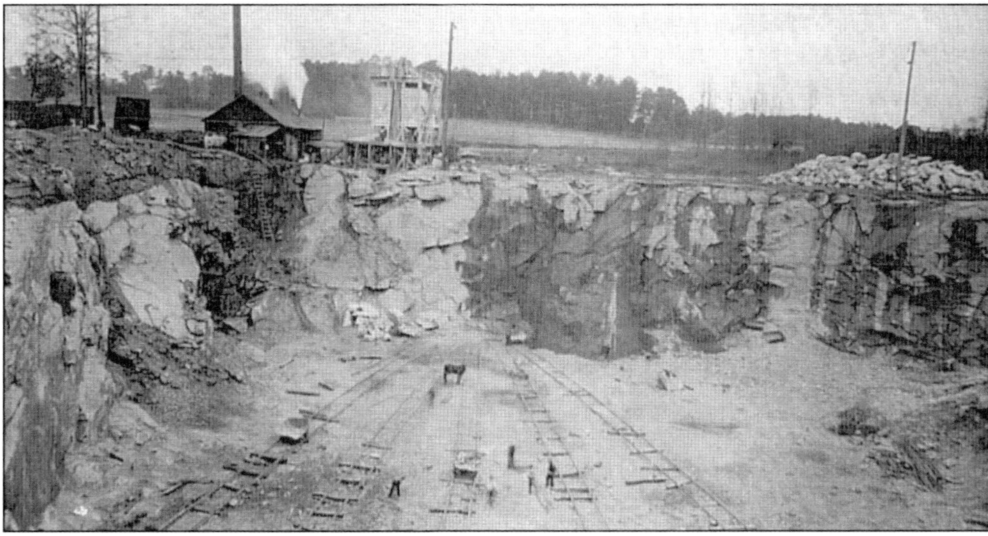

[**LEXINGTON QUARRY, *c.* 1910.**] James Wade Corley owned the property on which the rock quarry (seen here) was located, about 1.75 miles east of the court house on US 1. Corley leased this site to Dr. Crawford Long of Atlanta from 1901 to 1907 and then to Caspari's Stone Company from 1907 to 1914 for the purpose of producing both crushed and block granite. A spur line linked the quarry with the main railroad system. The work force included 15 to 20 men. The 100-foot-deep quarry, which has since filled with water and functions as a pond, is situated behind the Lexington School District One headquarters building on Tarrar Springs Road in the Corley Woods subdivision.

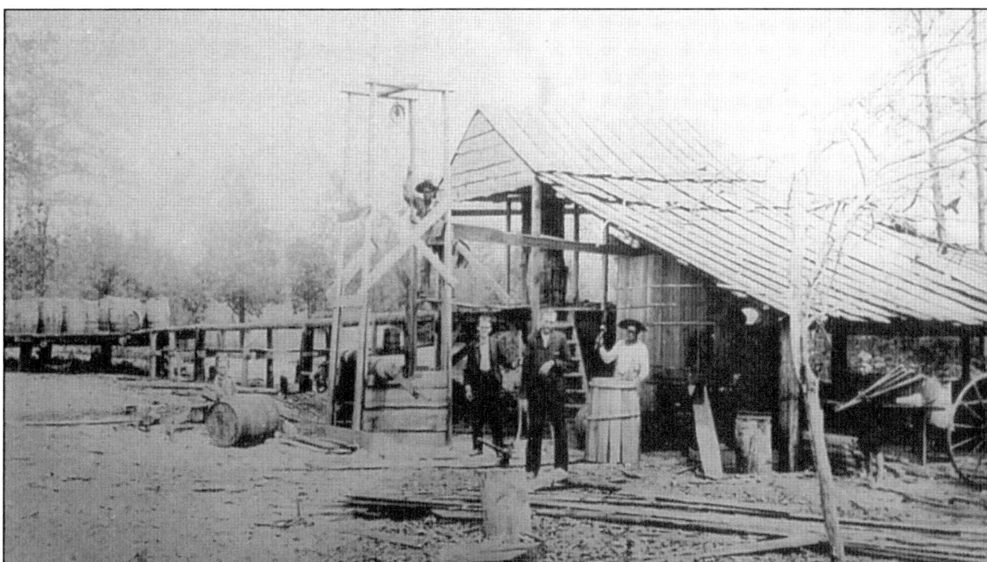

[**HENRY STEELE'S TURPENTINE STILL, ROUND HILL, *c.* 1900s.**] Some of the turpentine stills, like Henry Steele's turpentine still, were occasionally large-scale factories. Lexington farmers found that their rural pine forests could be a major source of income both by tapping the pine trees for sap, which could be continually collected and distilled into turpentine, and by harvesting the lumber that could be used in homes, barns, and commercial products. Many farmers considered their pine trees a second crop.

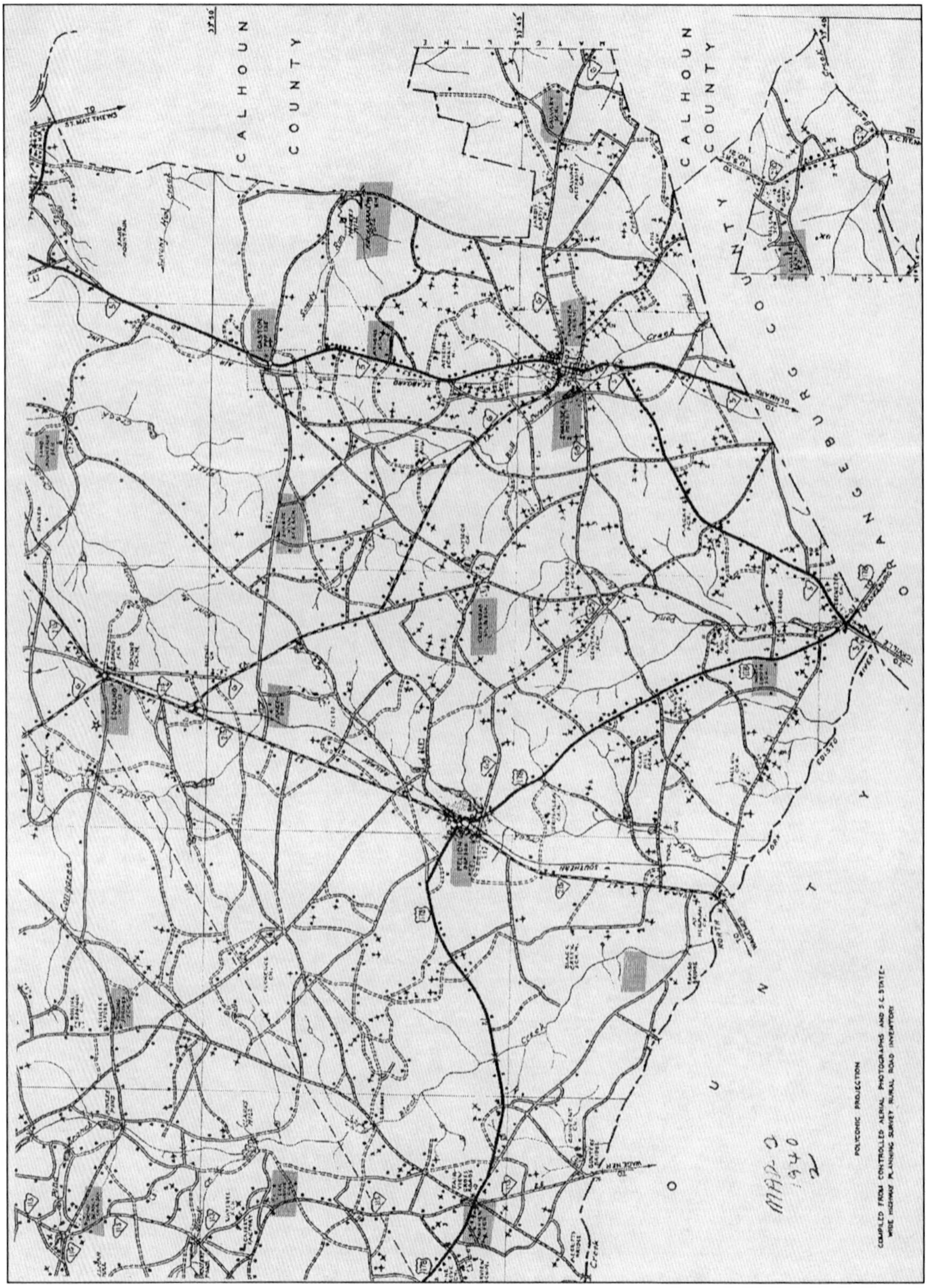

[Map of Southeastern Lexington County, 1940.] This enlarged regional section of a 1940 highway map of Lexington County covers the geography of chapter two. The small dark strips indicate the location of school sites. Highway jurisdictional abbreviations used in the captions are as follows: LC (Lexington County), SC (South Carolina), and US (United States). Other map sections are found on pages 8, 52, and 80.

Two

SOUTHEASTERN REGION

The lower quarter of Lexington County—extending from Gaston south to Swansea and the Horse's Neck, back over to Thor, up to Pelion, and on to Fairview Cross Roads and the Richton Community to the north—is a territory of perhaps greater topographic and economic diversity than any other part of the county. The resourceful inhabitants of this area, aware of their isolation from the more developed and thickly populated precincts to the north, nevertheless capitalized on the assets at hand—trees, ponds, creeks, and soil—to fashion their own distinctive world. Their southern sphere was one of lumbering and of sawmills, gristmills, and turpentine stills. It was also a land of cotton, especially in the rich rural neighborhoods bordering Calhoun, Orangeburg, and Aiken Counties.

Furthermore, it is a land of myth and legend, reflected in its very names: Pelion and Thor—the lower two of the four stops on the Southern Railroad were taken from ancient mythology; and Swansea—did its name derive from some association with old Wales (which would also explain the town's use of Cardiff and Monmouth for street names), or was it a popular corruption of the German word for twenty ("zwanzig"), thus symbolizing the strange happenstance of the town's equidistance from Columbia, Lexington, and St. Matthews? There is the legendary quality of the region's water, the clarity of which determined the railroad stops along the line. And there is the legendary tenacity of the people themselves who, despite the relative isolation and late development of their section, and their subjection to an often unforgiving land, have managed to create a vital and viable way of life.

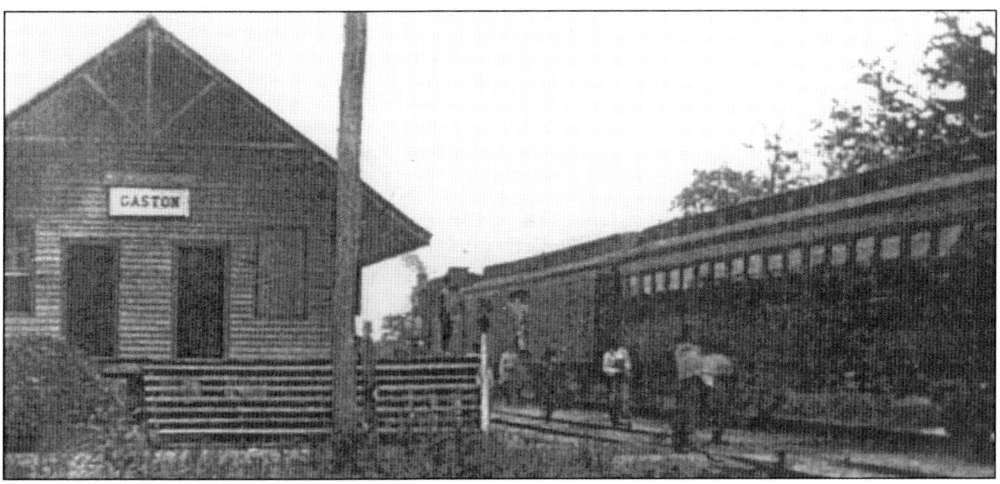

[RAILROAD DEPOT, GASTON, *c.* 1920.] The town of Gaston was incorporated on December 28, 1894, its limits extending half a mile in each direction from the depot. By 1910, it had a population of 125. The depot shown here is probably the initial one that served the old Florida Central & Peninsular Railroad, which connected Columbia with Savannah and was eventually absorbed by the Seaboard Air Line. This early depot was later replaced by another that was moved and subsequently destroyed by fire.

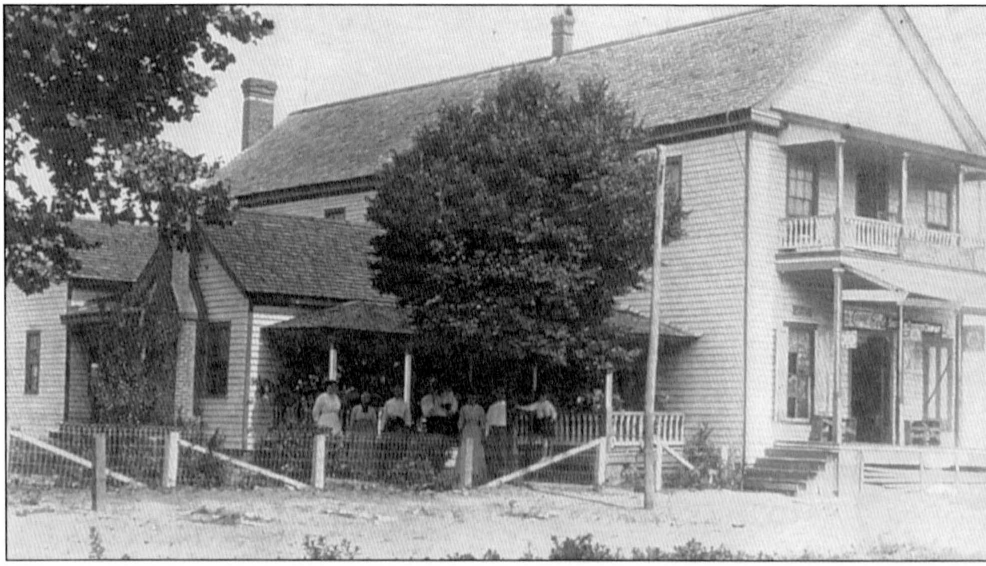

[J.F. FALLAW'S STORE, GASTON, *C.* 1910.] One of the few landmarks remaining from old Gaston, the J.F. Fallaw Store still stood in 2000 (as a private residence, minus its porches) at the corner of Meadowfield Road and Carlisle Street. The town's early post office was once housed on its first floor, while its second story was used for various community functions, events, and activities—even as a skating rink. Joseph Forrest Fallaw (1868–1941) married Idella Craft in 1889 and served as Gaston's postmaster from 1911 to 1941. He was a very active and loyal member of nearby Sandy Run Baptist Church.

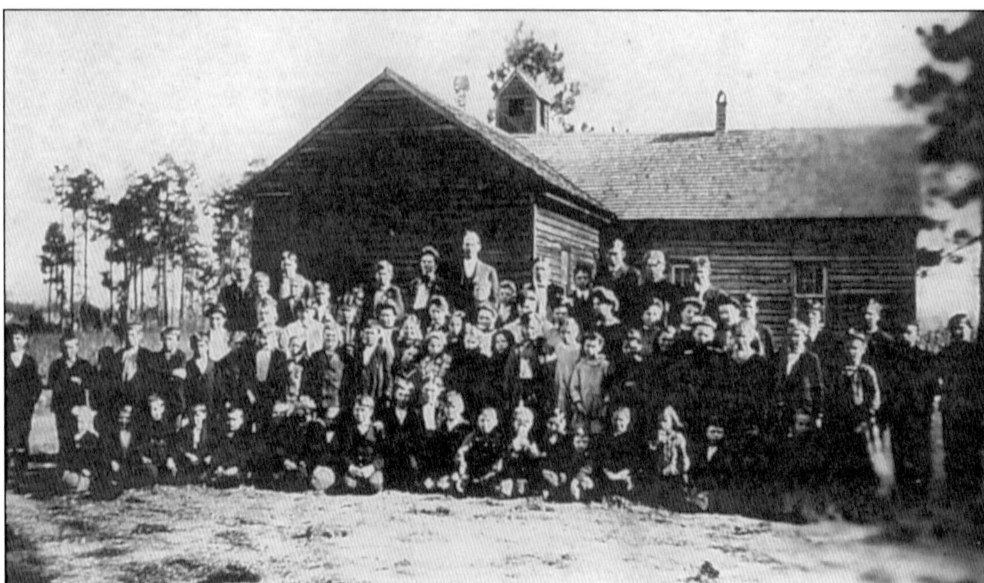

[GASTON SCHOOL, *C.* 1905.] Although this school was named the Gaston School, it was called Oakey Springs by the town's residents. Along with the Sandy Run Baptist Church, it was located on Oakey Springs Road, built on a tract of land (on the far side of the present Boy Scout Road) owned by James Reynolds. In Gaston in 1900, one teacher taught 57 students for a 20-week session. The students and their teacher posed for this picture at the rear of this L-shaped schoolhouse.

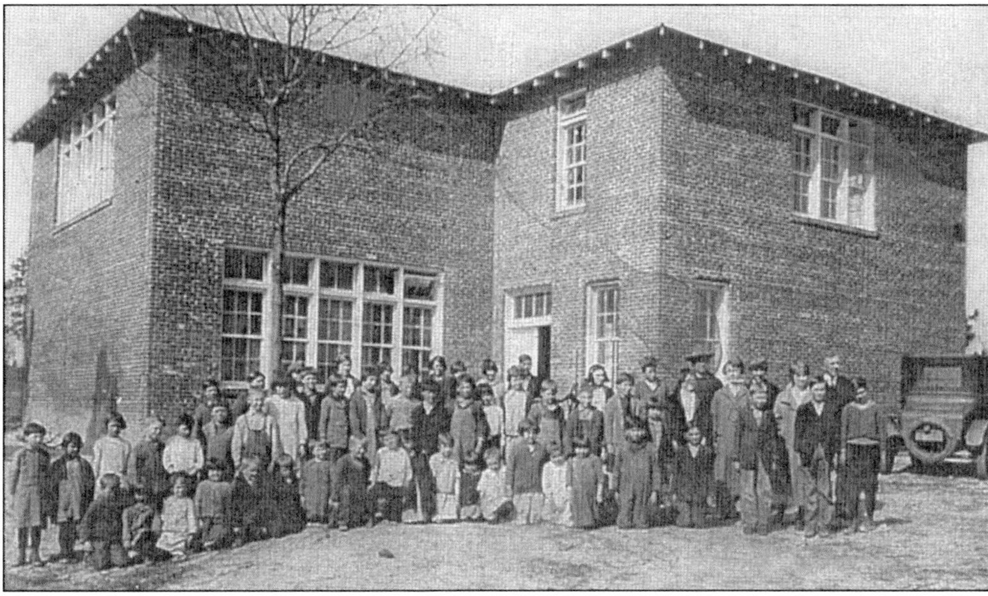

[Gaston Elementary School, c. 1922.] The two-story brick schoolhouse shown here, which by 1922 had replaced an oblong, two-teacher frame structure, still stands in much-altered condition near the corner of Carlisle and Oakey Springs Road. The second floor came to be considered a fire hazard and was removed. Through the years additional rooms were added as the student body grew. In 1984, the building was deeded back to the town, and since then it has been used as a civic center and museum.

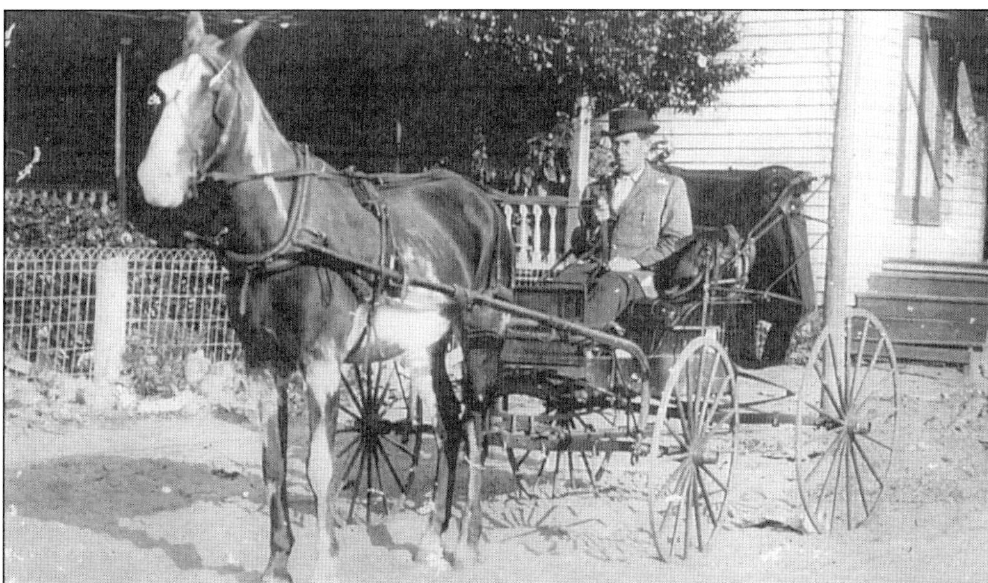

[Rural Mail Carrier Newlin B. Mack, Gaston, c. 1915.] Rural mail carrier Newlin B. Mack is shown here in his delivery buggy in front of J.F. Fallaw's Store, in which the Gaston post office was located and where Fallaw himself served as postmaster. Rural Free Delivery [RFD] began in 1896 with rural delivery inaugurated in Lexington County in 1901. Mack was a mail carrier for over 30 years.

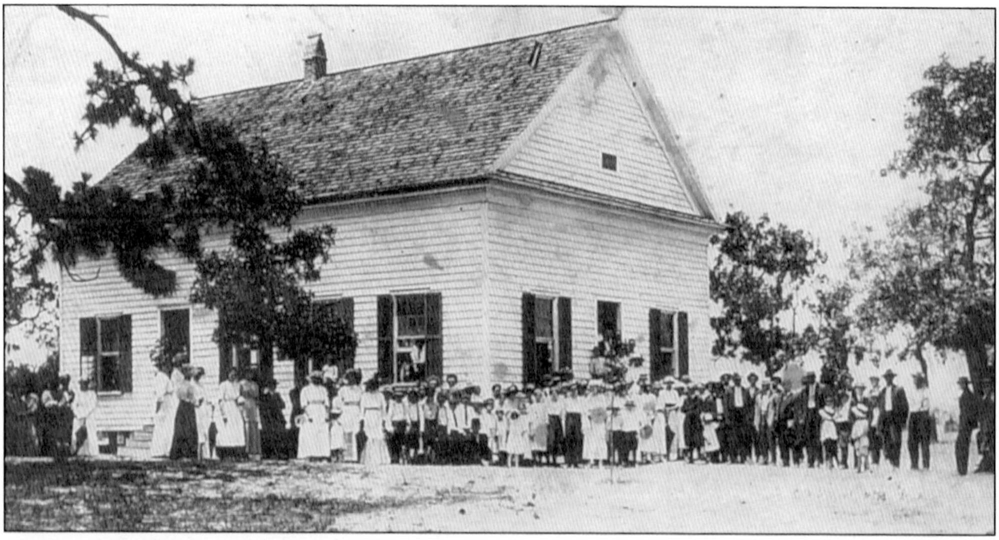

[SANDY RUN BAPTIST CHURCH, GASTON, *C.* 1912.] The Sandy Run Baptist Church had its beginnings in 1824 and by 1910 had a congregation of 198 members. The early sanctuary shown here was constructed in 1887 and could still be seen in 2000 at a new site on Oakey Springs Road near the turn onto Boy Scout Road. It was boarded up awaiting implementation of adaptive plans. The Sandy Run Baptist Church changed its name to the First Baptist Church of Gaston in 1954. Successive sanctuaries have been built on the original site with the current one erected in 1985.

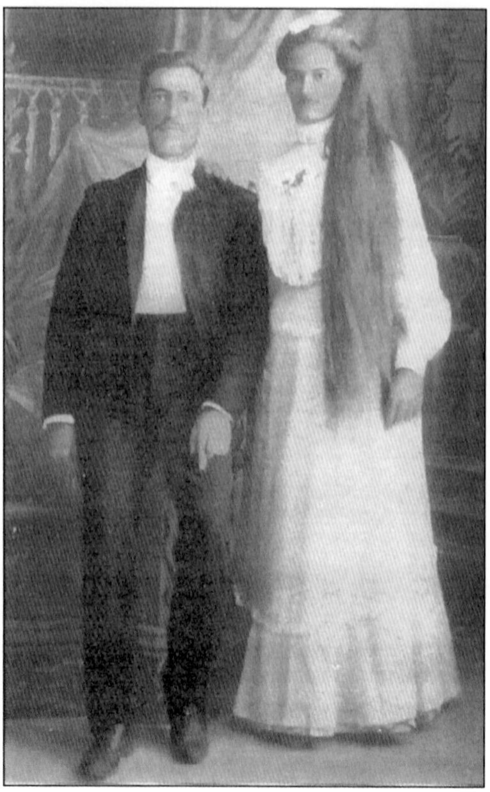

[PORTRAIT OF MR. AND MRS. CHARLES S. WALSH, *C.* 1905.] Charles Shuford Walsh (1879–1951) and Lula Arabelle Craft Walsh (1877–1928) lived off W.E. Jeffcoat and Sharon Church Road in the Cross Roads section about 3 miles west of Swansea. Their church was Antioch Baptist, and their children attended the Cross Roads School. Lula Walsh's daughter remembers that her mother could actually sit down on her hair.

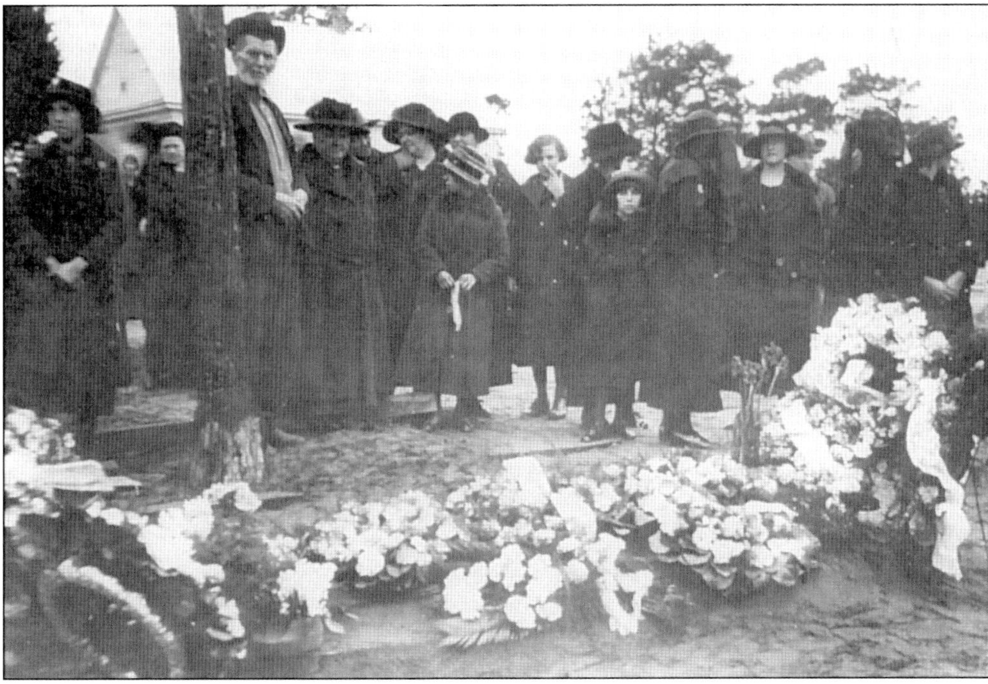

[Funeral of James E. Price, Gaston.] February 7, 1925, Sandy Run Baptist Church, Gaston, SC. This image documents the funeral of James E. Price (1903–1925), who was a policeman in New Brookland, where he was killed in the line of duty. His body was returned to his family home in Gaston for a funeral at the Sandy Run Baptist Church and burial in the family plot in the church's cemetery.

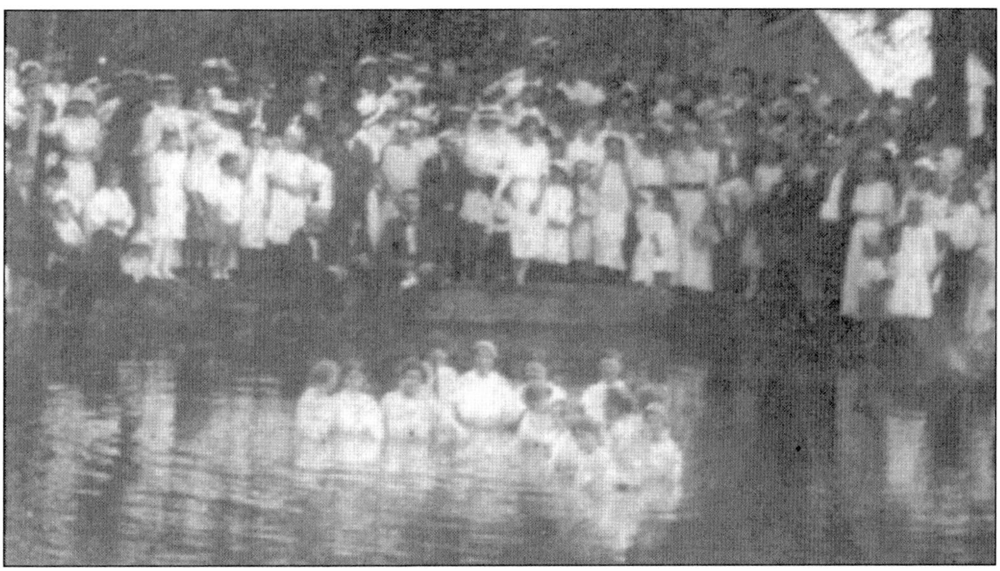

[Baptism at Huckabee's Pond, *c.* 1915.] The Sandy Run Baptist Church preferred to travel the 3.5 miles down Mack Street to Huckabee's Pond on Sandy Run Creek for their scheduled outdoor baptismal services. The entire congregation attended, dressed in their Sunday best. A building was located at the pond for changing into and out of the baptismal clothing.

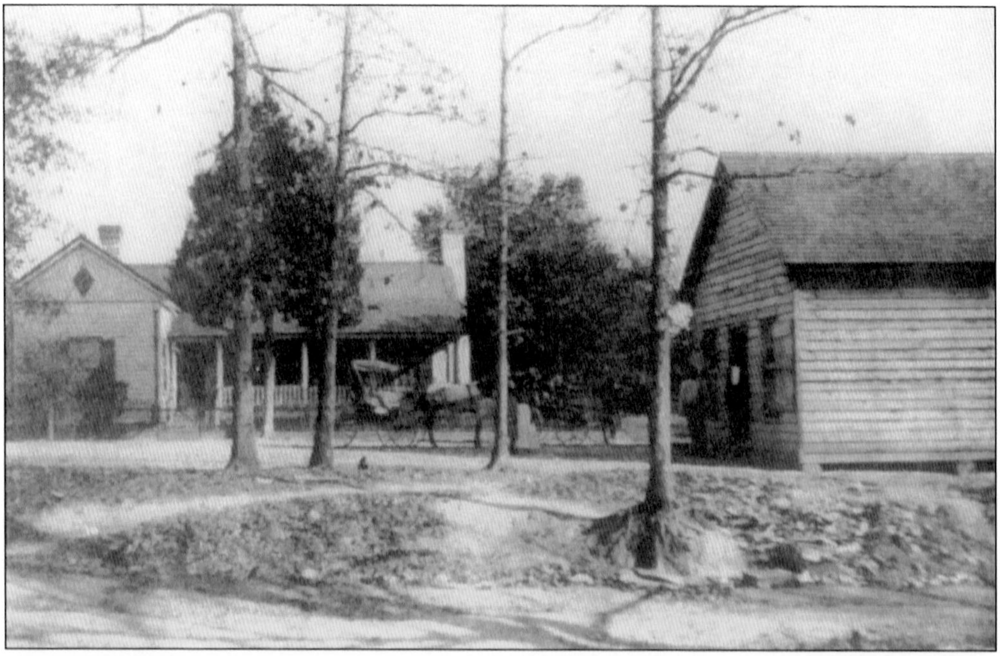

[Hallmans' House and Store, c. 1920.] The Hallman residence seen at left above—formerly owned by the Huckabee family—continued in 2000 to occupy its original site on Pine Plain Road. The store on the right, which sold Huckabee's flours and other milled products during this early era, was moved to a site about a quarter of a mile north and also still stood on Pine Plain Road.

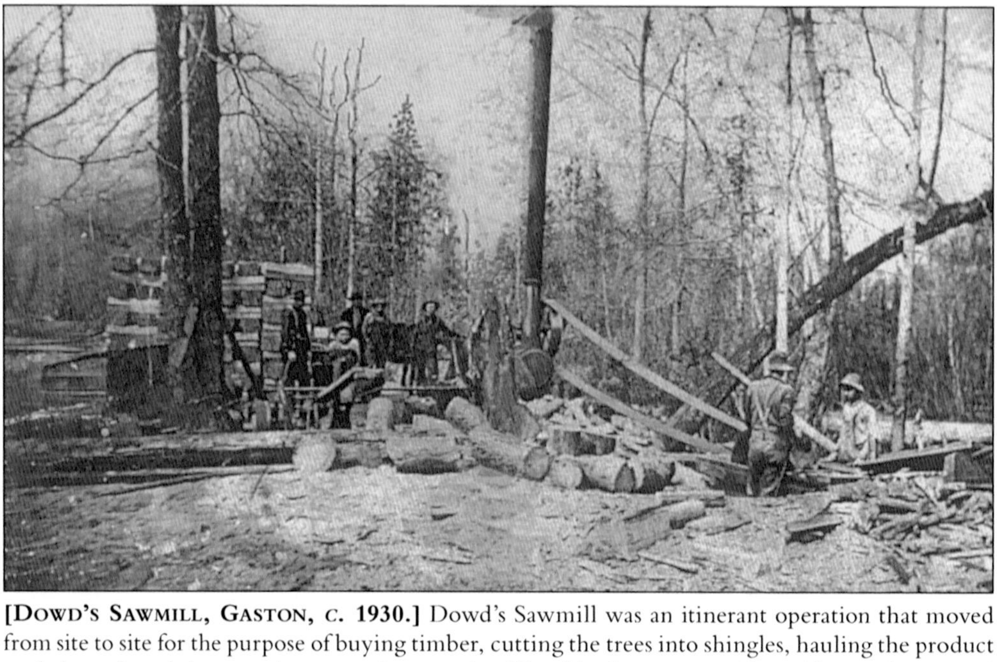

[Dowd's Sawmill, Gaston, c. 1930.] Dowd's Sawmill was an itinerant operation that moved from site to site for the purpose of buying timber, cutting the trees into shingles, hauling the product to their yard, and then moving on to the next site. The shingles were used in residences, barns, and other buildings in the area. The men pictured above, from left to right, are as follows: John H. Dowd, Loan Dowd, Harry W. Dowd, Belton Dowd, Ben Spires, Henry Dowd, and Gary Dowd.

[Portrait of the Craft Family Men with Musical Instruments, c. 1920.] Portrayed here with banjo and guitar in an unidentified venue are (seated, left) Thomas J. Craft (1882–1970), (seated, right) David I. Craft (1884–1949) and (standing, left) Samuel M. Craft (1880–1949), sons of the Loyd Harrison Crafts, who had a farm on Bachman Dykes Road (near Sharon Church Road) in the Cross Roads section. Standing at right is their brother-in-law, Charles S. Walsh (1879–1951). The family attended the Antioch Baptist Church (where the brothers are buried) and the children went to the Cross Roads School, which their grandfather helped to establish. The young men enjoyed providing musical entertainment for church events and community dances, or "frolics."

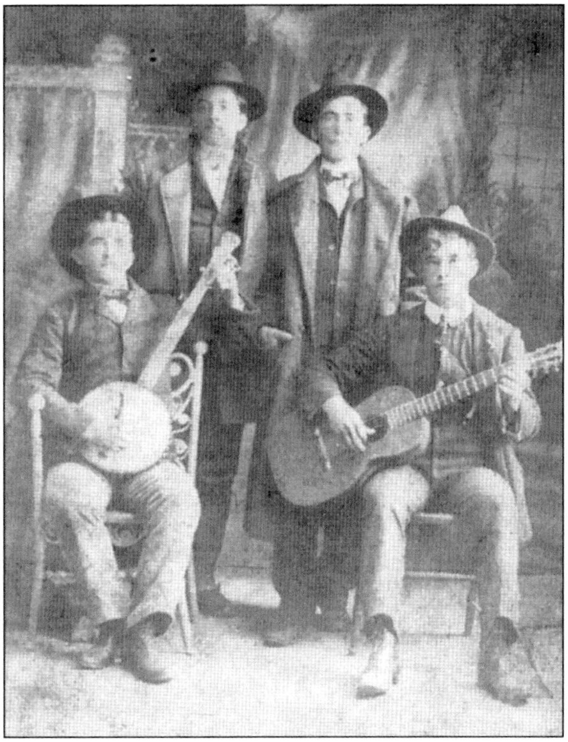

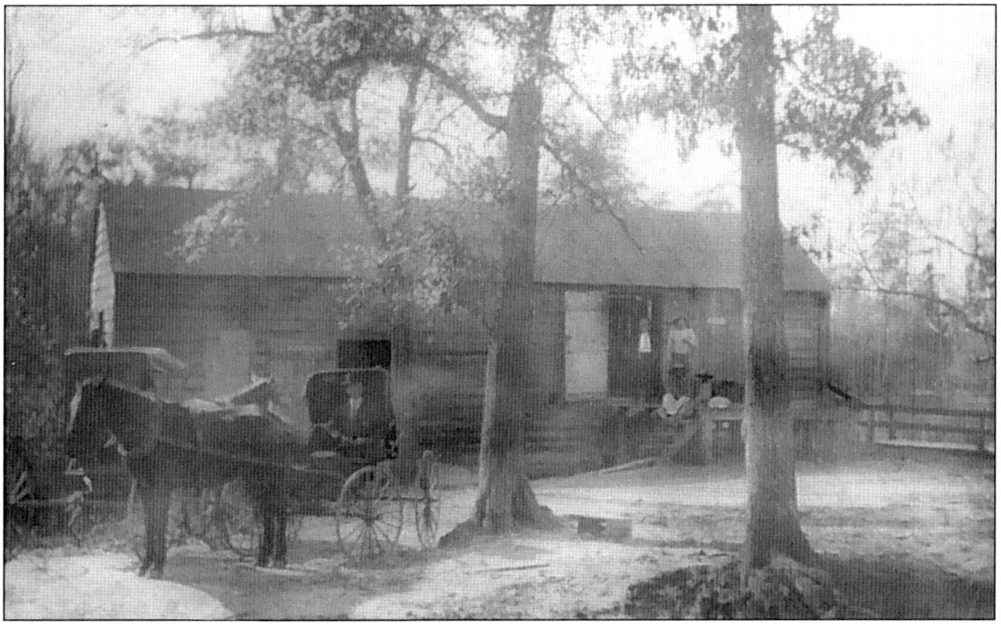

[Huckabee's Gristmill, c. 1918.] According to Elsie Rast Stuart, Huckabee's Mill, located about 3 miles southeast of Gaston and 3 miles northeast of Swansea on Huckabee's Pond, was a working mill until the 1930s (see "Roads, Railroads, and Bridges in Southern Lexington County" in *Names in South Carolina*, Winter 1981). Owned by the Hallman family, it still stood on Pine Plain Road in 2000.

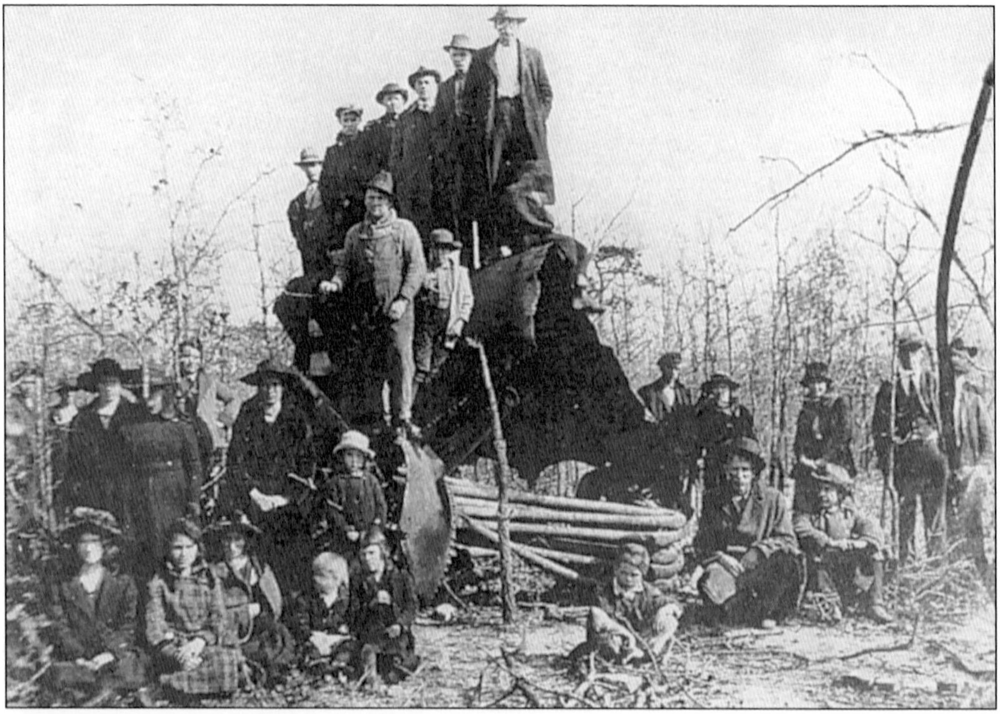

[Mourners in Aftermath of Sawmill Explosion, Gaston.] On Monday afternoon, February 11, 1922, the explosion of a 40-horsepower-type boiler at Sightler and Guignard's sawmill and shingle factory at Gaston took the lives of two workers—35-year-old James Griffin and his 14-year-old nephew, Burnett Griffin—and injured a third. The boiler was blown about 100 yards and some 50 feet into the air. This image presumably shows a crowd of friends and relations with the remains of the boiler on site at the sawmill.

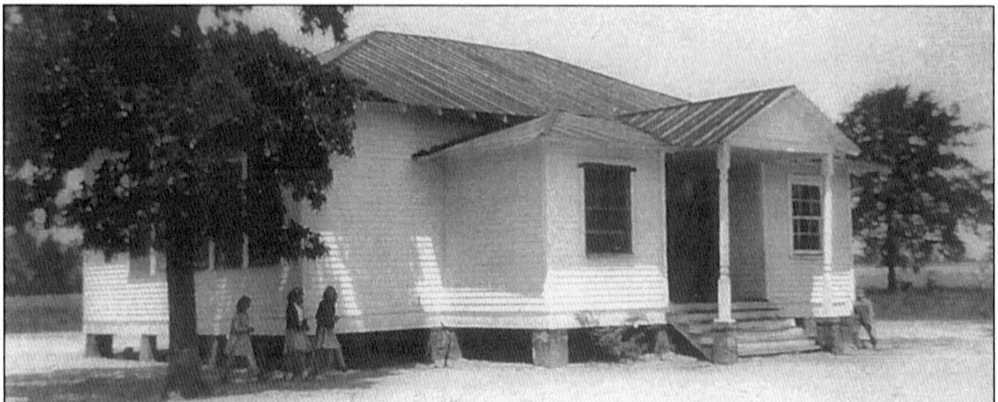

[Cross Roads School, c. 1920.] The schoolhouse pictured here replaced a timber one that may have existed on this site as early as 1849. In 1900 it served 40 students. By 1916 Lueco Gunter described this structure as "a very poor building with poor teaching equipment" and reported the district (#40) needed a new two- or three-room building to house its 91 students and 2 teachers. The "new" school building that was then erected could still be seen in 2000 near the Antioch Church a short distance from the junction of W.E. Jeffcoat Road and Sharon Church Road in a wooded area on the property of Barbara Poole. It is currently used to store hay.

[PORTRAIT OF TIMOTHY AND SARAH ANN CRAFT, MACEDON, *C.* 1905] Timothy Walter Craft (1842–1925) and Sara Ann [Wise] Craft (1843–1910) lived at Macedon, where they had a farm, kept a store, and operated a gristmill on Cedar Creek. Walter was also postmaster and station master at nearby Macedon Depot. He had served in the Confederate Army under General Johnson Hagood.

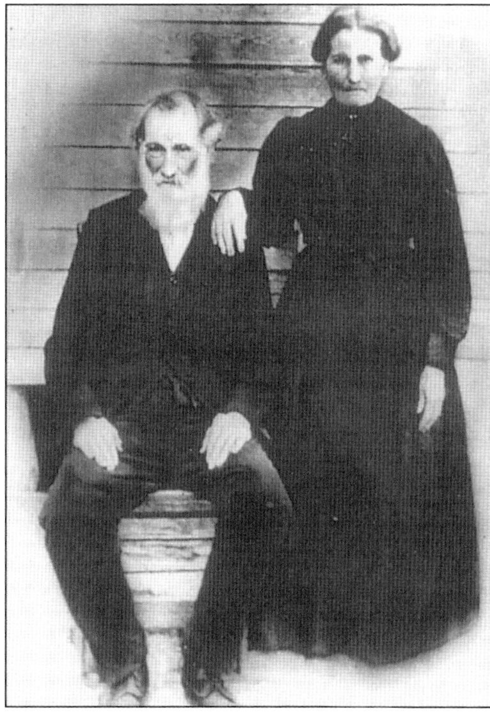

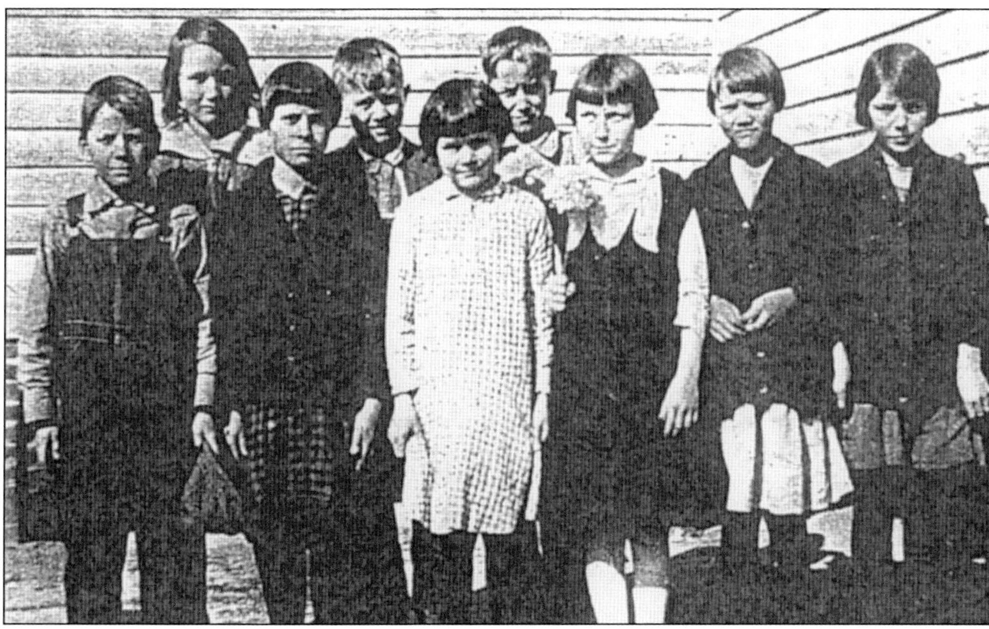

[CROSS ROADS SCHOOL STUDENTS, *C.* 1929.] This group picture of sixth grade pupils shows students who walked to school from various farms in that community. Early rural schools were placed in localities that did not have a school within a 3-mile radius. Because the teachers for these schools usually lived in distant towns, they had to find room and board with a family having extra rooms in the community for the number of weeks that the school was in session. Like the children, they would walk the 2 or 3 miles to the schoolhouse.

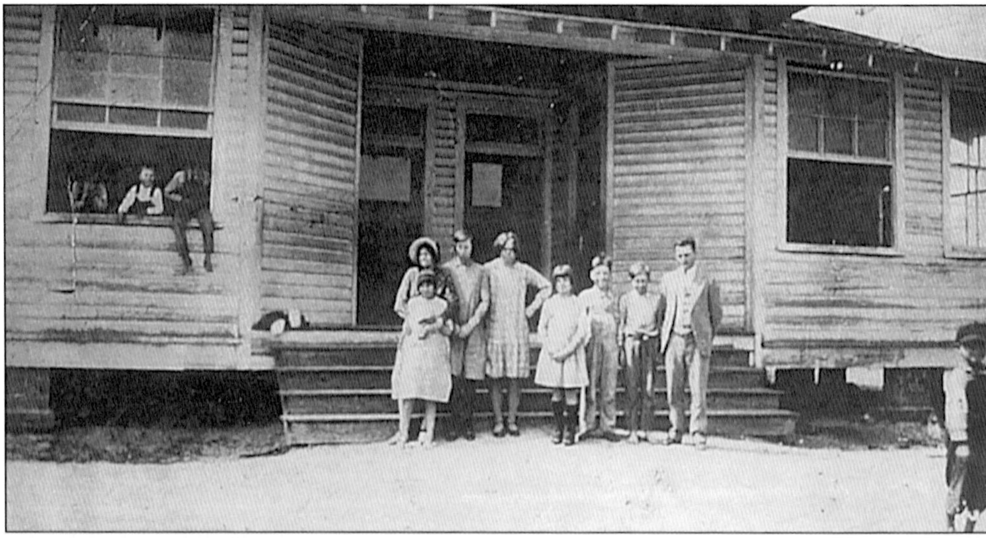

[Sharp's Hill School, c. 1920.] Sharp's Hill School served this community located about 3 miles west of Gaston near the intersection of Sharp's Hill and Meadowfield Roads. Since this building appears to consist of more than one room, presumably it is the one that Lueco Gunter refers to when he states that "the old [one-room] building is to give place to a new, modern one with the next session." Enrollment during the 1914–1915 session was 47 boys and 40 girls, with an average daily attendance of 53 students for a session of 100 days. The school was supported by a special tax. A small community building was founded on the site in 2000.

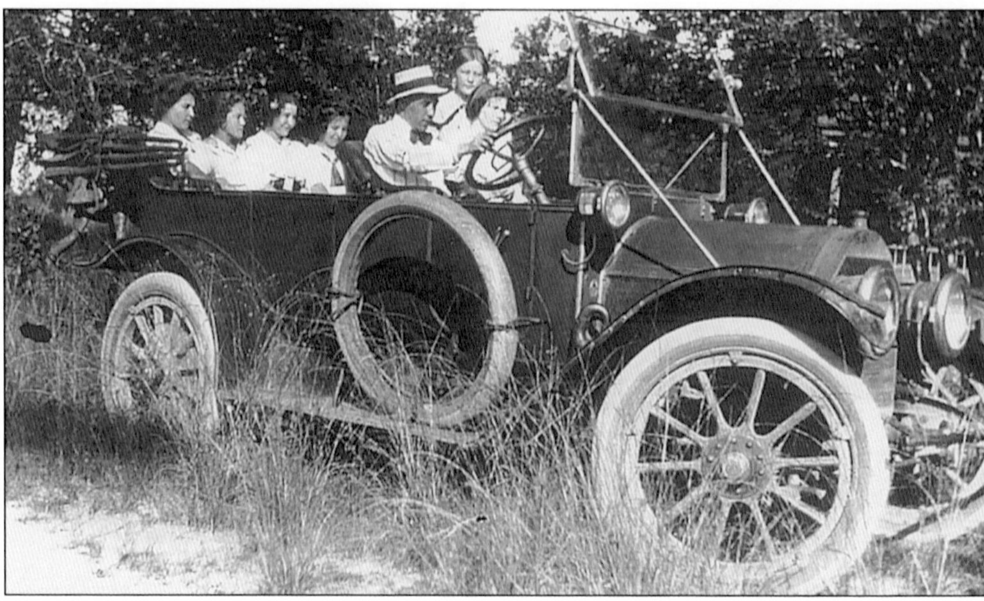

[Portrait of Grover C. Goodwin and Friends in His Automobile, Gaston, c. 1918.] Viewcards after 1910 often depicted individuals or groups of friends around their automobiles, which by then were becoming not only essential means of conveyance, but status symbols as well. Shown here behind the wheel of his car is Grover Cleveland Goodwin (1886–1941), a farmer as well as a photographer who documented the people, sites, and activities of southeastern Lexington County and elsewhere.

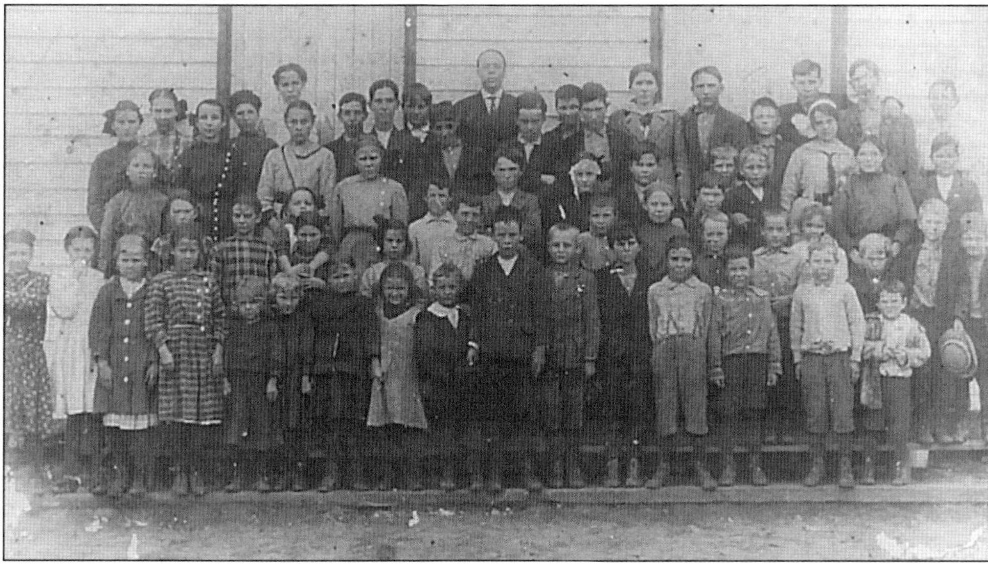

[Athens School Class Picture.] The old one-teacher Athens schoolhouse, which had 50 students in 1900, had not changed much in 1912 when this picture was taken. By 1916, Lueco Gunter called it "one of the best in the county . . . a well arranged, modern, two-room building" that had an enrollment of 54 boys and 40 girls taught by 2 teachers in a session of 120 days. Located on US 321 halfway between Gaston and Swansea, it still can be seen with the rooms that were later added to each side to make it usable as a motel. It has also served as a community center and as a church mission. In 2000 it was under repair.

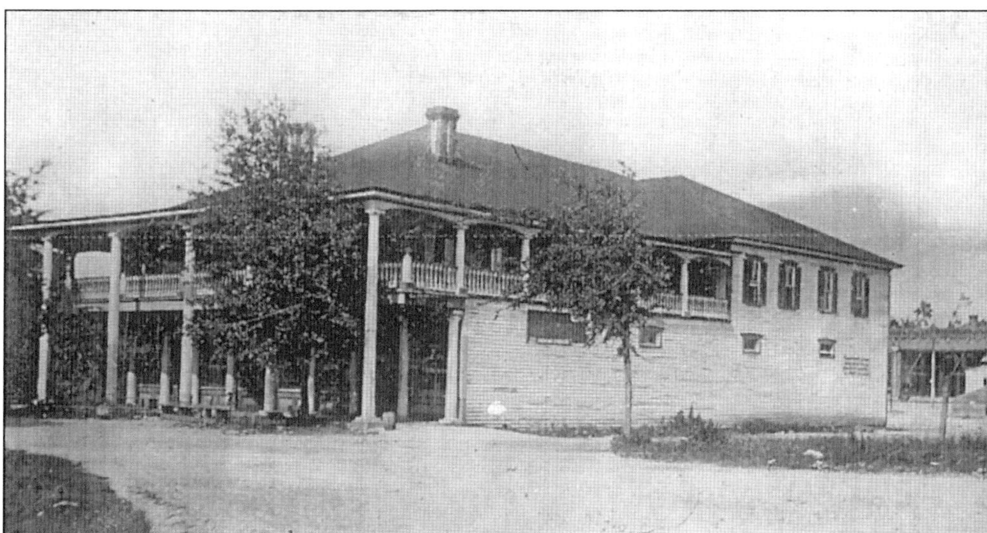

[Swansea Hotel, c. 1909.] The Swansea Hotel, which stood across from the railroad depot on Cardiff Avenue between West Second and West Third Streets, was in operation by 1913. The hotel's private rooms and a dining room were located on the second floor, which featured a long hall and porch that extended around much of the building. On the ground level were various stores and a barbershop. Once a center for area political gatherings, the hotel was destroyed by fire before World War II.

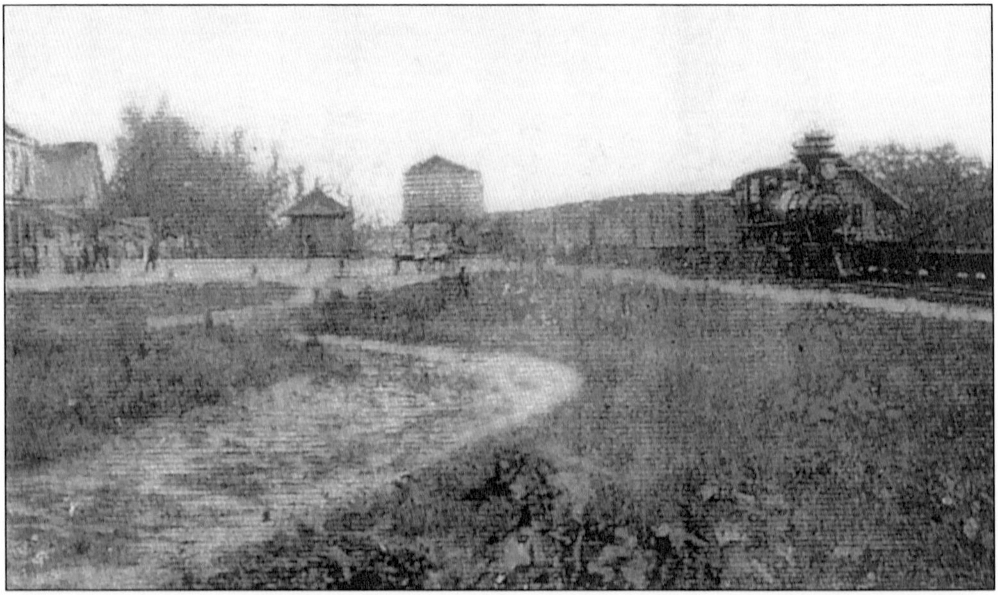

[Depot, Swansea, c. 1905.] An 1895 Rand, McNally map shows the old Florida Central & Peninsular Railroad (FC&P)—the third rail line to cross the county at the time and the first to take a southern route operating between Savannah and Columbia via Swansea, Gaston, and Dixiana. The FC&P was later absorbed by the Seaboard Air Line. The depot shown above is probably the one built in 1890, two years before Swansea was incorporated.

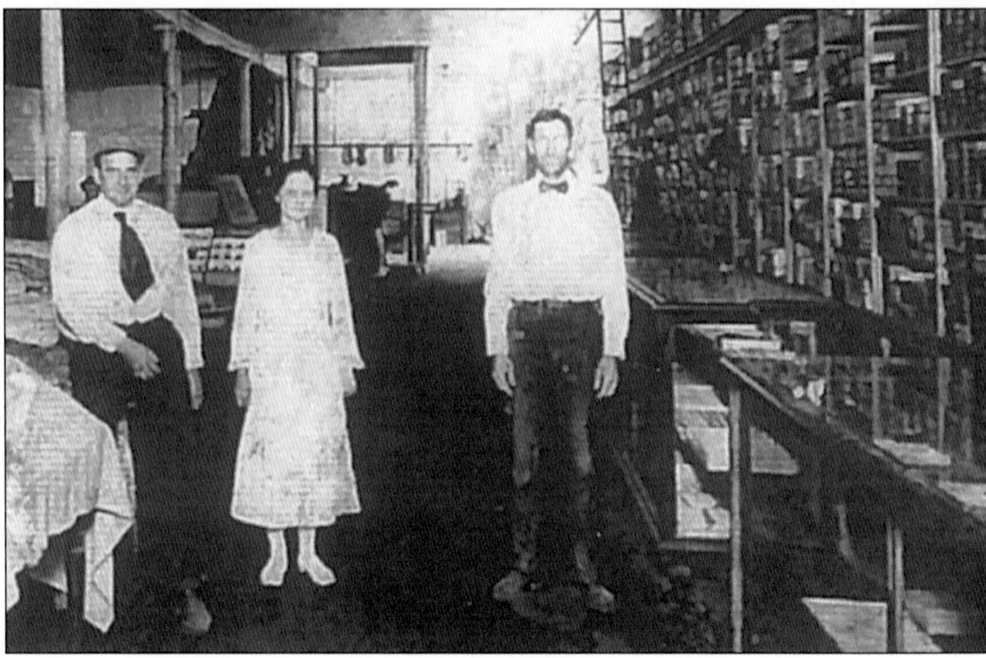

[Rubin and Shecter Dry Goods Store, Swansea, c. 1910.] Rubin and Shecter's on Monmouth [Main] Street catered to Swansea's 700 residents (1910) and area farmers, turpentiners, and millers for whom the town was the banking and mercantile center. Pictured here in the store, from left to right, are Thurston Williams, Minnie Shecter, and B. Shecter.

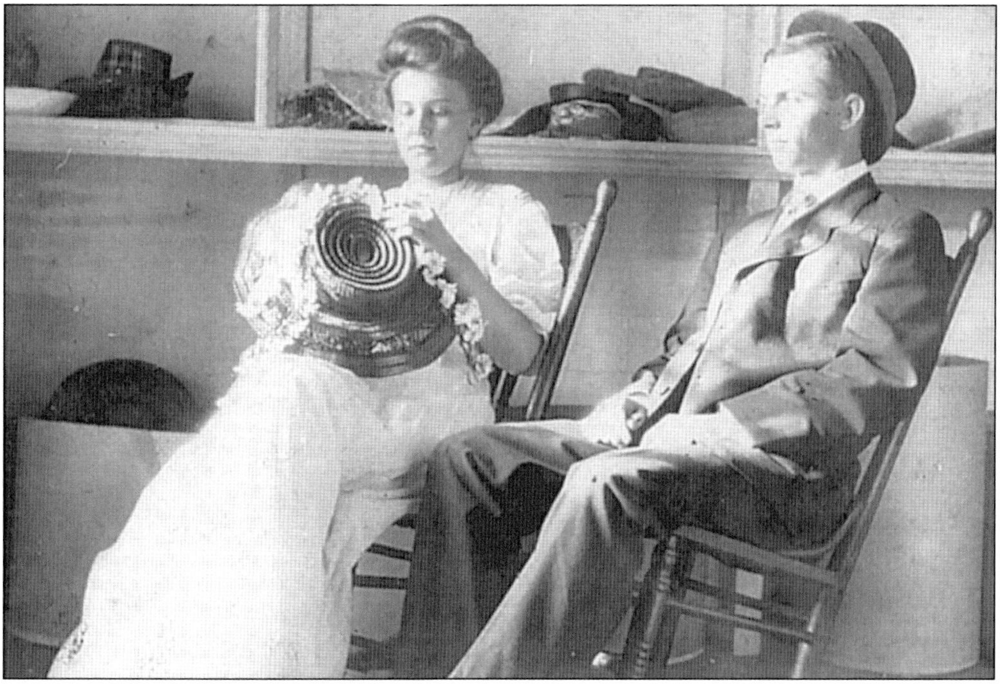

[Sallie Craft in Her Millinery Shop, Swansea, *c.* 1908.] Sallie Craft (1885–1954) operated a millinery shop on Monmouth Avenue during the first decade of the century. In this picture taken with an unidentified friend, she is shown fashioning one of the flower-trimmed hats popular at the time. J.H. Summer, a prominent resident of neighboring Newberry County during the late 19th century, made the remark that "no women worked outside the home except as a milliner, which was respectable." Although this photograph was not found in postcard form, its subject matter is of a kind often portrayed on viewcards during this era.

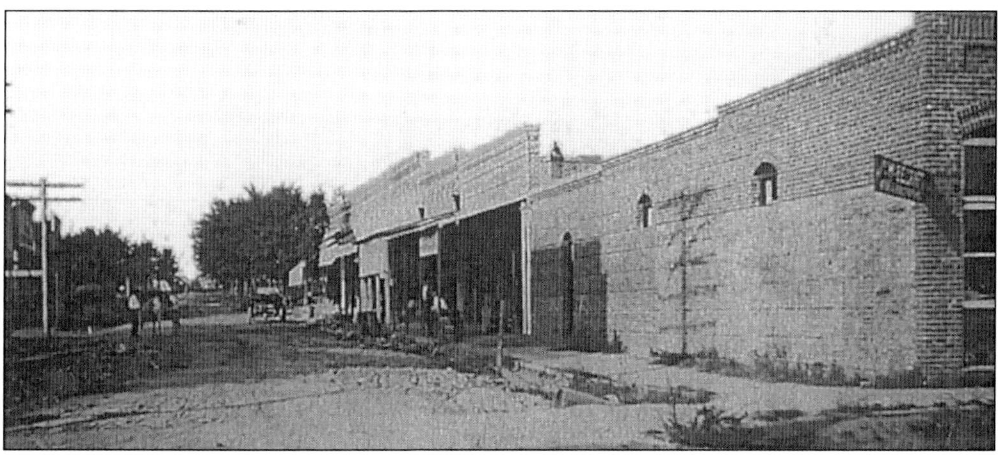

[Monmouth Avenue (Main Street), Swansea, 1910.] This view of the east side of Monmouth Avenue, looking north, shows what the block looked like prior to its destruction by fire in the 1920s, when Swansea had a population of some 800 inhabitants but no fire department. The building to the right, at the corner of Third Street, is remembered as the site of a Chevrolet car dealership. Beyond it was Bernstein's dry goods store, and farther up the block were Sharpe's grocery store and meat market, and Rubin and Shecter's dry goods store.

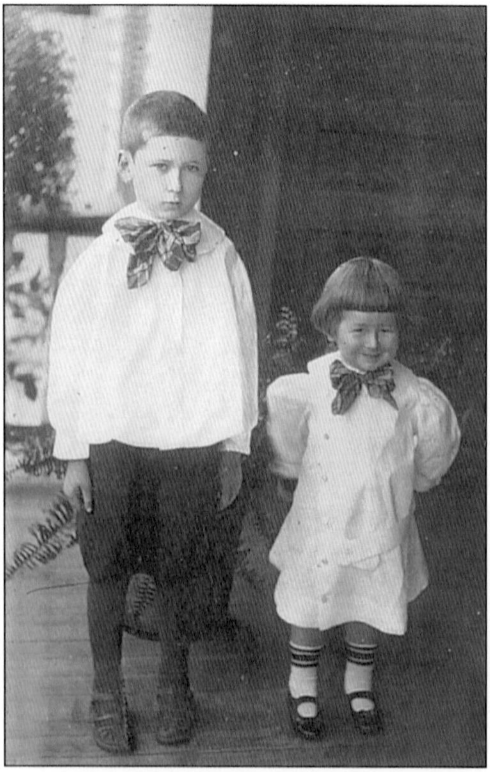

[Portrait of Harold and Ralph Witt, Swansea, c. 1929.] This portrait of Lee Harold Witt (1905–1949) and his brother, Ralph Wannamaker Witt (1909–1964), was taken on the steps of their home on Church Street (US 321) in Swansea, the site of the BB&T Bank in 2000. Harold attended Wofford and Clemson, came home to farm, and became owner and partner of Witt Brothers, a supply store in Swansea. Ralph also attended Wofford, farmed, taught school in Swansea and Leesville, and became director and vice president of the Columbia Production Credit Association (1946 to 1961).

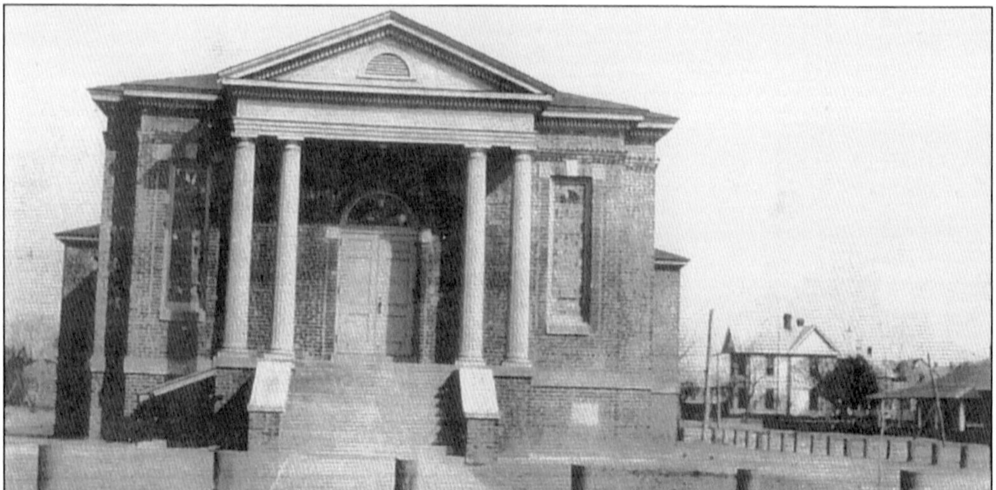

[Methodist Church and Residences on Lady Street, Swansea, c. 1909.] Built on land donated by Hilliard and Joanna Goodwin in 1894, the brick sanctuary seen here was erected between 1924 and 1926, replacing an earlier timber "Swansea Mission." To the right, on Lady Street, can be seen the large two-story, six-bedroom frame residence of Boynton E. and Sallie Rast Craft, who boarded the local schoolteachers (and at one time the school superintendent and his wife, Mr. and Mrs. William T. Wade). To the far right is the home of William Carlisle Rast, which burned in 1934. The Crafts' home burned on June 6, 1977.

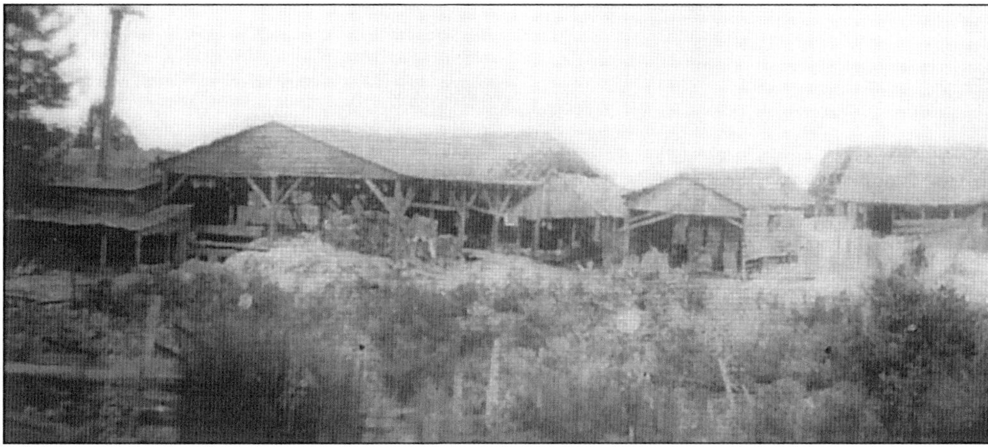

[W.B. Rast Sons Manufacturing Company, Swansea, *c.* 1920.] The Rast "basket factory," which was established by Mr. W. Bartowe Rast in 1914, faced Monmouth Avenue between Third and Fourth Streets. Swansea's only industry for many years, the Rast factory produced fine veneers, baskets, barrels, boxes, and vegetable crates. The view above shows the initial manufacturing sheds that no longer exist. The enterprise later included cotton ginning, seed buying, general milling, and ice manufacturing. L.O. Rast eventually joined his father in the business and operated the factory until 1964, even after a fire in 1946 destroyed much of the plant. Townspeople still remember the sound of the factory whistle, which blew at 7:00 a.m., at noon, and whenever there was a fire. Some of the factory's post-1946 structures still survived in 2000.

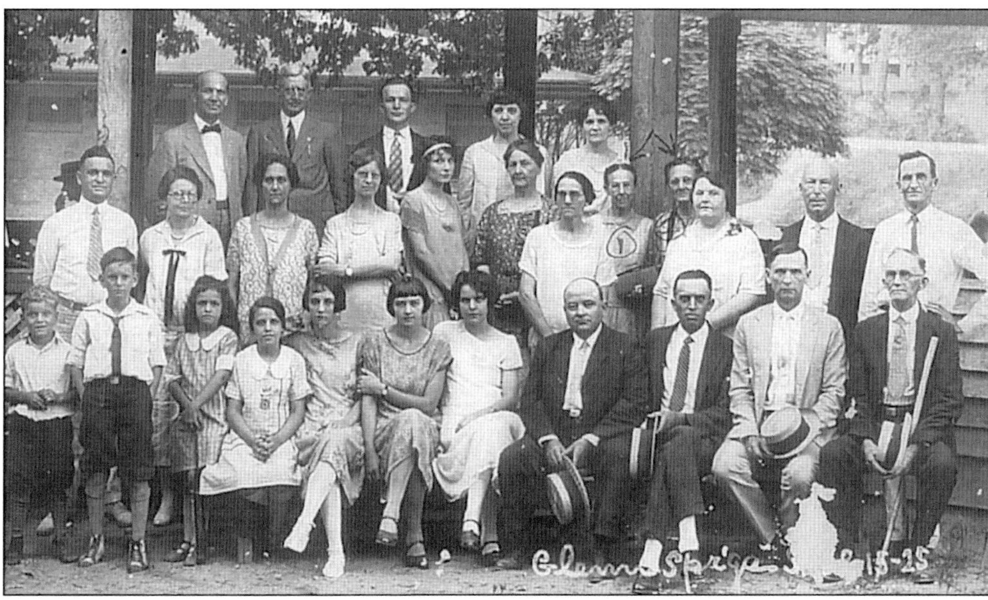

[Oliver and Rast Family Reunion at Glenn Springs, 1925.] In this era before air conditioning, those South Carolinians in the lower regions of the state who could afford to do so resorted to the Upcountry for as much of the summer season as they could manage. Members of the Oliver and Rast families from the Swansea area are shown here at a family reunion at Glenn Springs, a popular old mineral spa and vacation retreat in Spartanburg County. Located midway between Spartanburg and Union, Glenn Springs advertised itself as "one of the great human repair shops of the South."

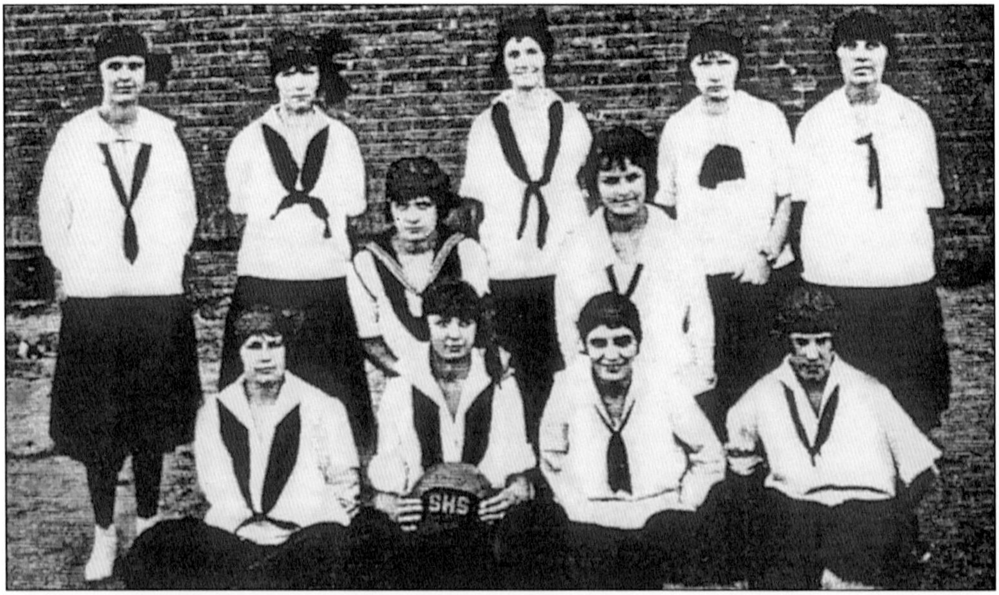

[Swansea High School Girls' Basketball Team, 1925.] This portrait of the Swansea High School girls' basketball team was taken against the backdrop of the school. The team members on the squad include A. Johnson, M. Rhoden, L. Dowling, L. Hutto, M. Rucker, H. Redmond, I. Craft, K. Chaplin, G. Roberts, B. McCullough, M. Johnson, and M. Rowell. The games were played on a cement court behind the school.

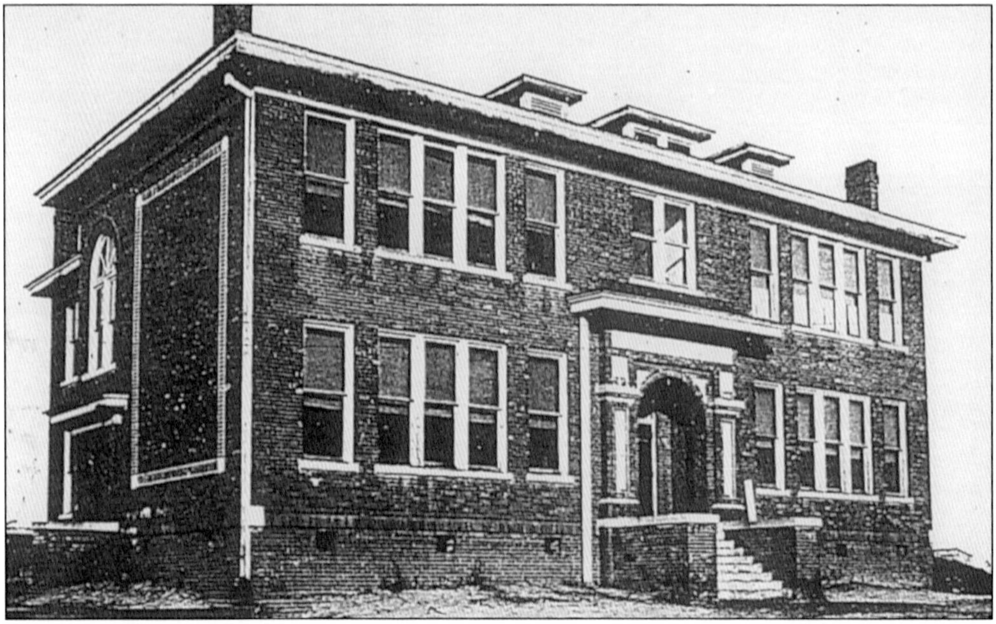

[Swansea High School, *c.* 1918.] The two-story brick school building above, which was erected on N. Lawrence Avenue by 1917, at first housed grades seven through ten. In 1919, Swansea ranked as a third-class high school with two full-time teachers and was one of the county's six regional high schools. When a new high school was constructed south of this one on the same block in 1926, the 1917 structure then became the grammar school. It was torn down *c.* 1953.

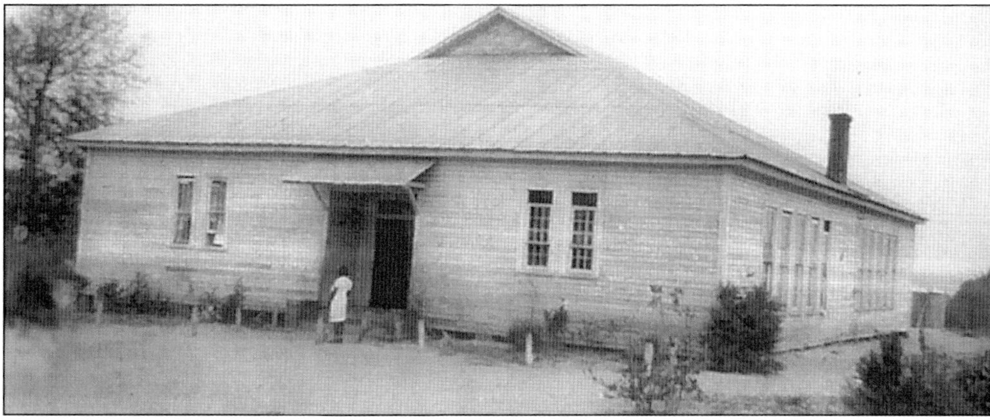

[Swansea School, c. 1930s.] This is the frame schoolhouse that once served Swansea's African-American community during the early era of educational segregation. Erected in 1953 on Redmond Mill Road (LC 692) on the southeast side of town, the school building is now utilized as the Lexington County School District Four headquarters. It bears the name of Monroe Pinckney, a lifelong resident of Swansea, graduate of Benedict College, and a prominent member of the community.

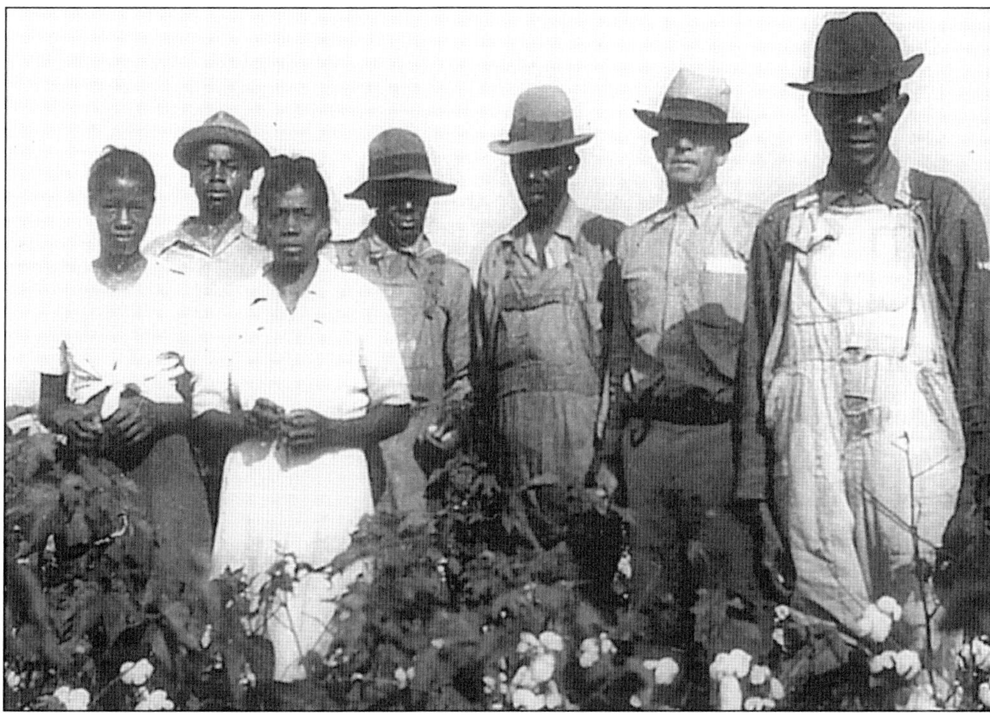

[John ("Jake") Lucas with a Group of Sharecroppers, Swansea, c. 1920.] As much as any other picture in the collection, this one shows the human and economic reality of the times in South Carolina, when cotton was still the county's major crop and sharecropping was one of the chief systems for providing farm labor. Shown here (second from right) with a group of sharecroppers is John Jacob Lucas (1880–1958), who sold part of his cotton field to the district when a new high school was built on Lawrence Avenue in 1926. The Lucas home still stands just south of the old school property, which has been adapted for residential use.

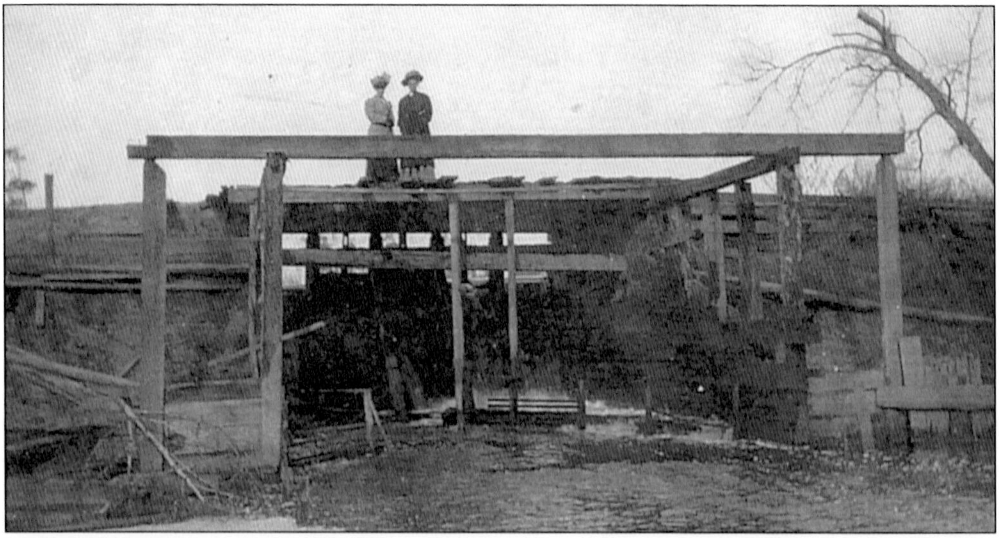

[Spillway at Gunter's Pond (Lake Swansea), c. 1900.] Gunter's Pond (or Lake Swansea, as it is also known by area residents), now owned by W.O. Shealy, is located just west of town on the Swansea Road (which goes to Pelion). In 1886, A.W. Martin, who built his residence near the future site of the railroad, proceeded to clear and dam Bull Swamp Creek so that timber could be floated down the creek to the Edisto River and on to market in Charleston. The pond became a popular site for swimming, boating, and fishing. The two women standing on the bridge above the dam and spillway are looking downstream (east).

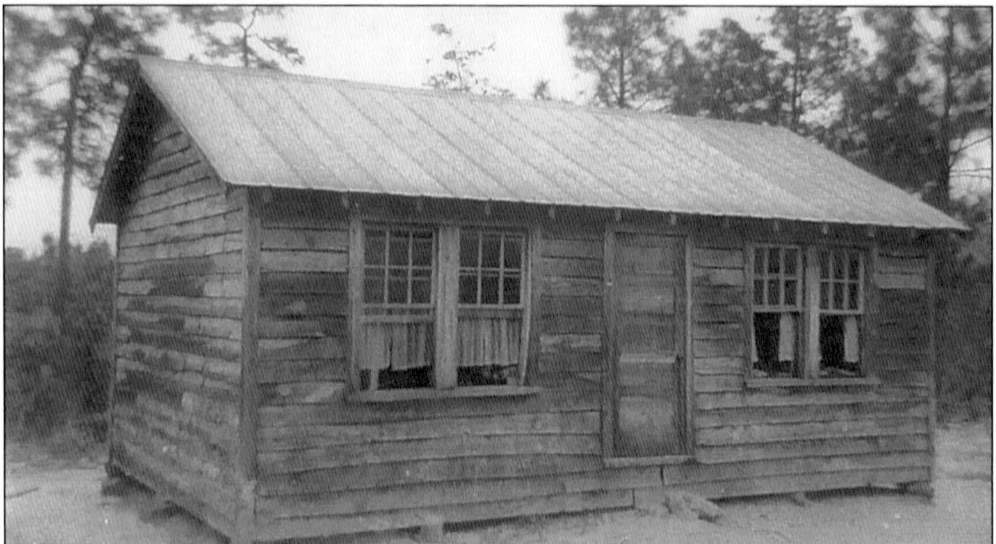

[Culler School, near Swansea, c. 1930s.] This one-room schoolhouse at Culler, a rural neighborhood east of Swansea on LC 164, was located on an unpaved road off Calvary Church Road and served the precinct's African-American community. "Only about ten percent of the colored schoolhouses in the state are respectable," wrote State Supervisor of Colored Schools J.B. Felton in his annual report for 1922. "Many of them are not only filthy and germ-breeding places but are so small that the children can hardly be packed into them and they can neither be kept warm in winter nor cool in summer."

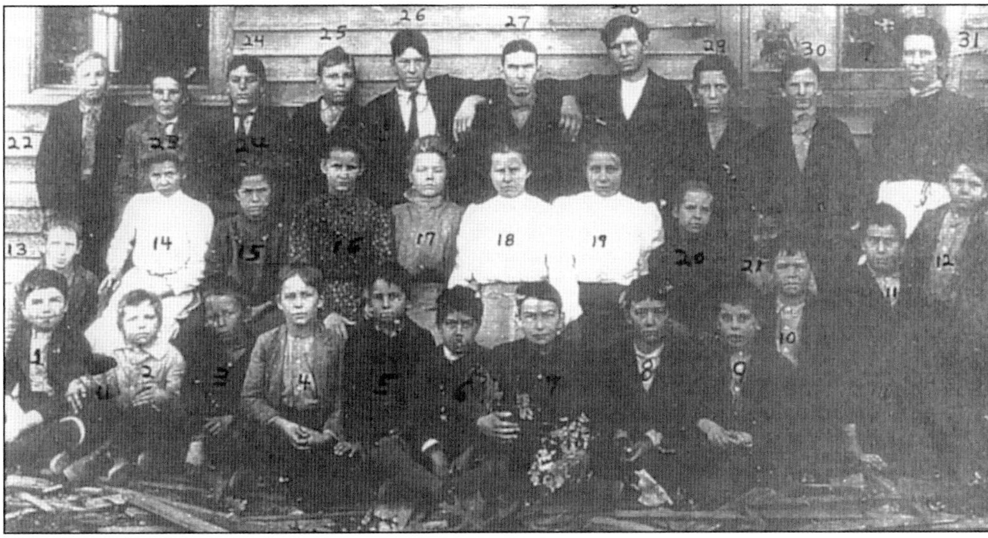

[Calvary School, near Swansea, 1908.] The one-teacher Calvary School was located about 4 miles east of Swansea near the crossroads of St. Matthews Road (SC 6) and Calvary Church Road (LC 164). At the time this picture was taken, it was taught by 1904 Leesville College graduate Dora Craft Redmond (1878–1962), shown here (second row, far right) with her 30 pupils. By 1915 Calvary had developed into a two-teacher school with 95 students. The building was considered substantial and well finished, but not altogether modern in its lighting and other appointments. Among the other teachers associated with this school were Mrs. Vivian Rast Wannamaker and Mrs. Splawn Rollins Davis, who in 1949, when Calvary was closed, moved with her pupils to the consolidated school in Swansea.

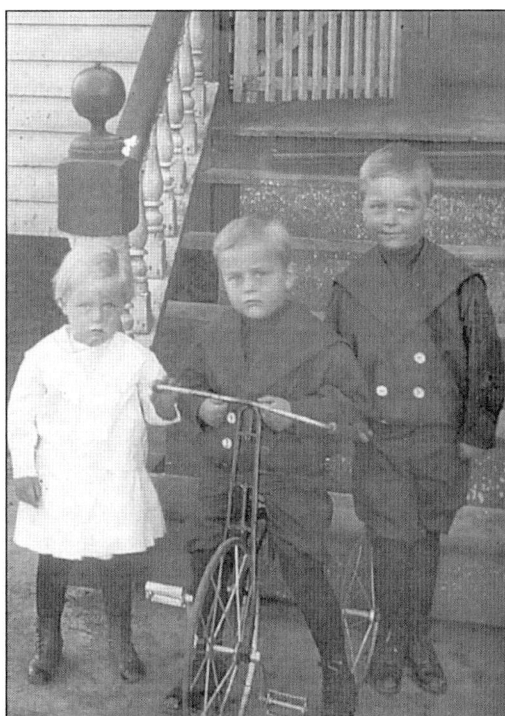

[Portrait of the Wannamaker Boys near Swansea, c. 1910.] Shown here at the front steps of their country home (which in 2000 was still standing) 6 miles east of Swansea are the sons of farmer Wade Hampton Wannamaker and his wife, Vivian Rast Wannamaker. Cecil V. Wannamaker (1909–1998), left, attended Clemson and became a farmer and rural mail carrier. Theron Rast ("Bill") Wannamaker (1908–1972), middle, graduated from Clemson and the Illinois Institute of Technology, served as an army officer in WW II, and retired as an executive with Hunt-Wesson Foods. Curtis H. Wannamaker (1907–1996), right, graduated from Wofford, served as an air force officer during WW II and the Korean War, and retired from Exxon Corporation in 1969.

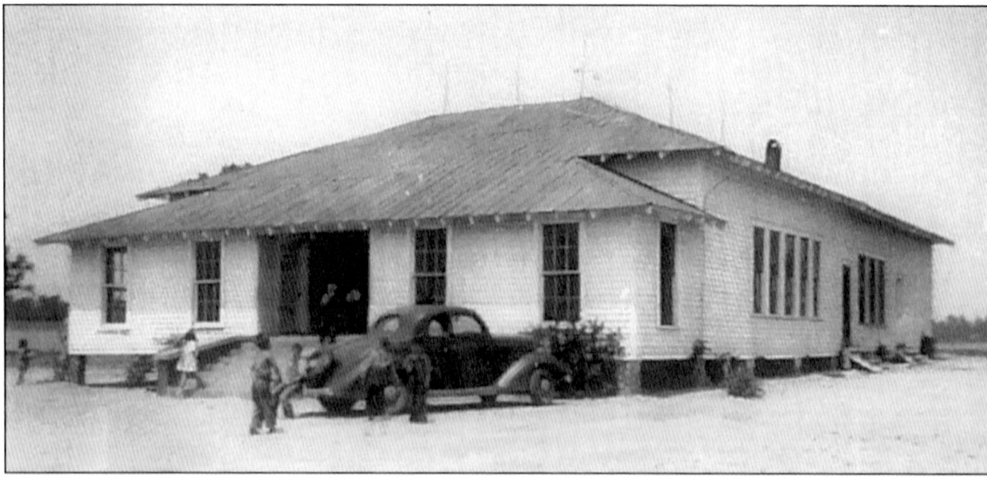

[North Edisto School, c. 1930s.] The North Edisto School (District #87)—the last of the expanded districts—was located off US 178 on Mack Edisto Road 7 miles southeast of Pelion near the county line. In 1916, Lueco Gunter described it as a one-man school with 94 students in a 110-day session. He advised the expansion of its teaching staff and school term, as well as the erection of a new building. The 1920s-era structure shown here no longer stands.

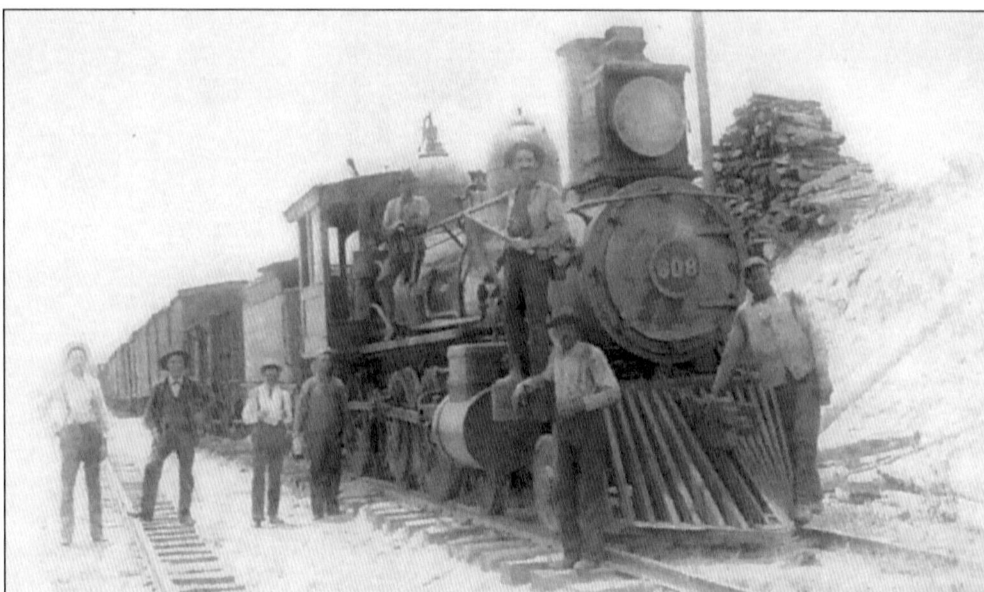

[First Train in Pelion, c. 1900.] The route begun in 1900 by the Carolina Midland Railway Company later became that of the Southern Railway, which created a string of rural depots south of Cayce. The daughter of a railroad official used her interest in mythology to name these five fuel and watering stops: Styx, Ossa (later changed to Edmund), Macedon, Pelion, and Thor. Pelion, a site selected for the pure filtered water of the Fort and Cedar Ponds that was needed for steam engines, became the only permanent town on the line. Its population grew from 75 in 1910 to 184 in 1920. In 1966, the old station was sold and moved to the property of Lt. Col. James F. Rast.

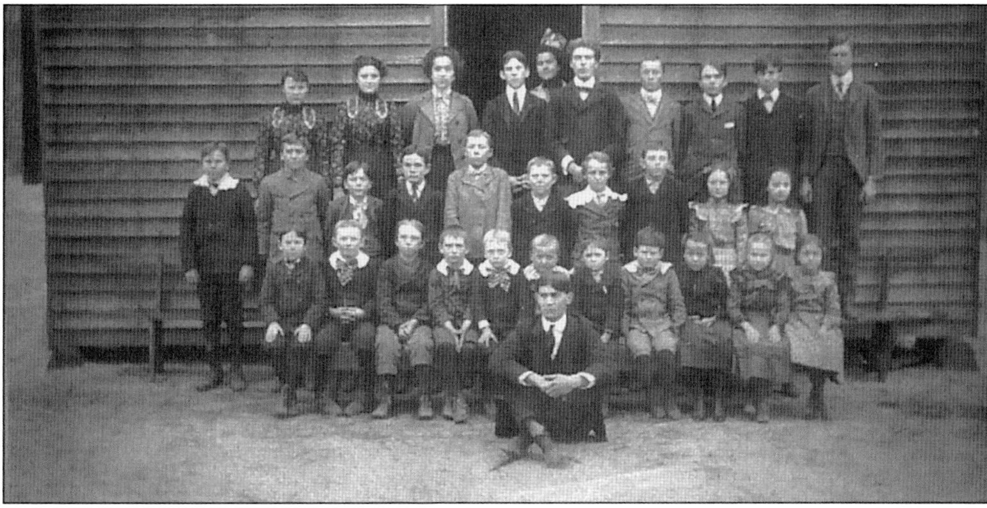

[Black Creek School near Thor, c. 1905.] In 1900, this one-teacher frame school building on the west side of Black Creek, 4.5 miles south of Pelion off Bub Shumpert Road, housed 17 students for a 20-week session that year. In 1915, when Gunter visited the school, little had changed. He described the structure that then served 23 students in a 120-day session as "one of the poorest in the county, a small, unceiled, frame house with inadequate lighting and in a rather dilapidated condition." Occasionally these small timber schoolhouses have been called "old field schools," a term that referred to their often dilapidated condition and rural location.

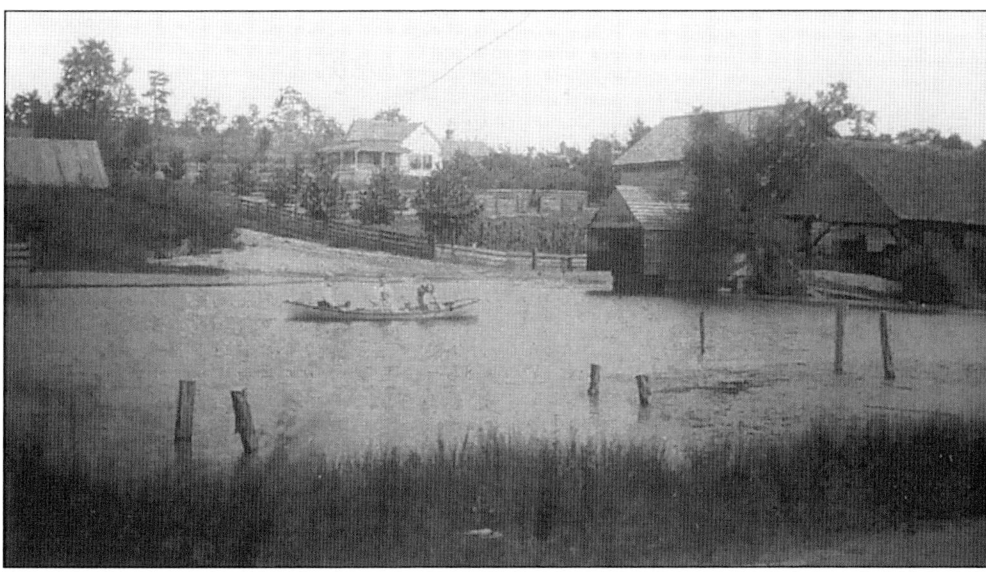

[Fort House and Pond, Pelion, c. 1910.] The Fort home site—pond, gristmills, and sawmills—was the homestead of James C. and Lessie Haltiwanger Fort, who owned the land that included the present site of Pelion. The scene above shows not only the Fort residence, barns, mills, and other buildings, but also the Fort children in the boat on the pond. Mrs. Fort granted the land for the railroad and depot, which became the hub for the town. She also had the town site surveyed and gave land for the churches and schools. The buildings seen here no longer stand.

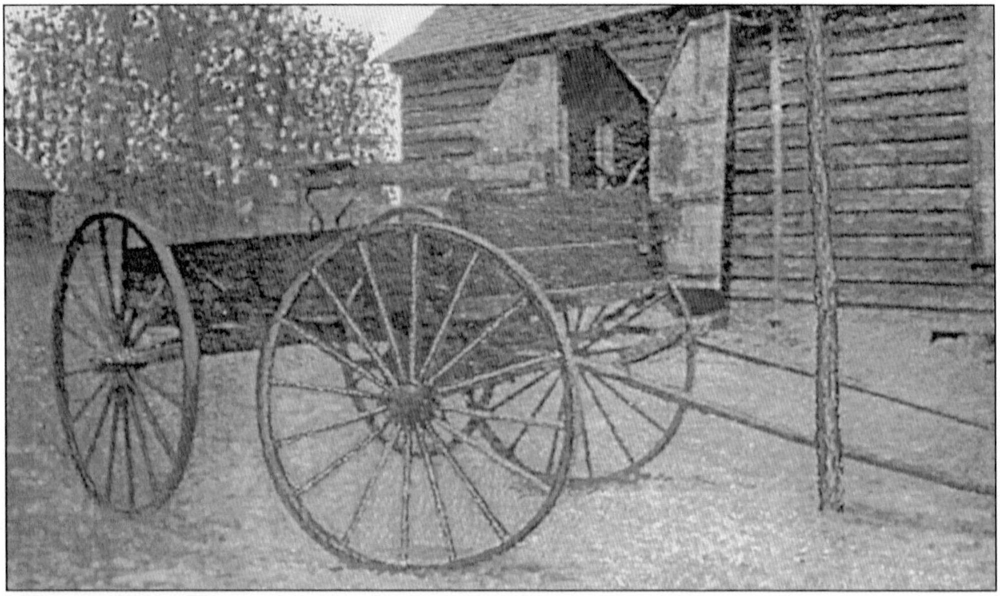

[WINGARD'S BUGGY MANUFACTURING COMPANY, PELION, C. 1911.] Founded in 1911, J.D. and Elzie Wingard's Wagon and Buggy Manufacturing Company produced custom-made wagons in a two-story building about 5 miles northwest of Pelion on the Old Charleston Road. The buggies were assembled on the ground floor and painted on the second. Later, at different times, Elzie operated both Ford and Chevrolet dealerships. The building eventually was converted into a tomato and peach cannery.

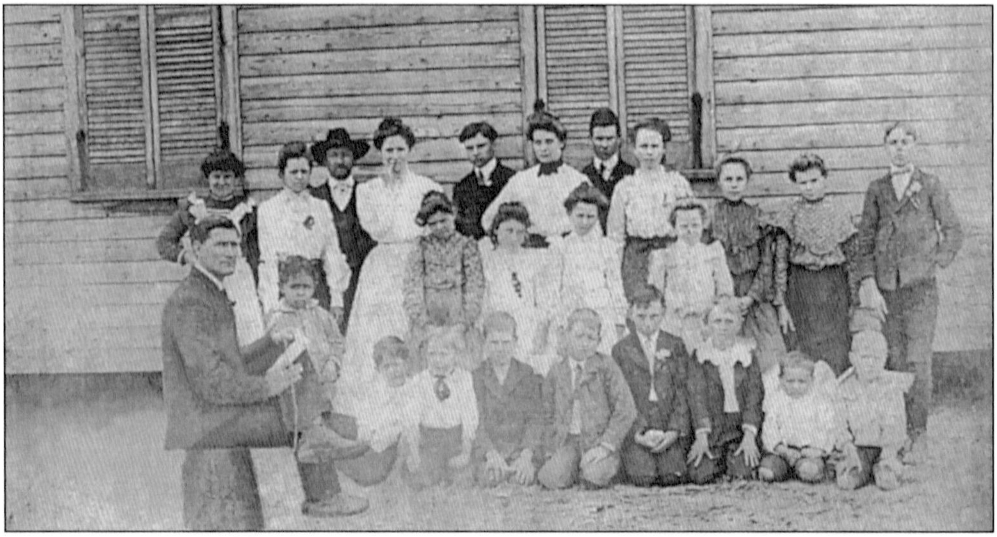

[SCHOOL PORTRAIT, PELION, C. 1905.] In 1900, Pelion constructed at the corner of Pine and Norris Streets an oblong, multi-purpose frame building with two front doors and a wood stove for heat. With its central interior partition, it could function variously as a schoolhouse (then serving 27 students), church, or community meeting hall. Students and their teacher are shown here in front of the building in 1905. By 1915, the limited eight-week school term of the earliest years had expanded to a 160-day session for the 90 students then being taught by a man and his wife. The structure no longer stands.

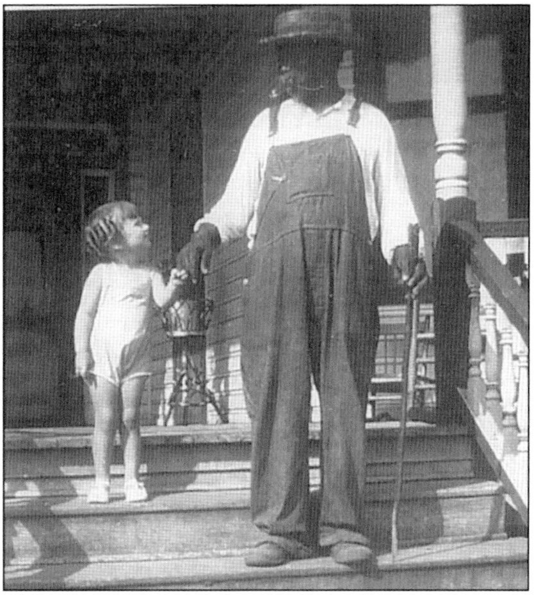

[Claire Eargle with Jim Austin, Pelion, c. 1930.] Young Claire Eargle was the daughter of educator Lionel Blanton Eargle, who was a teacher, principal, and later school superintendent at Pelion. Like many others during the difficult years of the Depression in South Carolina, they were forced to live very modestly. Their rented frame house lacked indoor plumbing and refrigeration, so they subsisted mainly on vegetables. Jim Austin, who lived at the Fort Pond, helped the Eargles do their chores and care for the livestock—a Jersey cow, some chickens, and pigs. Austin sold any extra eggs in West Columbia.

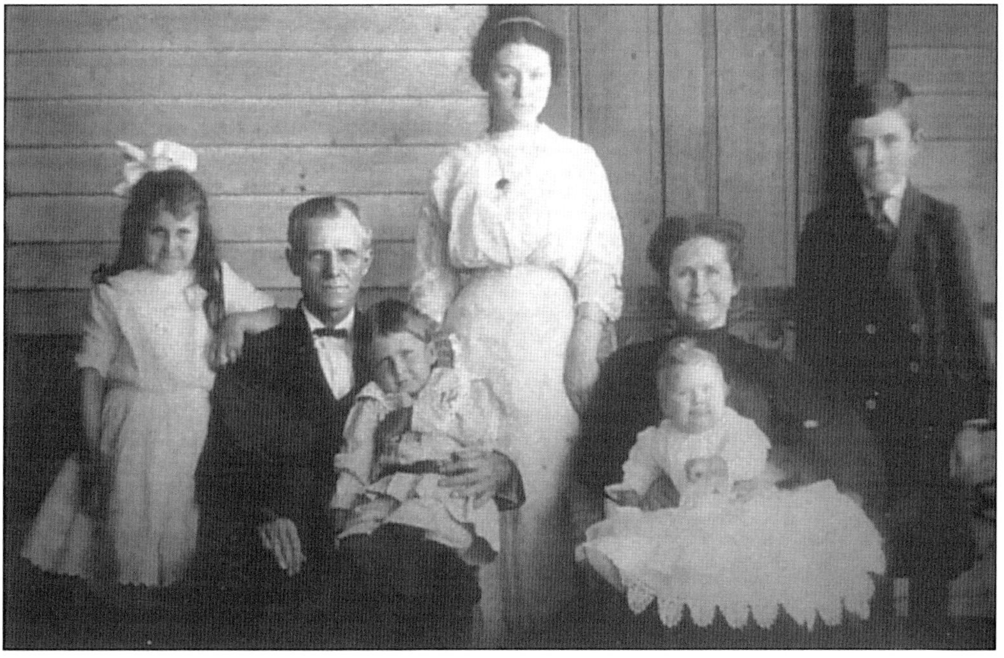

[Portrait of Mr. and Mrs. Daniel F. Shumpert Sr. and Children, Pelion, c. 1912.] Daniel Franklin Shumpert Sr. (1860–1937), originally from the Richton Community west of Pelion (near St. John's Lutheran Church), moved to Pelion in 1900 and became one of its earliest businessmen. He owned a general store (his merchandise included farm implements, coffins, and Sinclair oil and gas products), was co-director of the local bank in the 1920s, served on the school board, and was an active churchman. Shown in this family portrait are, from left to right, the following: Thelma; Shumpert holding his son, Horace; Viola; wife Sallie [Sarah Cornelia Lybrand (1876–1959)] holding Roseva; and Percy. Shumpert's store and other frame establishments in the business district were lost to a major fire in 1928.

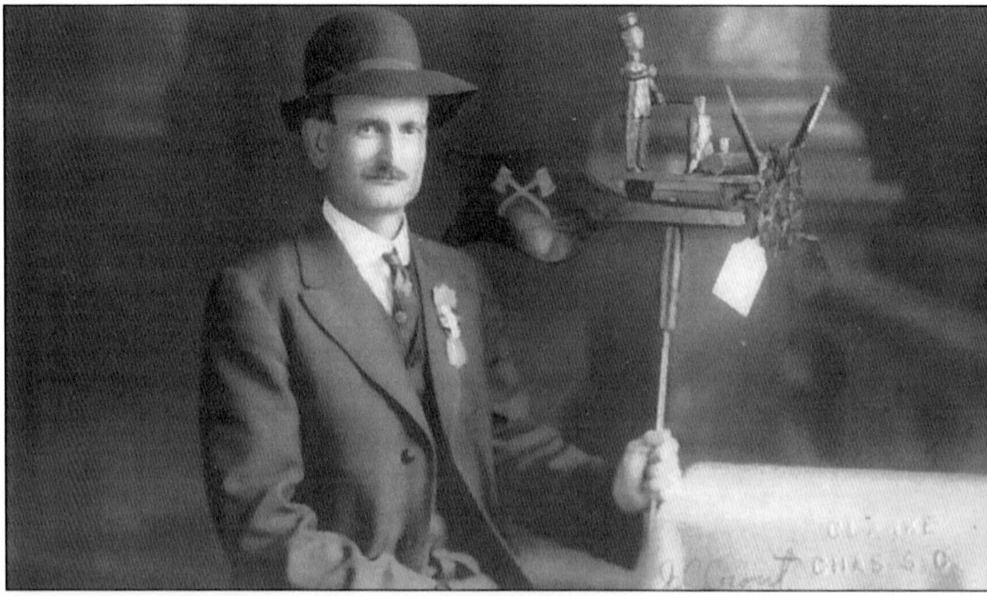

[Portrait of J.C. Crout, Pelion, *c.* 1910.] J.C. Crout (died 1930), son of Ephraim and Margaret Elizabeth Crout, was born near Holley's Ferry. Crout was a master builder and wood craftsman who made church furniture for the Holy Trinity Lutheran Church, where it is still in use. Scottish-born Charleston photographer William D. Clarke made this portrait.

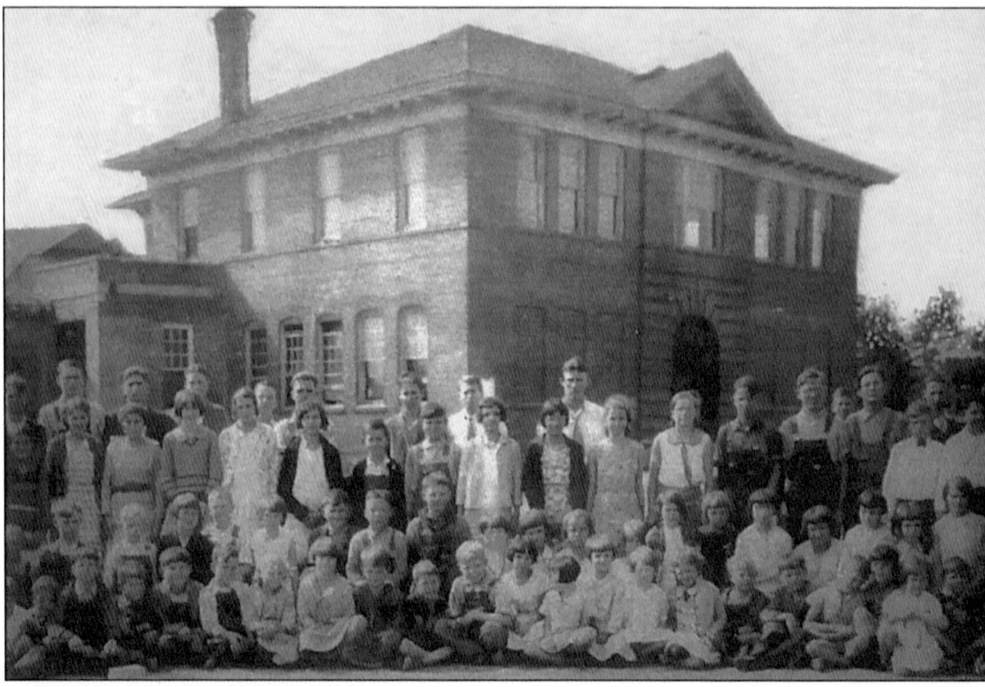

[Pelion School, *c.* 1930s.] When Lueco Gunter visited Pelion to inspect its school in 1915, the old frame building served 54 boys and 36 girls. Two years later a new brick building was erected near Magnolia and Fort Streets. This structure, which no longer stands, contained three classrooms on the ground floor and an auditorium on the second floor.

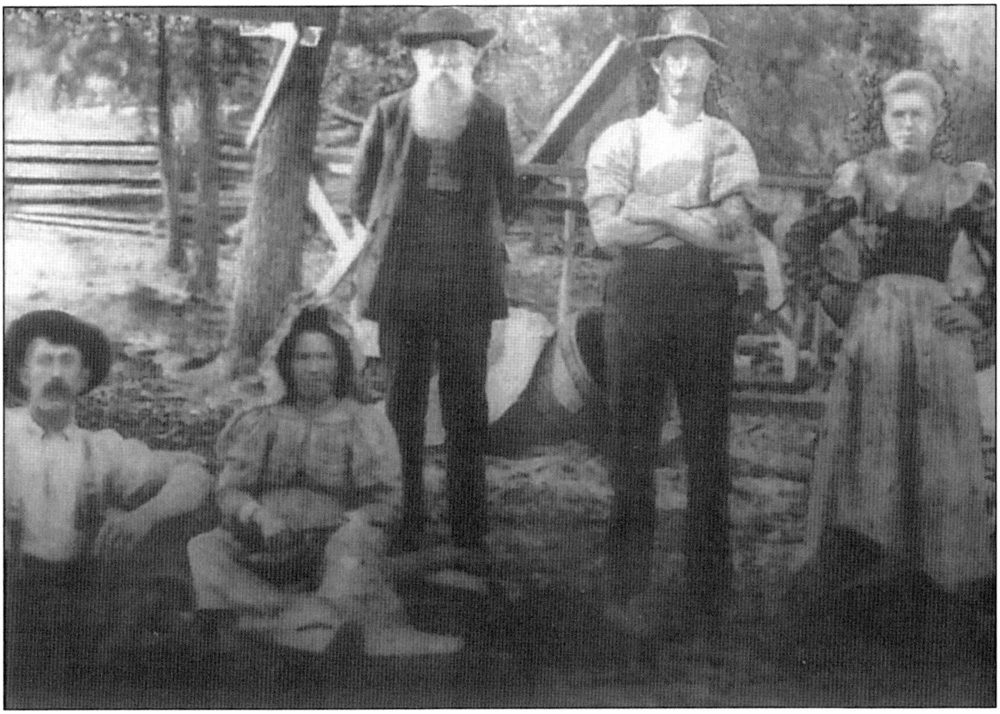

[Hog-Butchering Day near Pelion, c. 1910.] An important part of a farmer's program of diversification and subsistence was his growing of livestock. This scene shows a family during a day of hog butchering. Since refrigeration did not exist, farm families would join clubs in which they would take turns butchering hogs and distributing agreed-upon portions each month so that every family would have fresh meat throughout the year.

[Smith Branch School near Richton, c. 1910.] Once located 3.5 miles northwest of Pelion, off D.E. Clark Road, on a tributary of Black Creek, the one-room Smith Branch school had a ratio of 1 teacher to 70 students in a 24-week session in 1900. By 1916, it was still a one-teacher school with 54 students for a session of 120 days. Gunter described the school as "unusually well-proportioned for a one-teacher building of its kind." It was destroyed by fire in the late 1970s.

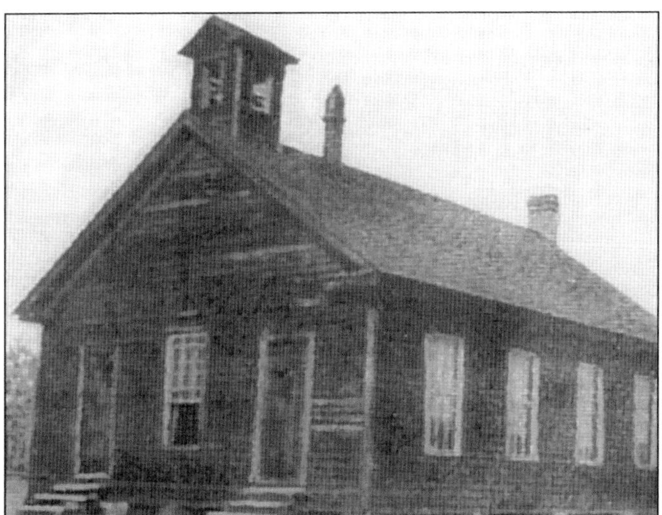

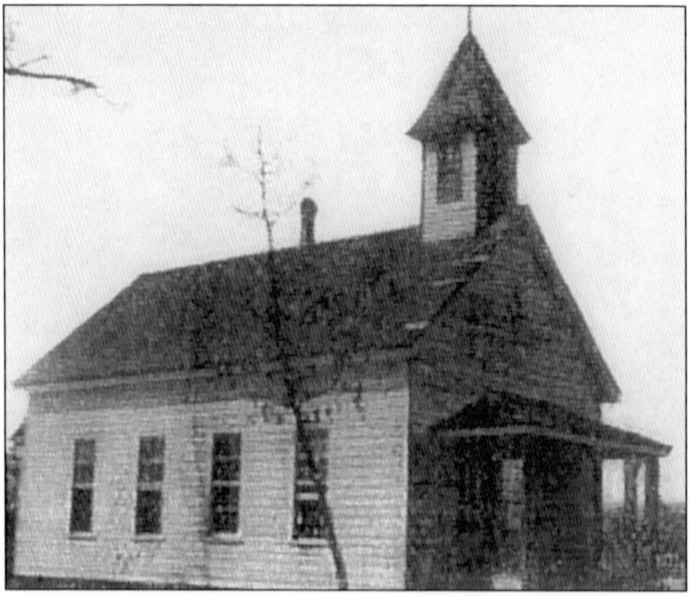

[Fairview School.] In 1900, this one-teacher schoolhouse, at the crossroads of Fairview Road (US 178) and Merrits Drive (LC 75) about 8 miles west of Pelion, initially served 32 students in a four-week session. Miss Dora Elizabeth Craft, a 1904 graduate of Leesville College, taught here from 1904 to 1907. In 1916, Gunter stated that the 53 students sat at homemade desks and used painted walls for blackboards.

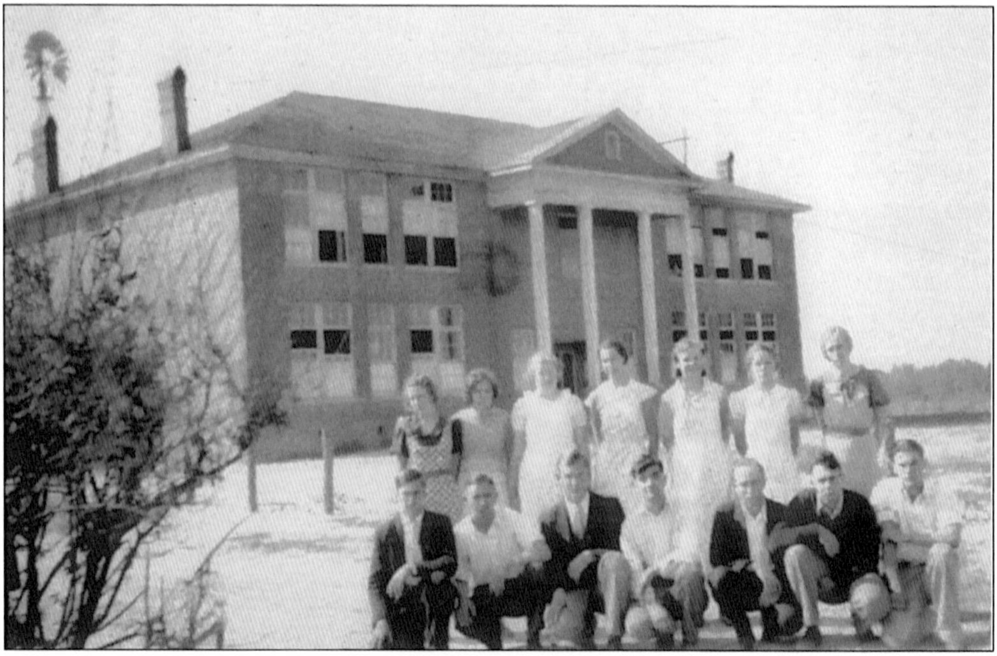

[Fairview HIgh School, 1934.] A new brick Fairview High School, which replaced the old frame grammar school, was opened during the 1922–1923 school term at the crossroads of Fairview Road and Merrits Drive. Shown above is the senior class of 1934 posing in front of the two-story building. Fairview was later consolidated with other regional schools and this building was closed and torn down.

[PORTRAIT OF DANIEL SHUMPERT, C. 1905.] Shumpert is one of the well-known names in Lexington County. The portrait at right is believed to be that of the Reverend Daniel Shumpert, a Pentecostal Holiness preacher in the Styx area. His branch of the family would have been identified with the old Richton Community—at Calk's Ferry and Water Tank Roads near Huffman's Mill on Black Creek. They would have attended St. John's Lutheran Church and gone to Smith Branch School. Some members of his family migrated east to Pelion; others farmed and operated a general store and post office at the junction of D.E. Clark and Water Tank Roads.

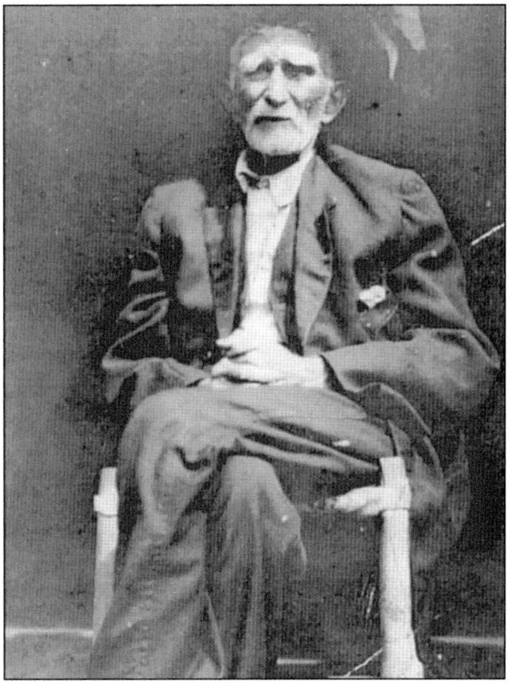

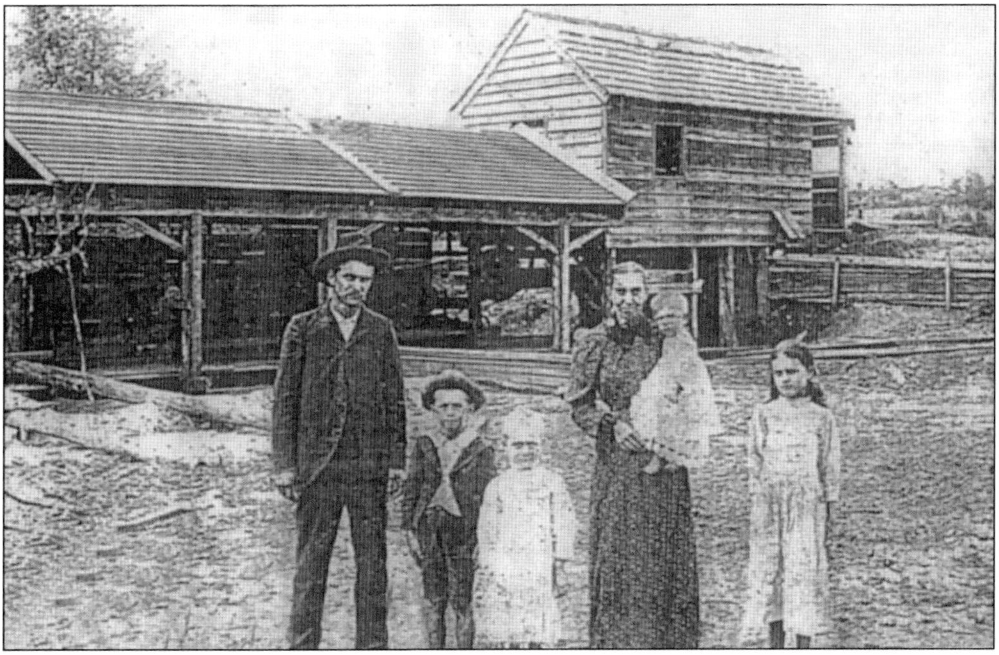

[HENRY SHUMPERT WITH FAMILY AND GRISTMILL, PELION, C. 1901.] Henry David Shumpert (1868–1927) built and operated a water-powered gristmill, cotton gin, sawmill, planer, shingle mill, and blacksmith shop on a 330-acre section on the banks of Cedar Creek several miles south of Pelion. Shown here in front of the mill are Shumpert and his wife, Minnie Lowman Shumpert (1870–1950), with their children, from left to right, as follows: Earl Bowers ("Bub"), Lola, Ernest, and Leila. The children attended Clay Springs School.

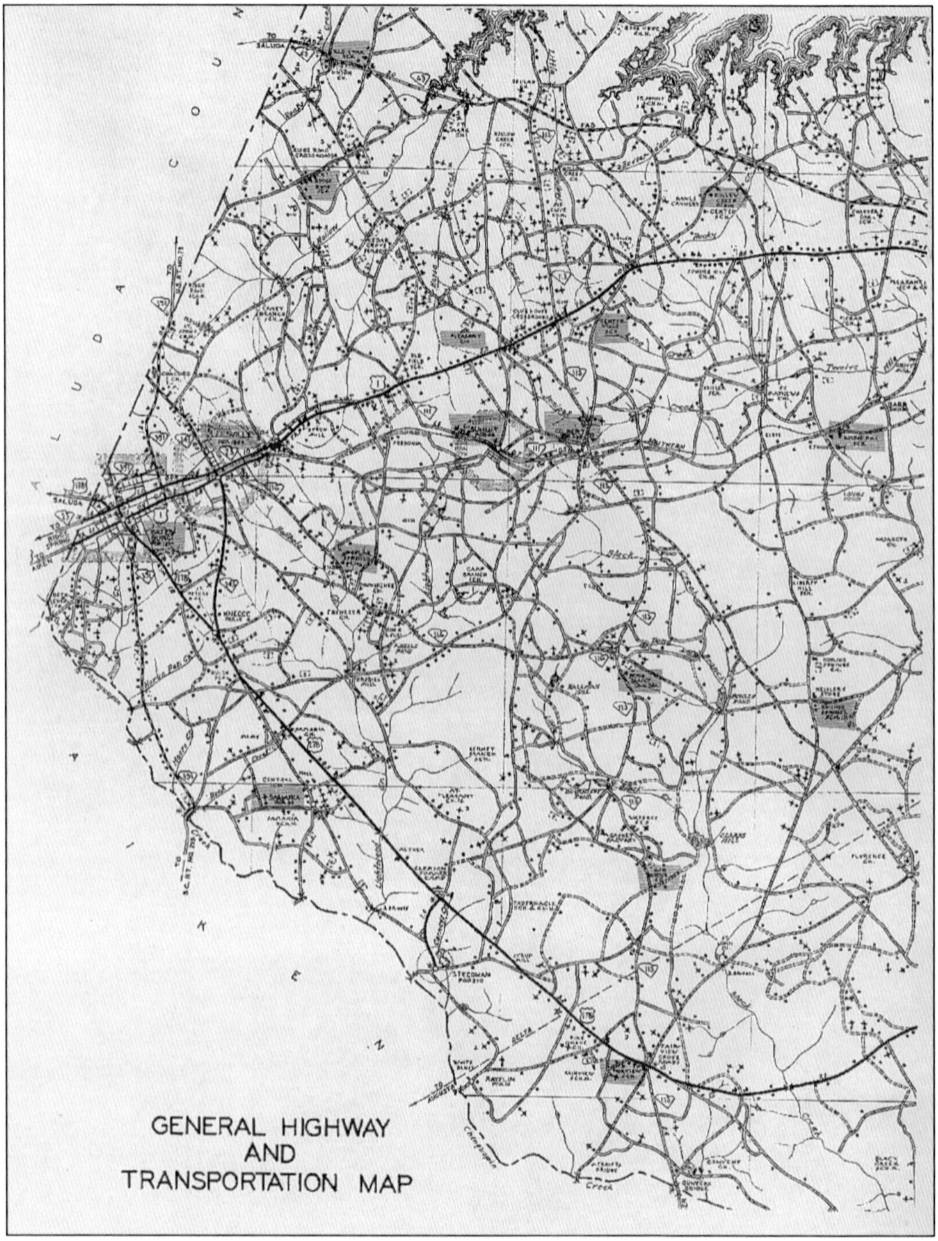

[MAP OF WEST CENTRAL LEXINGTON COUNTY, 1940.] This enlarged section of a 1940 highway map of Lexington County shows the region covered in chapter three. The darkened areas indicate the location of school sites. Highway jurisdictional abbreviations used in the captions are as follows: LC (Lexington County), SC (South Carolina), and US (United States). Other map sections are to be found on pages 8, 11, and 80.

Three

Western Region

"The remarkable Ridge section": such is the way this portion of Lexington County is characterized in the literature of the period. Extending some 35 miles from Lewiedale (Gilbert) to Trenton (in Edgefield County), the fruit ridge—as it is sometimes called—is that fall-line strip of high ground located midway between the mountains and the sea known for its fertile soil, pure water, healthful climate, and natural beauty.

The relatively early economic growth and development of this largely agricultural area can be credited mainly to the westward expansion of the Charlotte, Columbia & Augusta Railroad in 1869–1870, which led to the establishment of a string of depots that eventually spawned incorporated townships along the Ridge—especially Leesville (1875) and Batesburg (1877)—which took hold and prospered. As early as 1891 these two were placed among the first three in a ranking of the most prominent and prosperous towns in the county (see Lexington County and Its Towns, *1891) and by 1925 Batesburg, with a population of 3,500, claimed to be the largest and most progressive town in western South Carolina on the Southern Railway between Columbia and Augusta (see* The Twin-City News, *July 30, 1925).*

The rural, small-town way of life that defines the history and culture of this region has been shaped into fiction by Batesburg native Lodwick Hartley. Plum Tree Lane *(1978), a thinly disguised characterization of his hometown, may contain the kind of truth from the period that gives these vintage pictures their real meaning.*

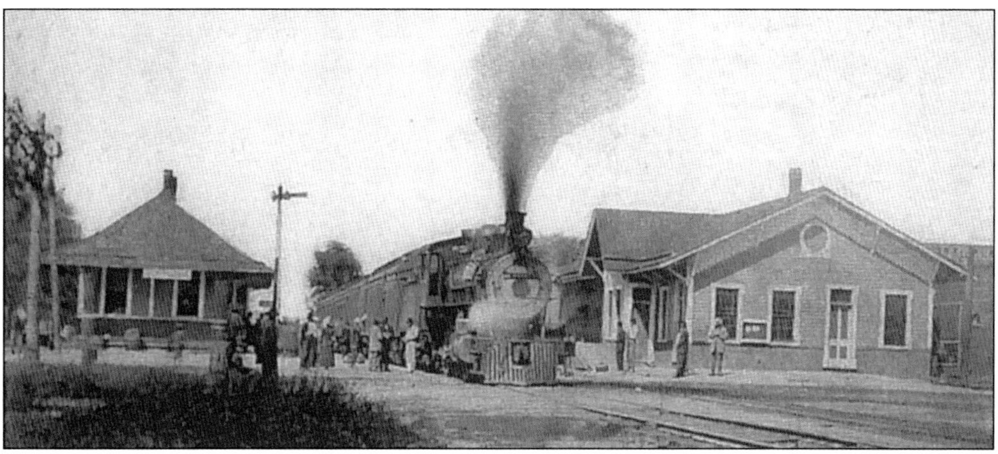

Southern Passenger Station on Right, Southern Express and Freight Office on Left, Batesburg, SC [1912]. For a century the arrival and departure of trains was an assumed part of the daily rhythm of life in both Batesburg and Leesville—an essential part of their sights and sounds. Four passenger trains once ran between Augusta and Columbia each way, the last of them making its final run on October 14, 1967. The picture above shows an east-bound train stopped between the Southern's two Batesburg railroad structures. In 1982, the depot at the right, built in 1894, was moved to the farm of "Junebug" Oswald about 4 miles from Batesburg off the Wagener highway.

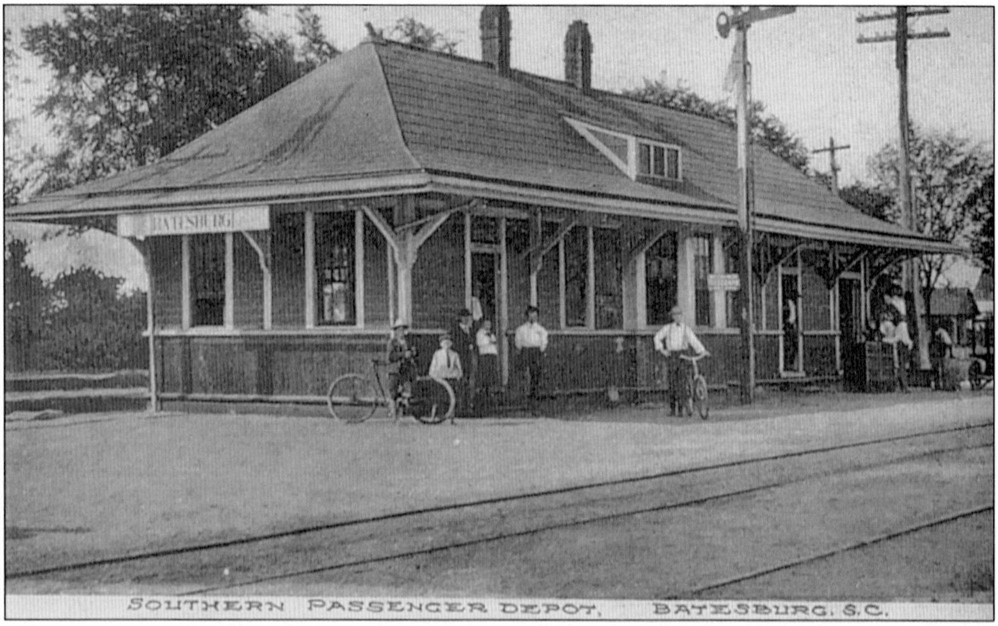

SOUTHERN PASSENGER DEPOT, BATESBURG, SC [*C.* 1910]. In 1869–1870 the Charlotte, Columbia & Augusta Railroad (absorbed by the Southern) constructed the second rail line to cross Lexington County. In 1908 Batesburg claimed to have almost perfect railroad schedules, with double trains running each day to and from Charlotte, Columbia, Augusta, Aiken, and connecting with all local trains in South Carolina. By then, a new passenger station had been built. It still stands on the west side of town in the municipal playground situated in the 400 block of Wilson Street, where it was relocated around 1960 by the Batesburg Women's Club. In 2000 efforts were undertaken towards its reutilization as a railroad museum, meeting hall, or welcome center.

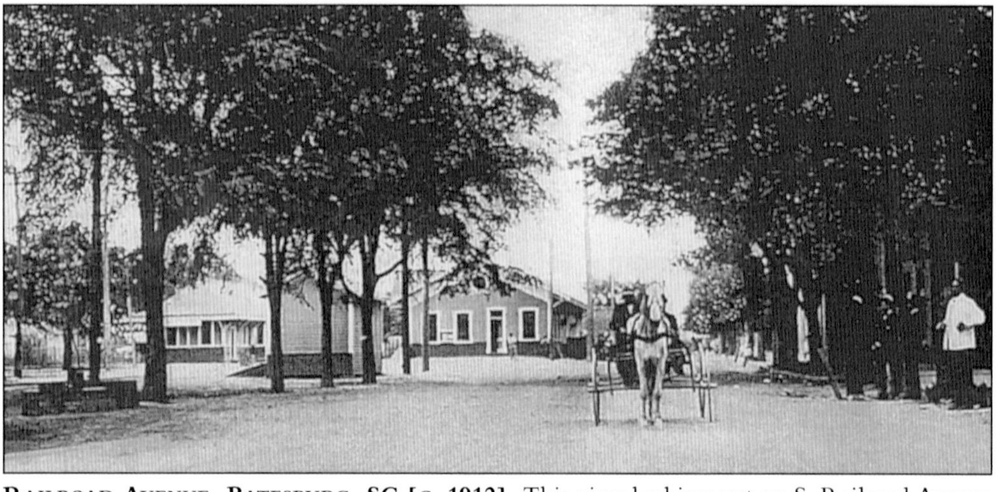

RAILROAD AVENUE, BATESBURG, SC [*C.* 1912]. This view looking east on S. Railroad Avenue shows the two railroad depots at the heart of a tree-lined downtown Batesburg. The little building closest to the camera functioned between 1904 and 1913 as a railroad baggage or tool house. By the 1920s Batesburg, with a population that had grown from 971 in 1900 to some 2,717 in 1920, had become the largest town in the county and the hub of its wholesale, retail, and banking enterprises. In 1923 it boasted 62 stores, 1 large wholesale house, and 8 medical doctors, dentists, and opticians.

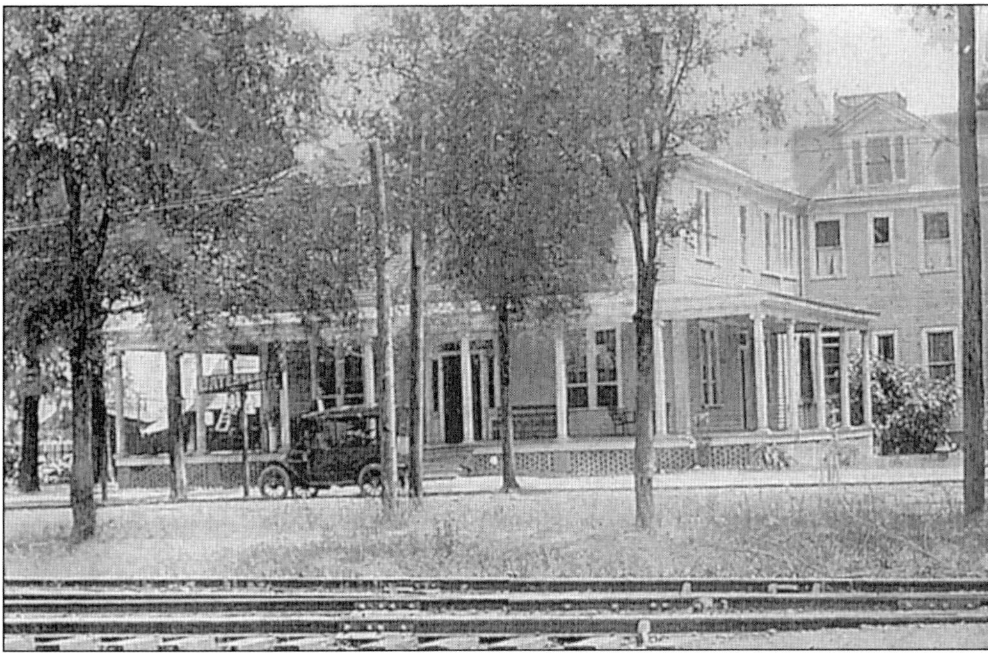

BATESBURG HOTEL, BATESBURG, SC [1909]. The Batesburg Hotel, established in the early 1870s, once stood at the corner of S. Railroad Avenue and S. Pine Street facing the railroad tracks, whose trains brought it much of its business. At one time it was designated as a railroad eating house, when the trains stopped for meals: 20 minutes each for breakfast, dinner, and supper. After the hotel burned, the site became the location of the Nutt apartments.

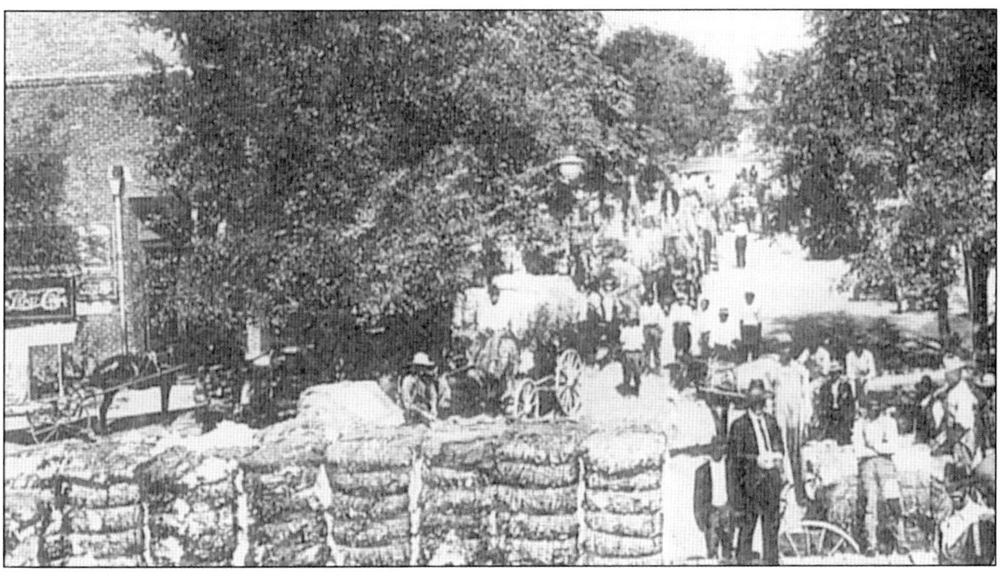

COTTON MARKET, BATESBURG, SC [C. 1910]. Taken from about the center of the wooden cotton platform on Railroad Avenue, facing north up Granite [Fulmer] Street, this photograph was probably taken from atop a railroad freight or passenger car. The bailed cotton, one of this rural area's staple agricultural commodities, is ready to be shipped out. As early as 1883 Batesburg was shipping an average of 3,000 bales annually.

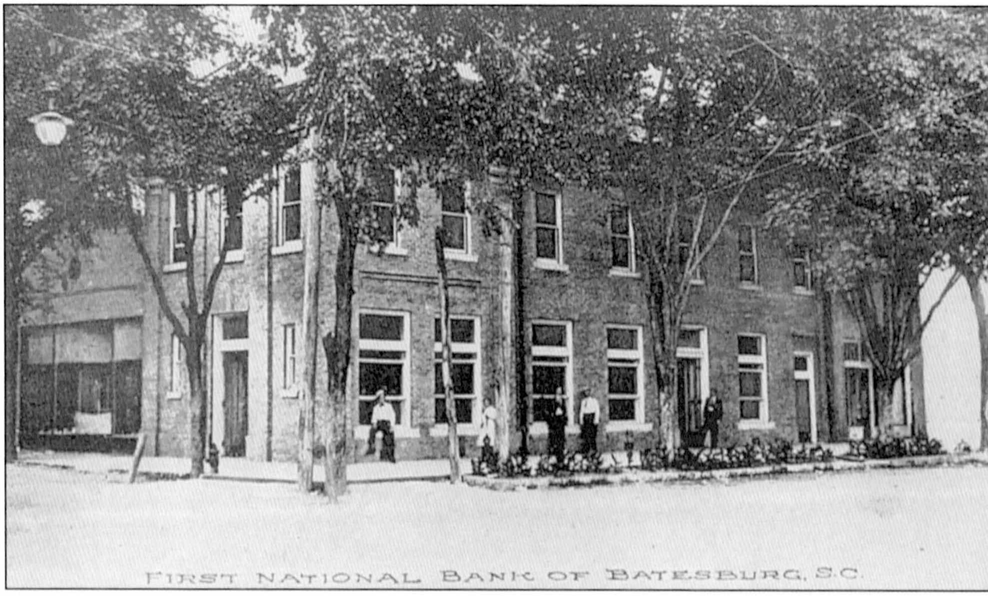

FIRST NATIONAL BANK OF BATESBURG, BATESBURG, SC [*c.* 1910]. Organized in 1900 with capital of $25,000, the First National Bank moved from its initial site into this yellow, two-story, granite and vitrified pressed brick building across Main [Oak] Street from Gunter's Drug Store in 1908. The building was later utilized as a restaurant by Nicholas "Chris" Christakos, who immigrated from Greece in 1898, moved to Batesburg in 1926, and operated Chris's Cafe until his death in 1965. The store to the left, known as Mae's in 2000, once housed Addy's Clothing Store.

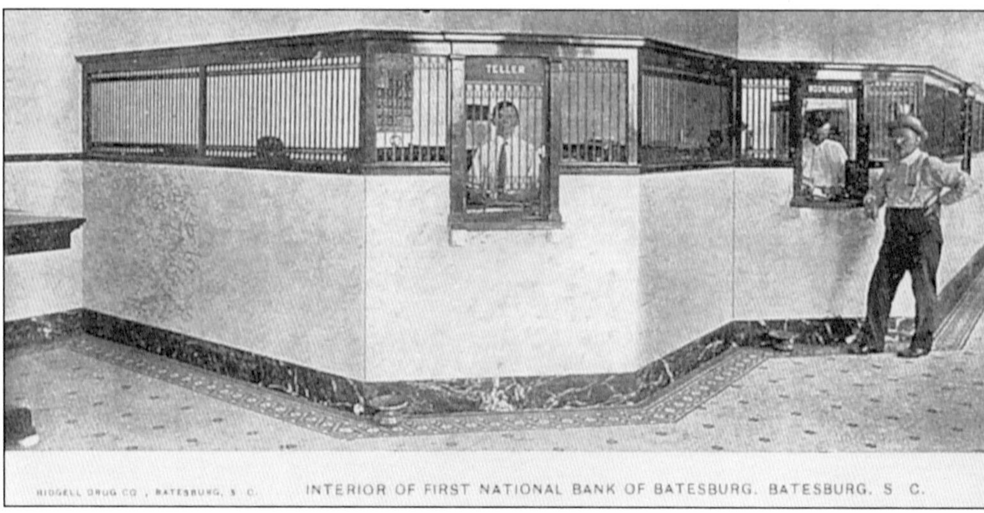

INTERIOR OF FIRST NATIONAL BANK OF BATESBURG, BATESBURG, SC [*c.* 1908]. A major article on Batesburg that appeared in *The State* (Columbia) on July 1, 1908, indicated that the First National Bank of Batesburg, which had begun its business "in a small room and with a small capital," had just moved into its new building, described as "one of the finest buildings in South Carolina, built especially for its own use." The bank's interior had marble wainscoting and solid mahogany woodwork. Its large modern vault was a manganese burglar-proof safe with double time locks. Furthermore, the entire building was equipped with electric lights.

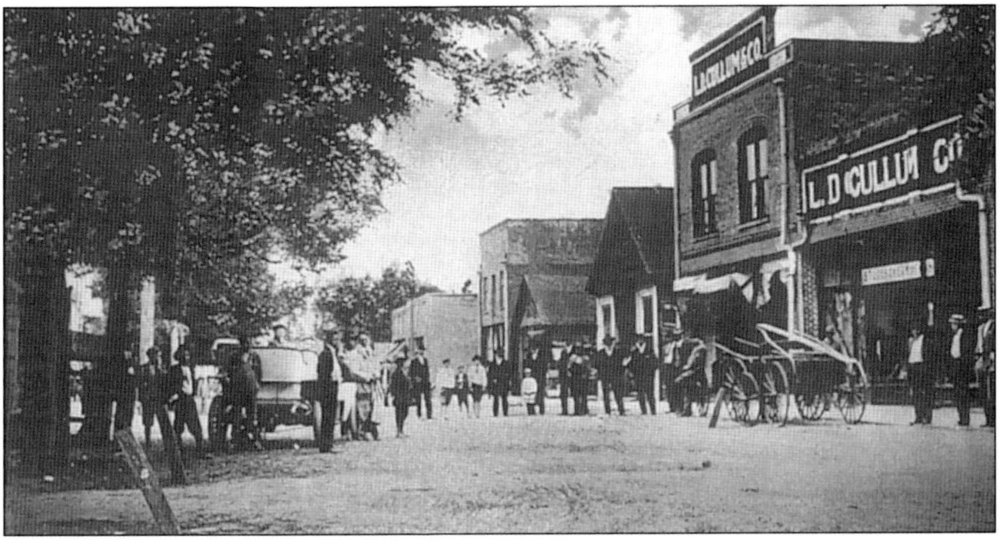

GRANITE STREET, BATESBURG, SC [*c.* 1912]. Running parallel with Main [Oak], Granite [Fulmer] Street was the second of Batesburg's principal banking and business thoroughfares extending north from the town's railroad complex of depots and warehouses. The commercial establishments of L.D. Cullum dominate the righthand side of this early view of Granite Street looking north. In 1919, the handsome Bank of Western Carolina, which still stands, would be built on the northeast corner of Granite and Railroad.

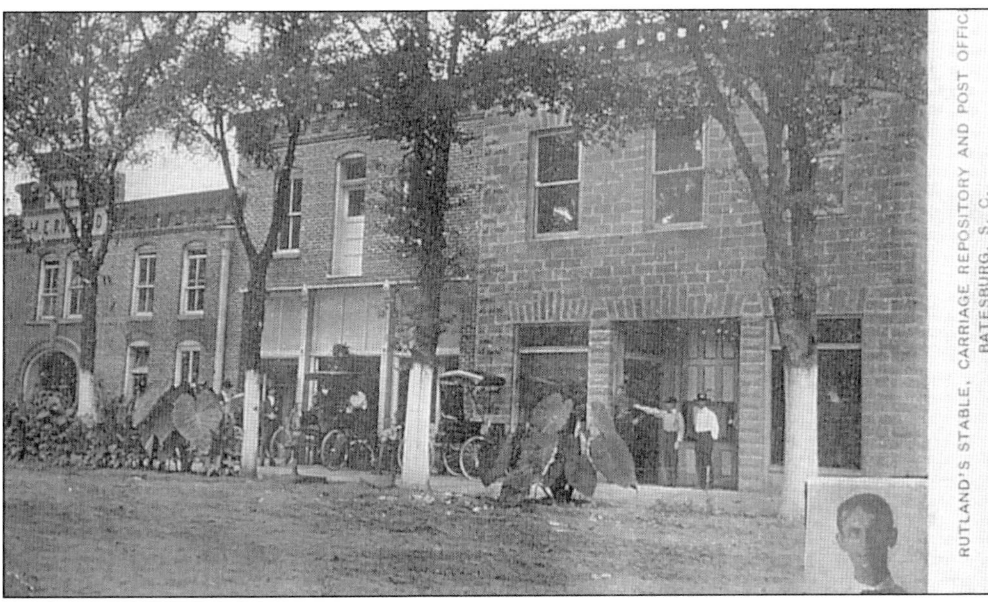

RUTLAND'S STABLE, CARRIAGE HOUSE, AND POST OFFICE, BATESBURG, SC [*c.* 1908]. An editorial in the *Batesburg Advocate* of September 1, 1905, mentions "the large up-to-date hollow block building, being erected by Mr. M.E. Rutland, next to his stables, and, which will be the future home of the *Advocate*." Three years later, in its July 1 feature on Batesburg, *The State* (Columbia) ran the above picture, including the small inset photograph of Rutland, who was one of the town's chief dealers in horses, buggies, and wagons—and who also may have established the first inter-urban taxi service between Batesburg, Leesville, and Johnston.

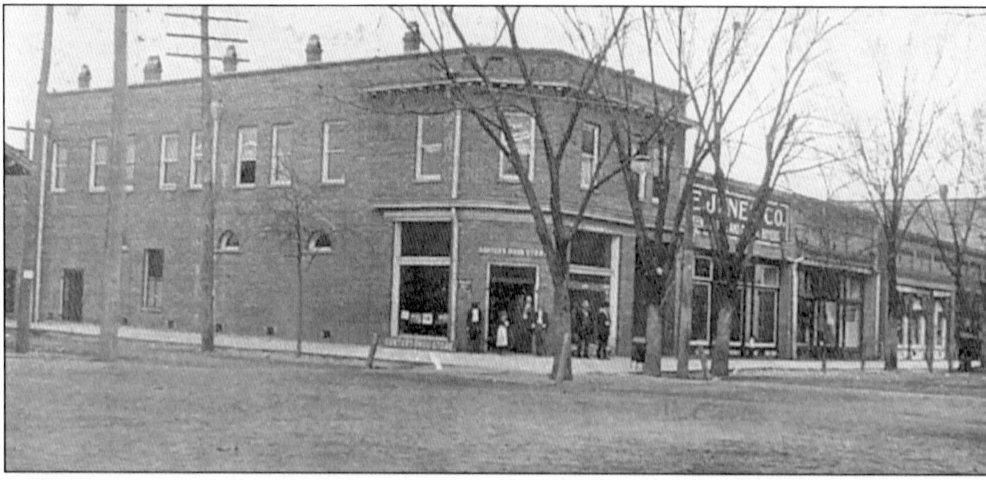

CORNER MAIN STREET AND R.R. AVENUE, BATESBURG, SC [*C.* 1908]. Gunter's Drug Store published this view of its own premises perhaps shortly after the move to its new location in the Fox Building across from the train depot in 1908. It subsequently became Ridgell's, and later the Fair Drug Company. By 2000, the building was vacant. The space occupied by the E. Jones Company, to the right, became Fox's grocery store and then, in 1925, the A&P. Roof Hardware has occupied the premises since 1993.

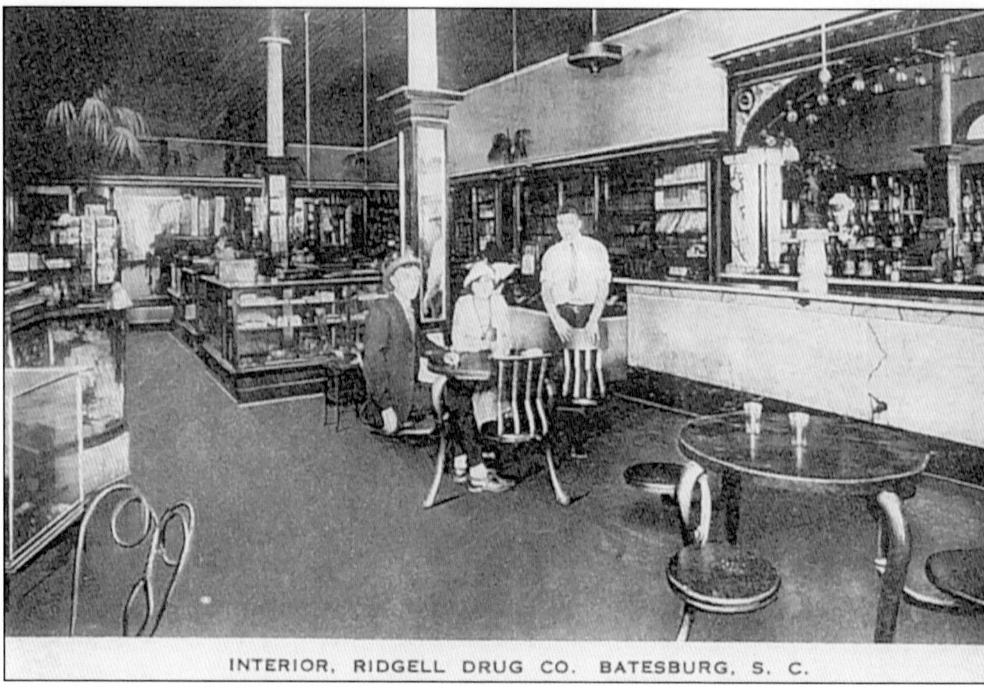

INTERIOR, RIDGELL DRUG COMPANY, BATESBURG, SC [*C.* 1918]. The well-appointed interior of the Ridgell Drug Company, depicted here with three unidentified persons (probably two customers and a store attendant), featured a potted palm and elegant furniture and fixtures, including lights with Tiffany shades reflected in a mirror behind a marble soda-fountain counter. The Tiffany fixtures, created to resemble flowers with multi-colored petals, reportedly still survive in private hands.

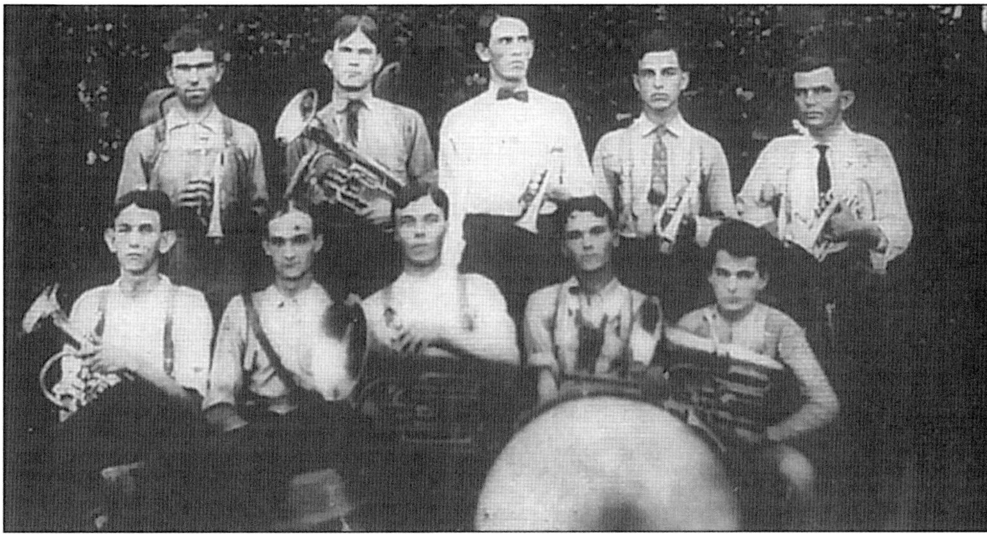

[Batesburg Brass Band, Batesburg, *c.* 1909.] This outdoor postcard portrait of the Batesburg Brass Band was mailed from "F.R." in Batesburg to Arthur Harman at the Lexington Manufacturing Company on June 29, 1909. "Our band is all OK," the sender wrote. "We will play on the 3rd." The venue referred to here was no doubt one of the several Fourth of July "first class" barbecues offered in the area on the third that year—perhaps the annual one furnished by D.E. Hammond and Lewie Hallman at Gilbert, to which everyone was invited in order to enjoy the music, "listen to the discussion of the [liquor] dispensary question," and pay a visit to "the photographer, Blanchard, of Columbia, [who] will be on hand to make your pictures" (see the *Lexington Dispatch*, June 30, 1909).

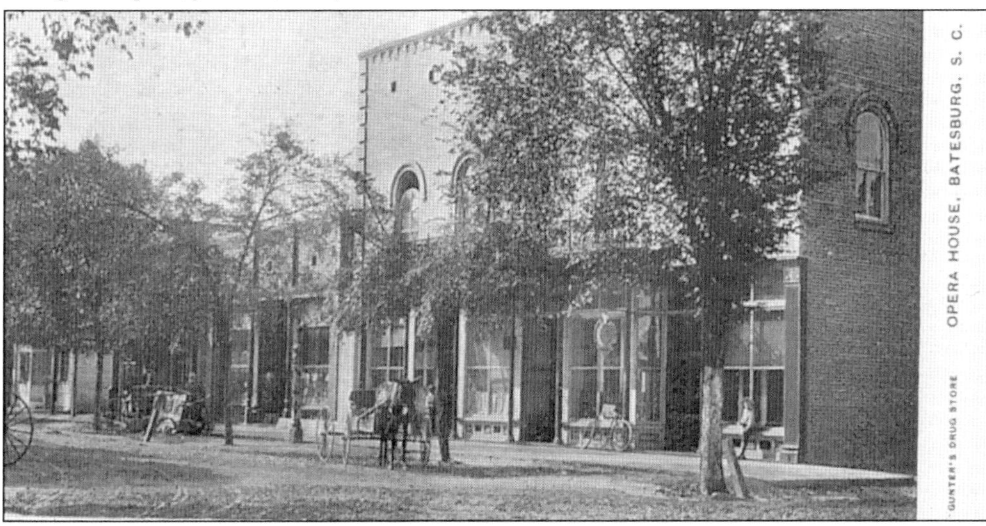

Opera House, Batesburg, SC [1909]. "Butt's Panorama and moving pictures were shown at the Opera House last night," a reporter wrote in the *Batesburg Advocate* on March 17, 1905. "No one, investing ten cents to see this exhibition, will come away regretting the outlay." Like other South Carolina towns, Batesburg by 1901 had an imposing opera house, which meant a multi-purpose building with a large second-story meeting hall usable for public programs and entertainments. Located at the corner of N. Oak and W. Church, it was often referred to as the Kaminer Building for the family that erected the structure. In 2000 its ground level continued to be used commercially.

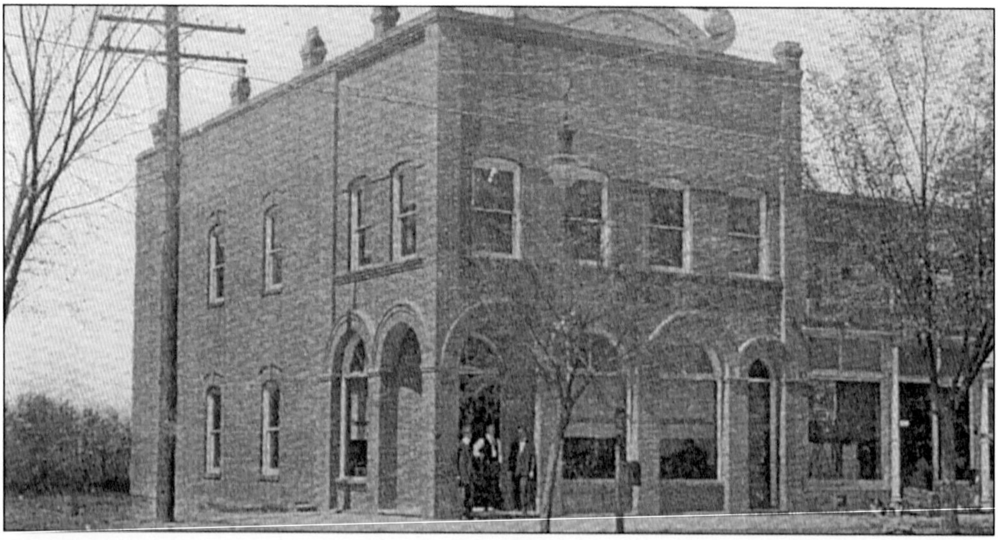

The Citizen's [*sic*] Bank, Batesburg, SC [1906]. In an ad in the local paper of December 15, 1905, the officers of the Citizens Bank of Batesburg invited friends and visitors to "call and see us in our New Handsome Brick Building—The finest and best equipped in the three counties." It later became the town hall and eventually housed the jail and fire department at the rear. Lodwick Hartley, in his book *Plum Tree Lane*, also indicates that several of its old offices once served as the Batesburg library. The structure was demolished in 1988, leaving vacant its lot at the corner of Lexington and Granite [Fulmer].

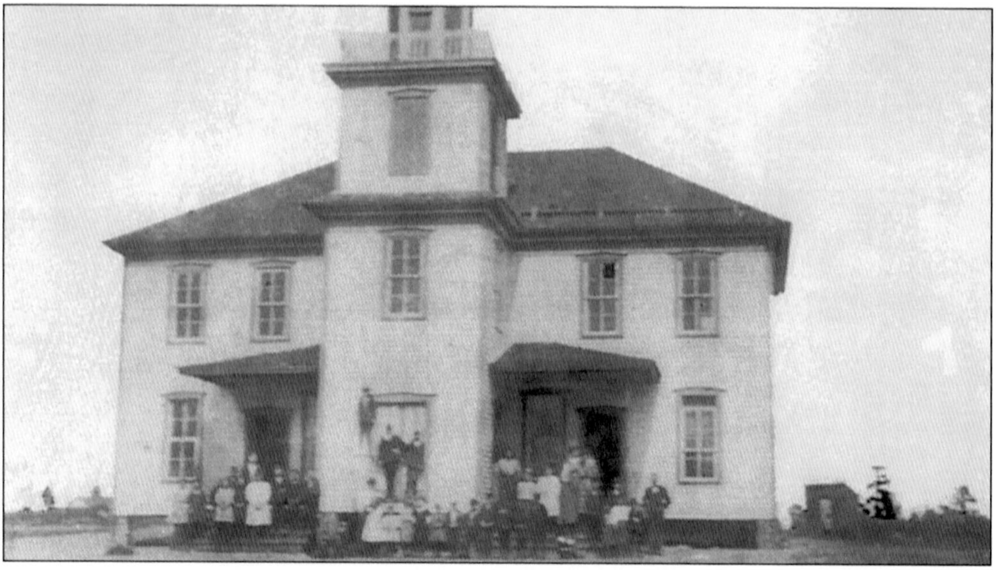

[Old Batesburg Baptist School/Batesburg High School/Batesburg Collegiate Institute, 1909.] The building shown here, once located half a mile south of the post office, has been identified as the old Baptist school, possibly built as early as 1886. Some called it the Batesburg High School in 1895, and it later became known as the Batesburg Collegiate Institute, which in 1902 advertised itself as "free to all the children in the district." In 1900, 142 pupils attended school here. It burned down in 1912 and was replaced by the "new" brick Batesburg Graded and High School (see p. 61).

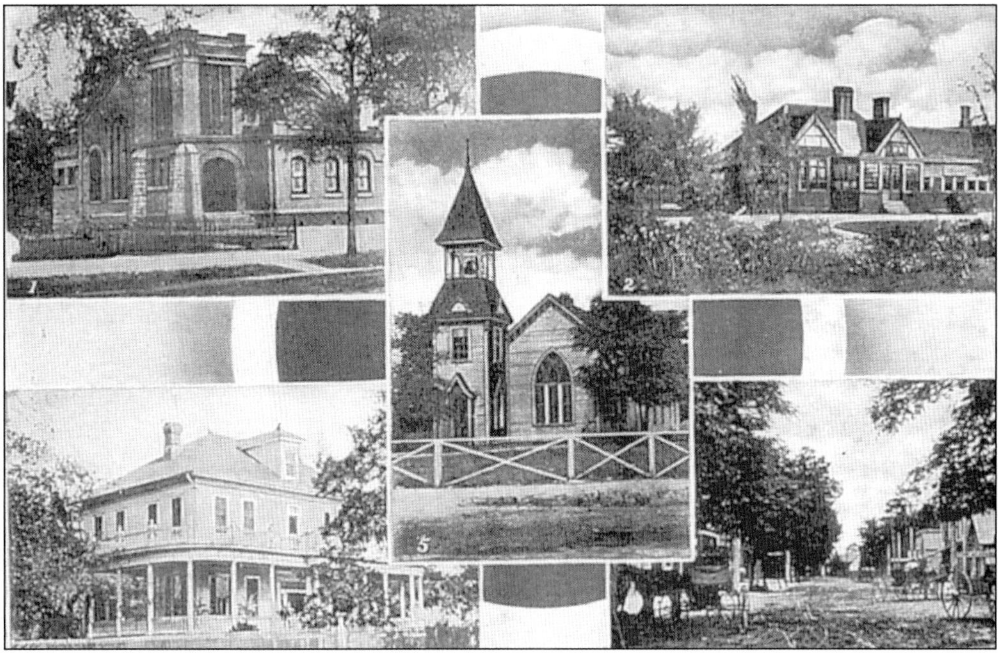

[Multi-view Card, Batesburg, *c.* 1910.] This photographic montage showcased what were considered Batesburg's principal locations of interest. Featured here are the following: the Baptist Church (upper left); "Green Gables," residence of the W.C. Farbers (upper right); "The Oaks," home of the N.A. Bates family (lower left); a portion of Granite [Fulmer] Street looking west (lower right); and the Methodist Church (center).

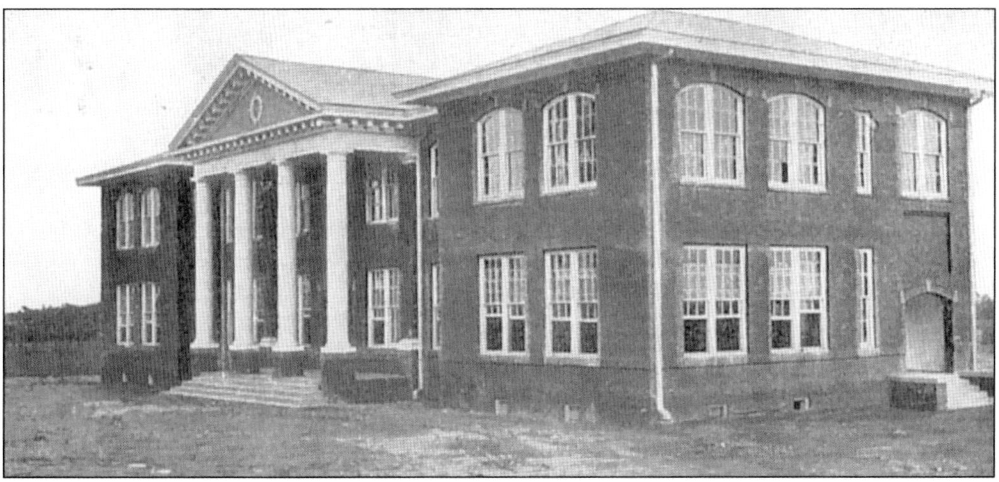

Batesburg Graded and High School Building, Batesburg, SC [*c.* 1912]. Facing north on Columbia Avenue (US 1), the "new" Batesburg Graded and High School was built for $15,000 in 1912, in time for the 1912–1913 school session. By 1920 its four-year high school curriculum had elevated it to the level of a second-class school. Batesburg writer Lodwick Hartley would later describe it as "a massive pile of bright red brick designed to be fire-proof" and featuring "an imposing portico with gleaming white columns. Victorian Gothic, or an attempt in that direction, had been succeeded by Classic Revival." It has survived in style to house administrative offices of Lexington County School District Three.

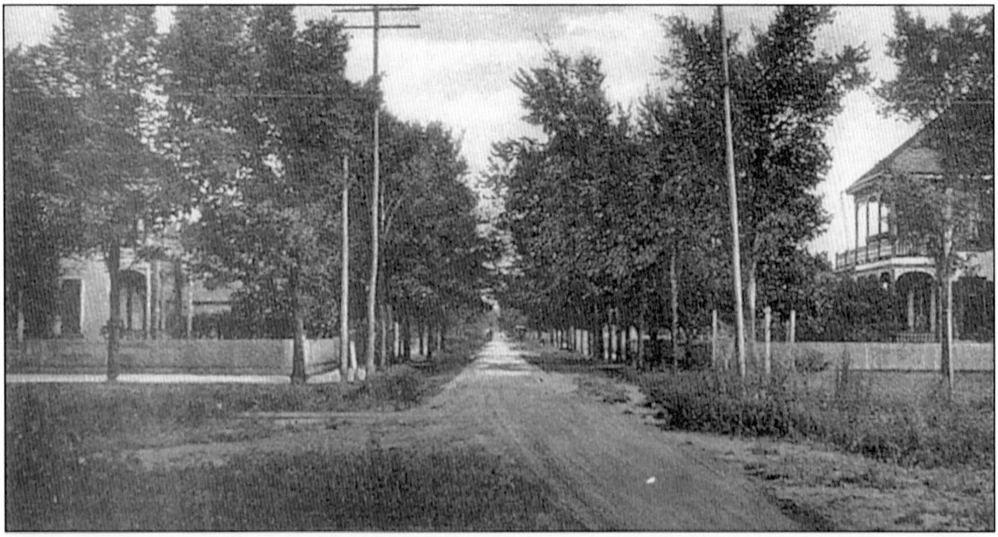

PEACHTREE STREET LOOKING SOUTH, BATESBURG, SC [*c.* 1908]. The two residences facing each other here across Peachtree Street at its intersection with W. Railroad Avenue belonged to members of one of Batesburg's leading mercantile families, the Cullums. Both houses, in altered states, still stand: at right, that of James Colwell Cullum (which served for many years as the Cullum Hotel), with its large front piazzas now removed; to the left, that of his brother, Lorenzo Dow Cullum, which in 2000 could be seen directly east at 550 W. Railroad Avenue. Peachtree Street would later become the fictional Plum Tree Lane of writer Lodwick Hartley (1906–1979).

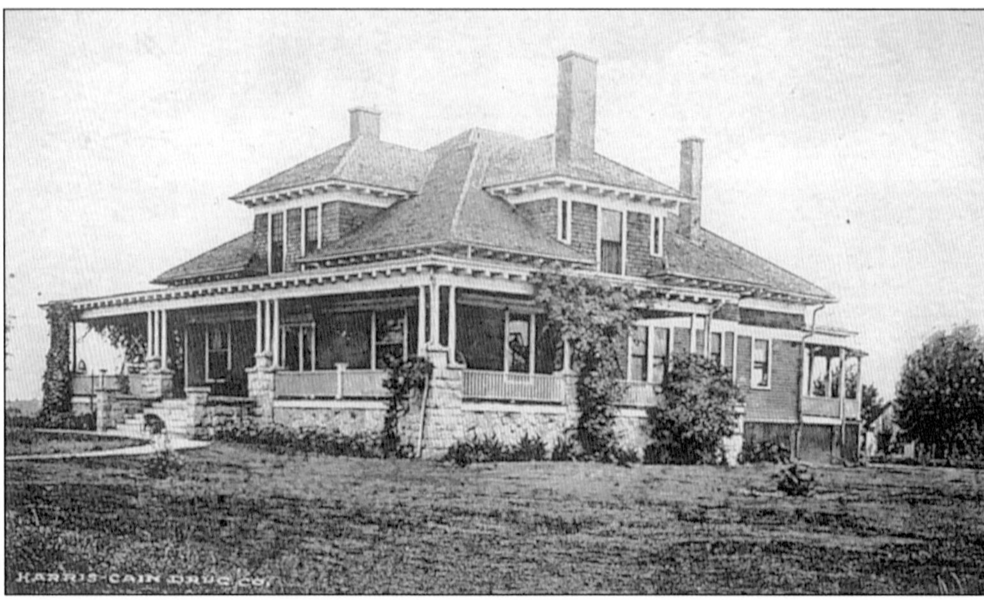

RESIDENCE, A.C. JONES, BATESBURG, SC [*c.* 1908]. This residence, now painted white and still standing on Fair Avenue, once belonged to Mr. Albert C. Jones, who was associated for many years with one of Batesburg's largest commercial enterprises, the Elisha Jones Company, and later became president of the Batesburg Fertilizer Company. The Sanborn maps of Batesburg, which begin in 1895, show Fair Avenue for the first time in 1908.

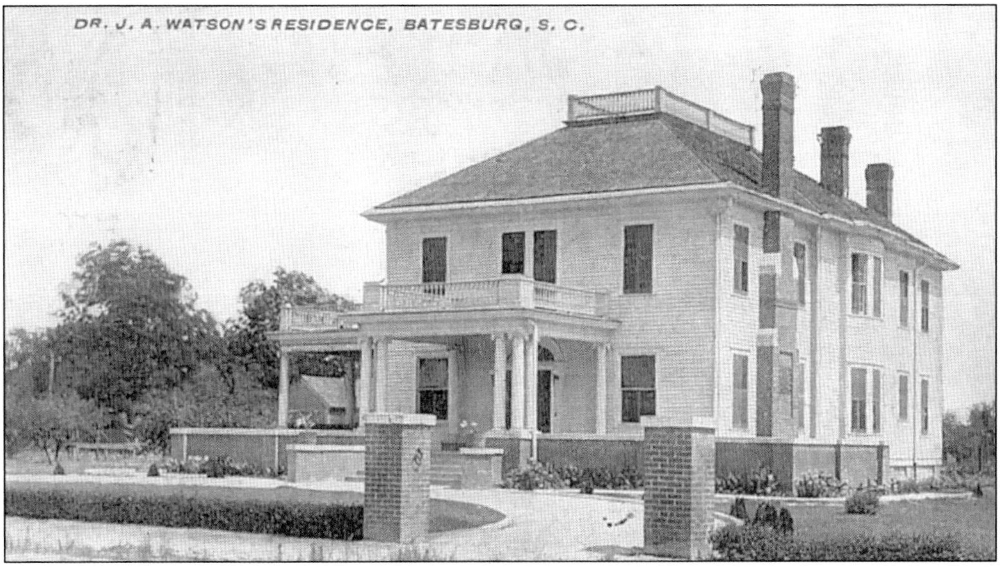

DR. J.A. WATSON'S RESIDENCE, BATESBURG, SC [C. 1910]. Following the death of Batesburg dentist James Arthur Watson (1880–1934), who built it, this huge residence became the home of jeweler, inventor, and manufacturer Elisha S. Copeland and his family. In 2000 it still stood on Lexington Avenue.

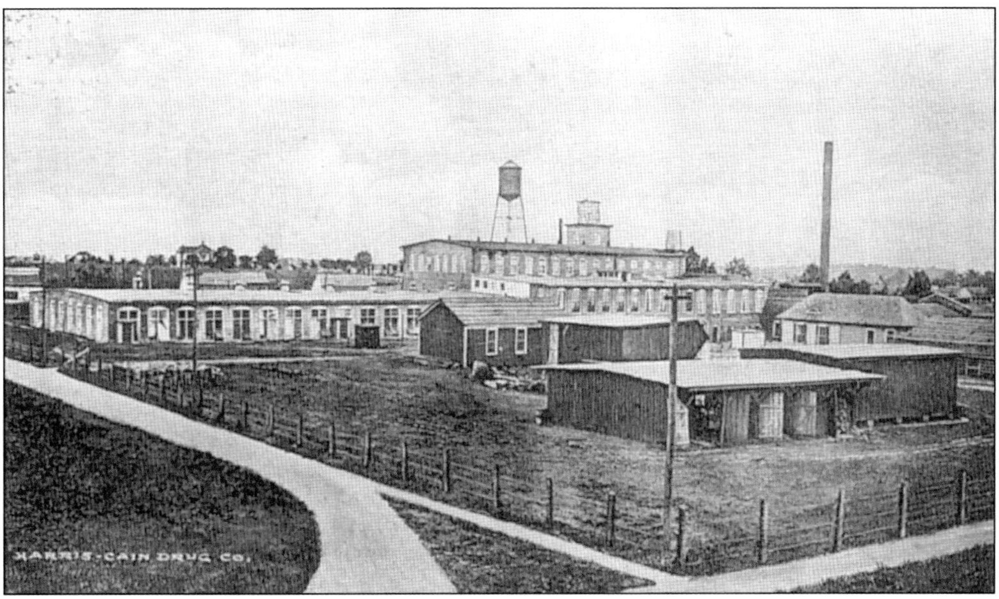

MIDDLEBURG COTTON MILLS, BATESBURG, SC [C. 1908]. Chartered in 1893, the Batesburg Cotton Mills began operations in 1895. By 1898 the mill had become one of a group owned by the Martel Corporation. Given the name Middleburg Mills, the Batesburg branch by 1908 was operating 300 looms and using 10,624 spindles to manufacture its cotton ticking, hickory shirtings, drills, and awning stripes. In 1925, still going strong, it boasted of never having experienced a strike or other labor trouble. Catlin Farish, a division of Burlington Industries, purchased the mill in 1957. The old brick three-story main building, seen beneath its water tower here, still occupies the original site.

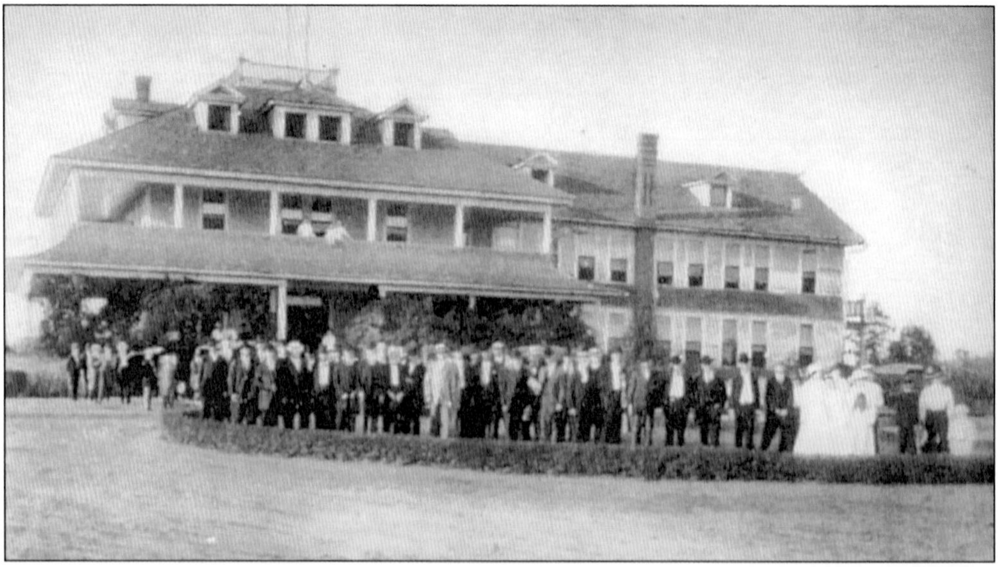

SUMMERLAND COLLEGE, BATESBURG, SC [*c.* 1913]. The building seen here as the main one of Summerland College actually opened as the Lexington Hotel in early 1906. Designed by Columbia architect Charles C. Wilson and built equidistant between Leesville and Batesburg, the two-story modern colonial inn became known as the Summerland Hotel. It boasted 40 bedrooms, 6 bathrooms, 3 parlors, 2 elevators, large lobbies, a billiard room, and a barbershop. It served as the central structure of this Lutheran college for women from 1912 to 1925, when it burned to the ground.

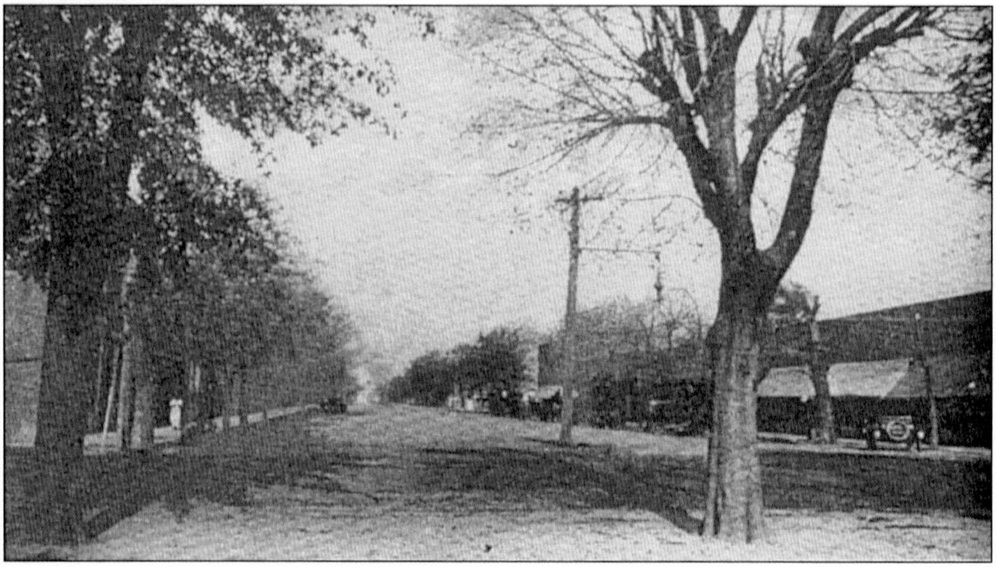

MAIN STREET LOOKING NORTH, LEESVILLE, SC [*c.* 1925]. Leesville College is barely discernible far up at the end of Main Street in this viewcard that shows the old central business district (minus its current median) with its original commercial blocks and the hackberry trees that once lined the street. It was laid out by brothers David C. and John Jacob ("Jake") Shealy on land acquired by their father, John Shealy, of the Chapin area. The railroad, constructed about 1869, crossed Main in the distance.

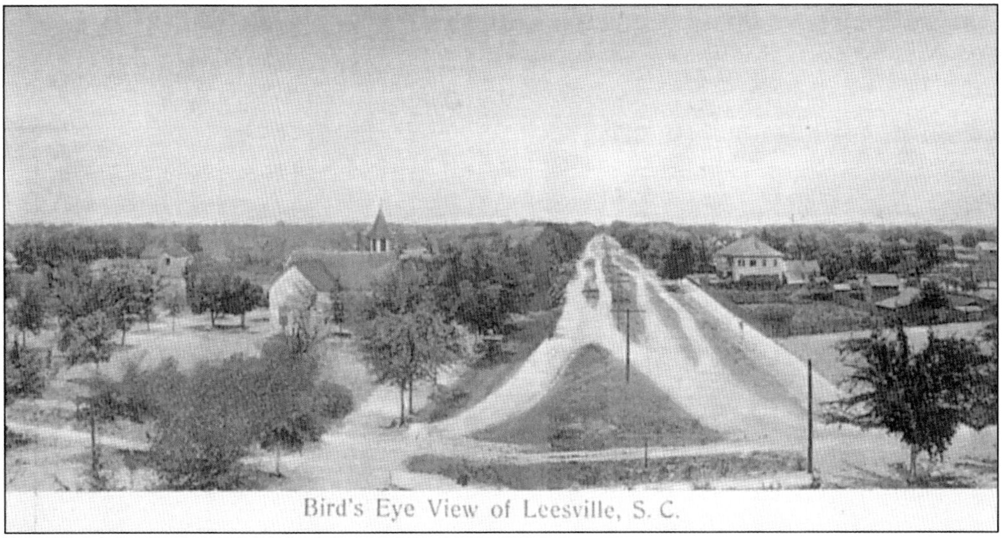

BIRD'S-EYE VIEW OF LEESVILLE, SC [C. 1909]. Looking south on a dirt Main Street, this view must have been taken from the bell tower of Leesville College after 1908, when Mr. Furman Brodie strung 4 miles of three-phase 2,300-volt line from his mill pond south of town to furnish Leesville with electricity. Its population in 1910 was 900.

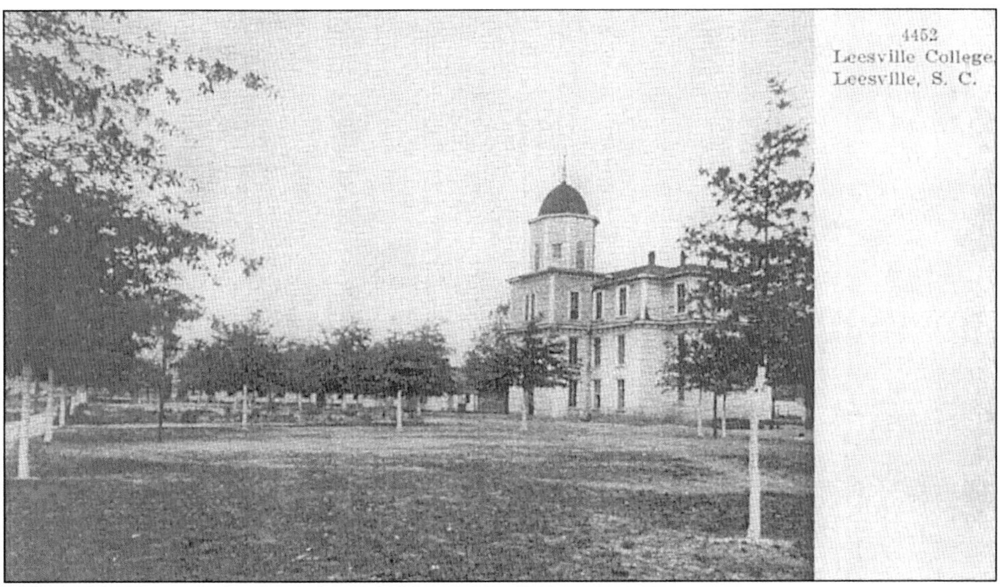

LEESVILLE COLLEGE, LEESVILLE, SC [1907]. The three-story concrete structure pictured above, hailed as "one of the most substantial and elegant school buildings" in South Carolina, served as the architectural centerpiece for Leesville College, which was chartered in 1890 and succeeded the Leesville English and Classical Institute, which had operated successfully for nine years. It was utilized as part of the town's school system and eventually became the property of Leesville. This building, minus its wooden top floor and tower (which were removed about 1935), still stands on College Street at the north end of Main and functions as headquarters for the Ridge Arts Council and the Batesburg-Leesville Historical Society.

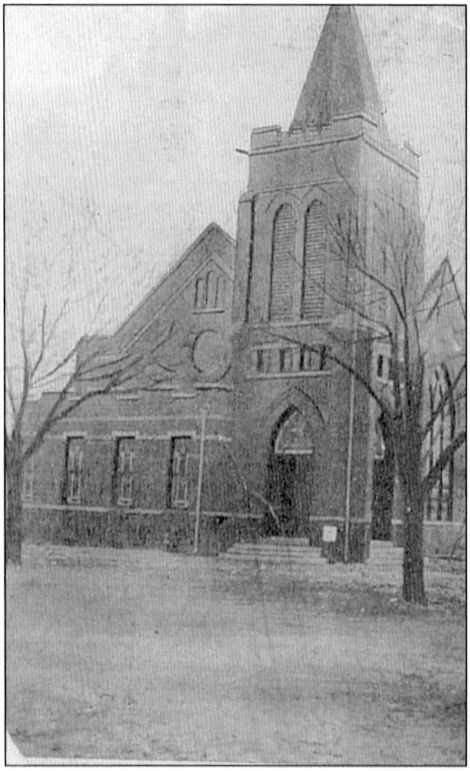

METHODIST CHURCH, LEESVILLE, SC [1909]. Now called the Leesville Methodist Church, this "new" brick sanctuary located on East Columbia Avenue was erected in 1908 under the leadership of the Reverend M.M. Brabham. According to the cornerstone, which can still be seen to the right of the front steps, as shown here, the building committee consisted of J.P. Able, J.H. Bodie, and C.D. Barr.

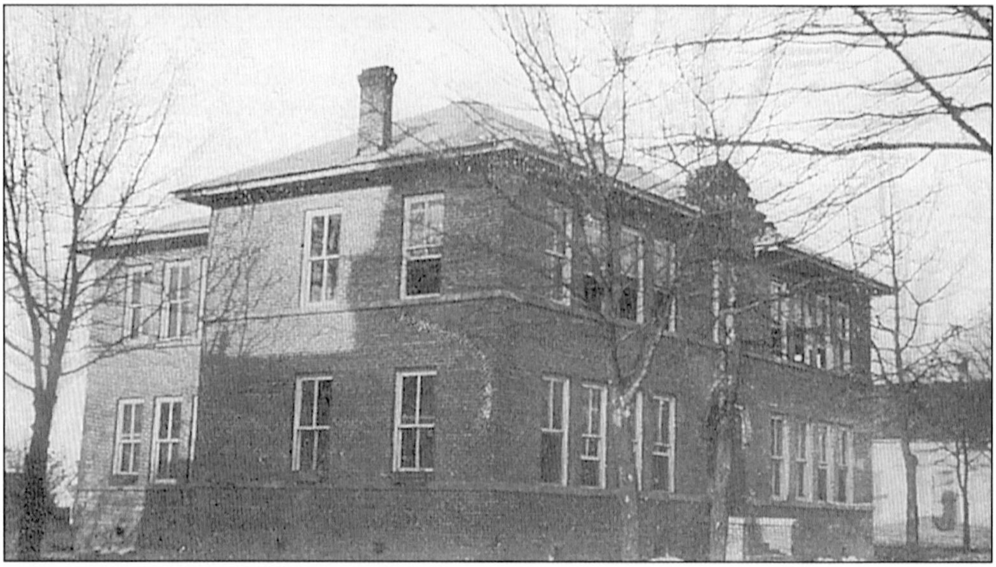

[HIGH SCHOOL, LEESVILLE, *C.* 1912.] One teacher served 97 students for a 16-week term in the public school of Leesville in 1900. By 1919, its high school ranked as a third-class type (two full-time teachers, a three-year curriculum, 32- to 36-week sessions and 12 to 13 units). J.W. Ballentine by then was in his fourth year as principal, with 17 years of teaching experience. By 1925 the school had received state accreditation. In 1922 the cornerstone was laid for the new Batesburg-Leesville Consolidated High School.

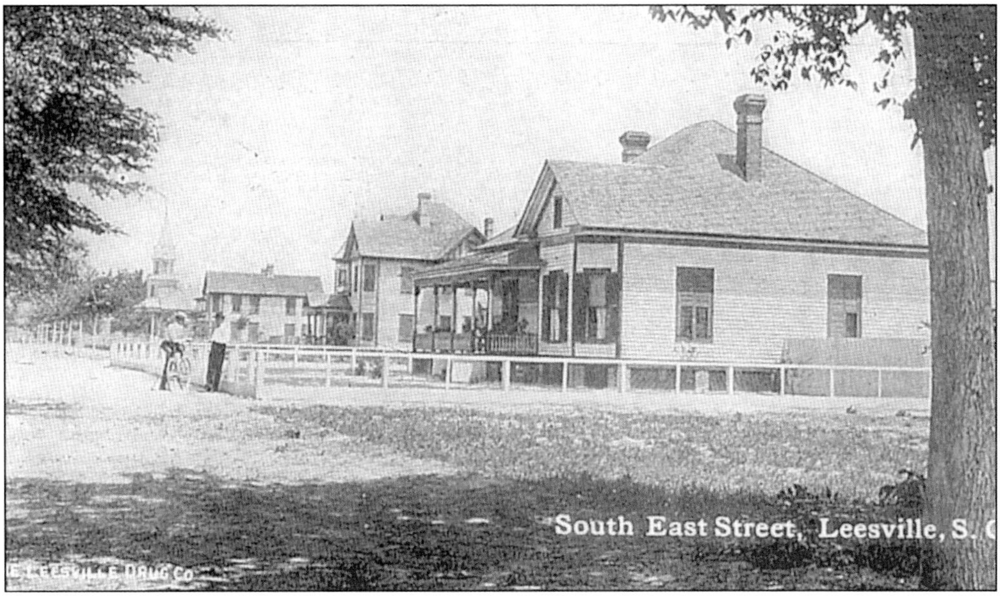

SOUTH EAST STREET, LEESVILLE, SC [1909]. South East Street crosses East Columbia Avenue just beyond the middle Quattlebaum House (no longer standing.) Facing north, with the pre-1908 timber Methodist Episcopal Church (visible in the distance at left), is a row of residences, two of which were identifiable in 2000. At the right is the old Meetze-Bouknight home, now much changed in its brick renovation, but recognizable by its original roofline, and in the middle distance is the Etheridge house, still carefully maintained.

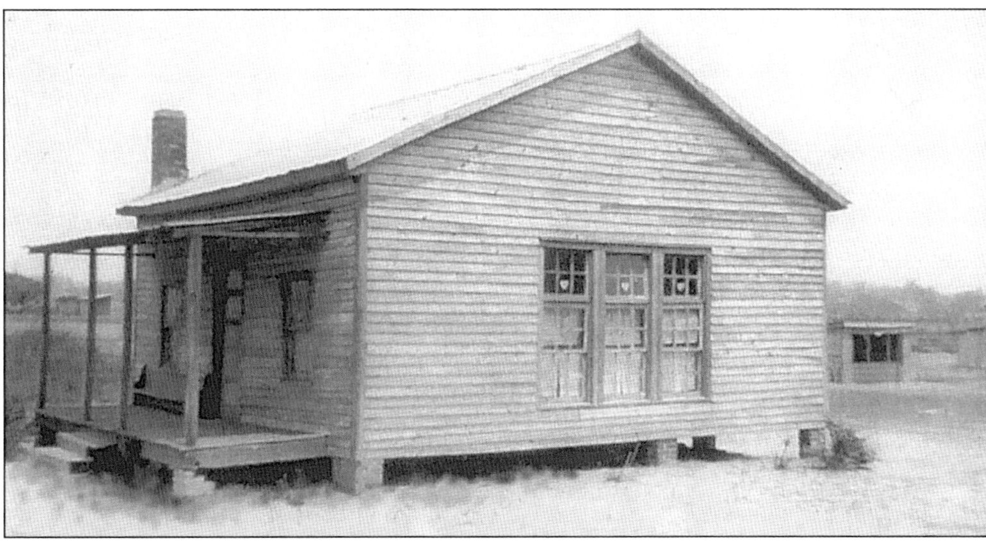

[LEESVILLE SCHOOL, *C.* 1930S.] Presumably the small schoolhouse shown above replaced the one that existed before 1900 and served the community's 85 African-American students. At one time located in the middle of Hall Street (now S. Lee) in Simmon Town, it reportedly continued to be used for pre-school and first grade after the Hampton School was built. Hampton was the Rosenwald School established largely through the efforts of the late Frederick Hampton Hendrix (1862–1947) for the use of children from the Twin Cities. The records show that Rosenwald spent $4,000 on school buildings in the county during 1922 and 1923.

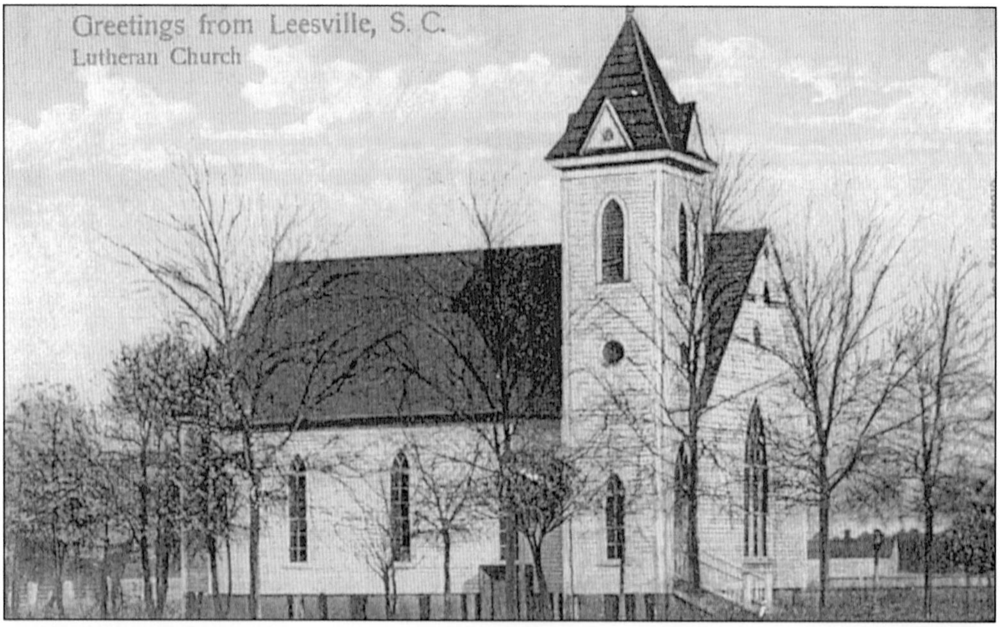

GREETINGS FROM LEESVILLE, SC. LUTHERAN CHURCH [1910]. The brick sanctuary of the Wittenberg Lutheran Church on N. Lee Street, completed in 1919, replaced the 1887 wooden structure shown here, with its Gothic windows and bell tower, constructed when the church was known as Luther Chapel (1870 to 1917). This card is postmarked 1914.

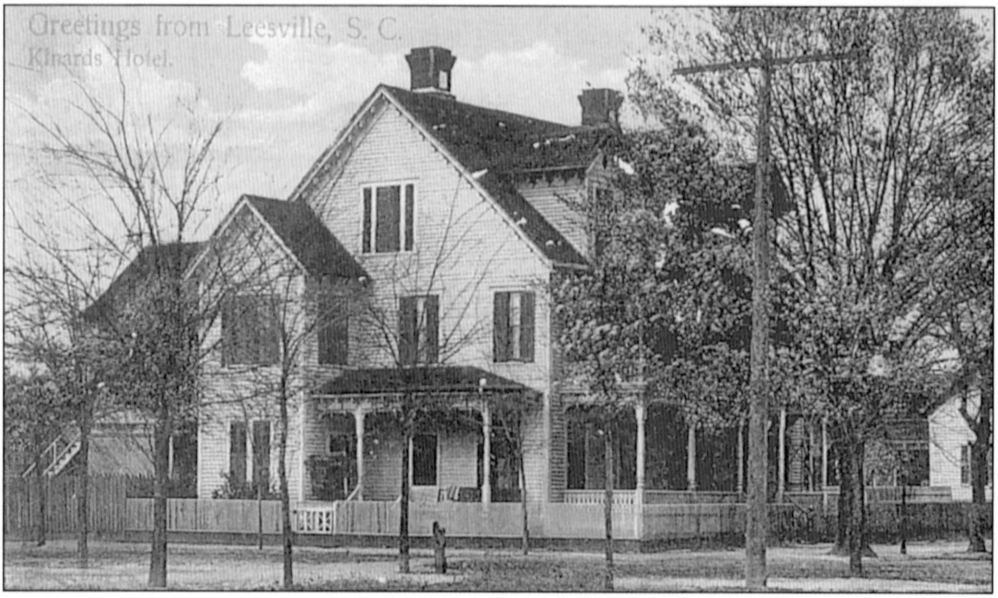

GREETINGS FROM LEESVILLE, SC. KINARDS HOTEL [1910]. Kinard's Hotel once stood at the northeast corner of E. Church Street (SC 23) at its intersection with N. Lee, a block from Leesville's business district. Built about 1899, the large frame house was operated as a hotel for many years by Mr. and Mrs. Jim Kinard; later, as the Leesville Hotel, by their daughter, Mrs. J.E. Black; and finally by the David Elkinses, who subsequently used it as a private residence before razing it in 1959 and building another house on the site.

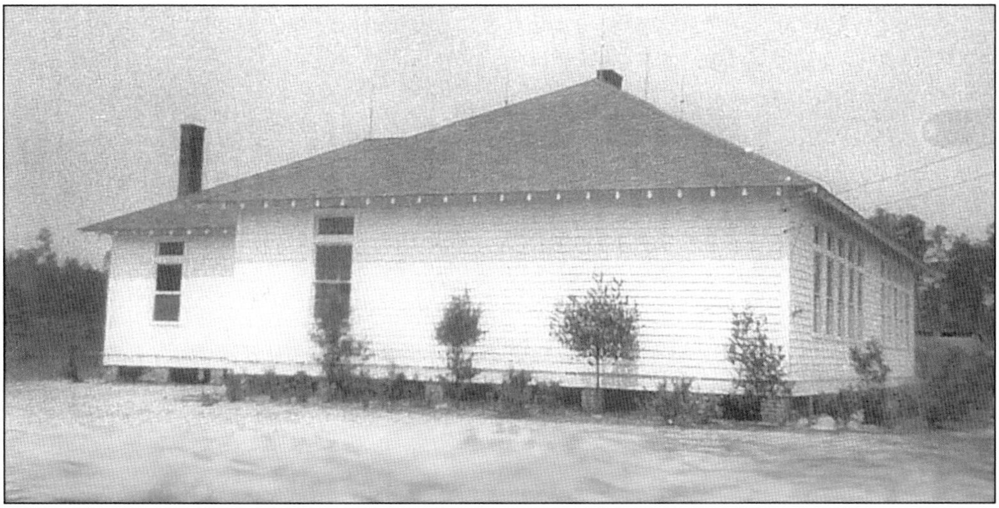

[SAMARIA SCHOOL, *C.* 1930S.] Samaria shows up on South Carolina maps as early as 1883. The rural Samaria School, near Haven Road and Oleander Road off US 178 about 7 miles southeast of Batesburg, served this community of 100 in 1910 near Chinquapin Creek on the Aiken County line. Gunter's visit in 1915 described the school as a "comparatively new one" with an enrollment of 78 students in a session of 110 days and taught by one lady. He recommended a larger modern school, three teachers, and a longer session. By the early 1930s, each of these requirements was met. This building no longer stands.

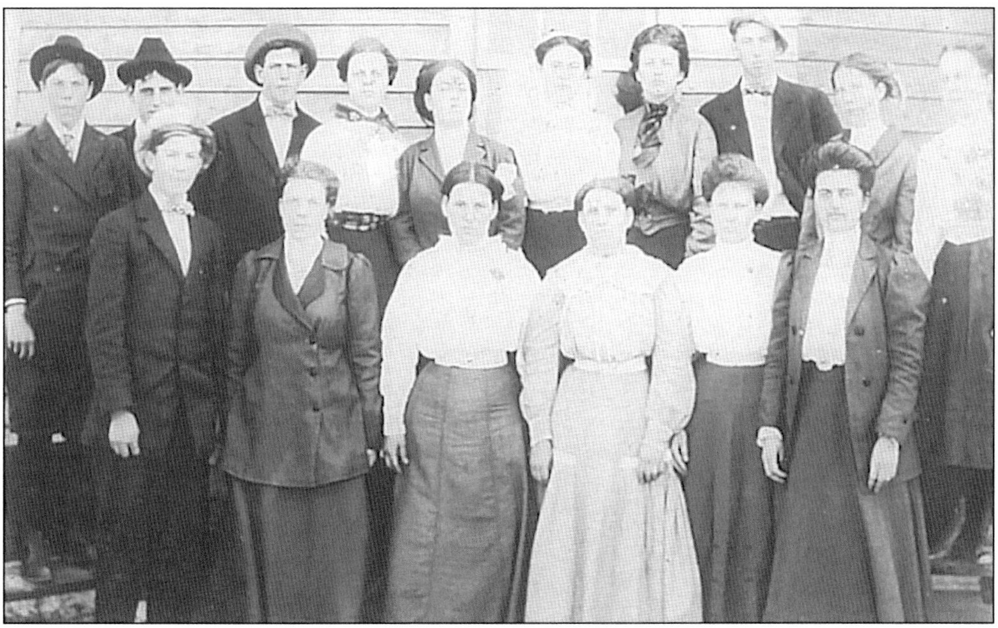

[SUMMER SCHOOL FOR TEACHERS, BOILING SPRINGS, *C.* 1910.] Public school teachers dressed up for this group portrait presumably after their successful completion of summer course work. Bertha Kleckley (Smith) is standing in the front row, far right. In 1915 South Carolina had 2,556 white schools; 1,701 of them had one teacher; 467, two teachers; 150, three teachers; and 238 had more than three teachers. There were 2,325 one-teacher schools for African-American children, 118 two-teacher schools, 30 three-teacher schools, and 42 with more than three teachers.

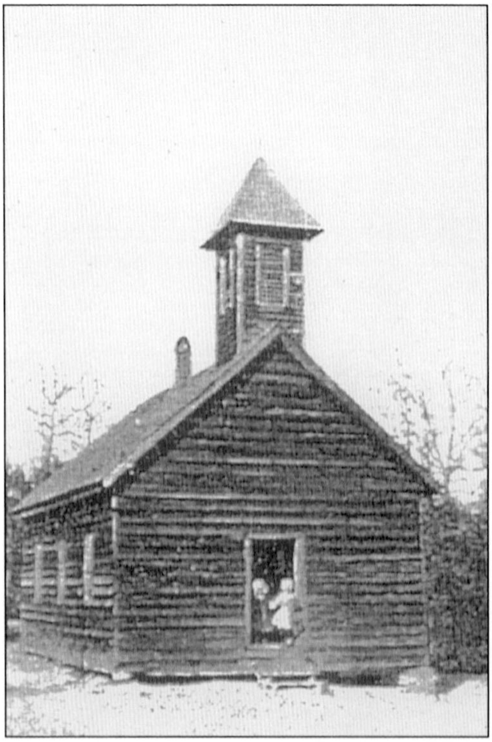

[Poplar Springs School, c. 1910s.] Daniel Senn conveyed half an acre of land to the Poplar Springs Academy in 1877, and the following year a 20-by-30-foot one-room schoolhouse was built. The school and the Enon Lutheran Church (organized in 1901) have long been closely linked. In 1900 this one-teacher school, located 3 miles east of Leesville on Pond Branch Road, had 39 students in an eight-week session. Gunter's visit in 1915 found 64 students in a seven-grade curriculum that "was well organized and gave evidence of good teaching." A modern schoolhouse replaced the initial building in the early 1920s.

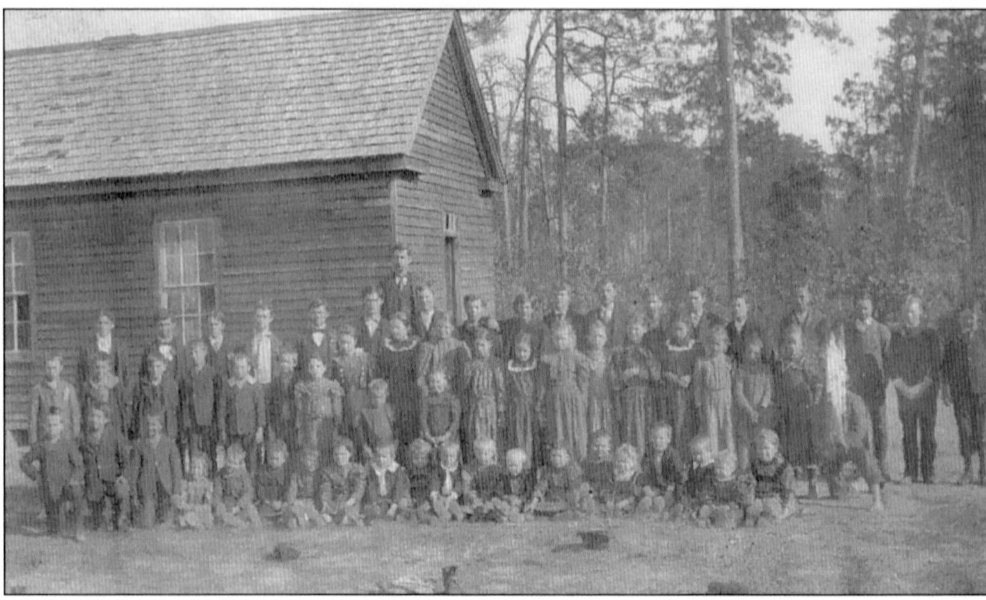

[Pond Branch School, c. 1906.] The turn-of-the-century one-teacher Pond Branch School, 4 miles south of Gilbert near the crossing of Pond Branch Road and Neely Wingard Road, served 41 students in a nine-week session in 1900. By 1915, when Gunter visited the school, it had expanded to two teachers and added a second classroom to house 46 boys and 40 girls in a session of 140 days. He suggested it needed a third teacher. In 1919 Mrs. Bertha Smith, with 16 years of experience as an educator, became the principal. Pond Branch students later attended the Gilbert School.

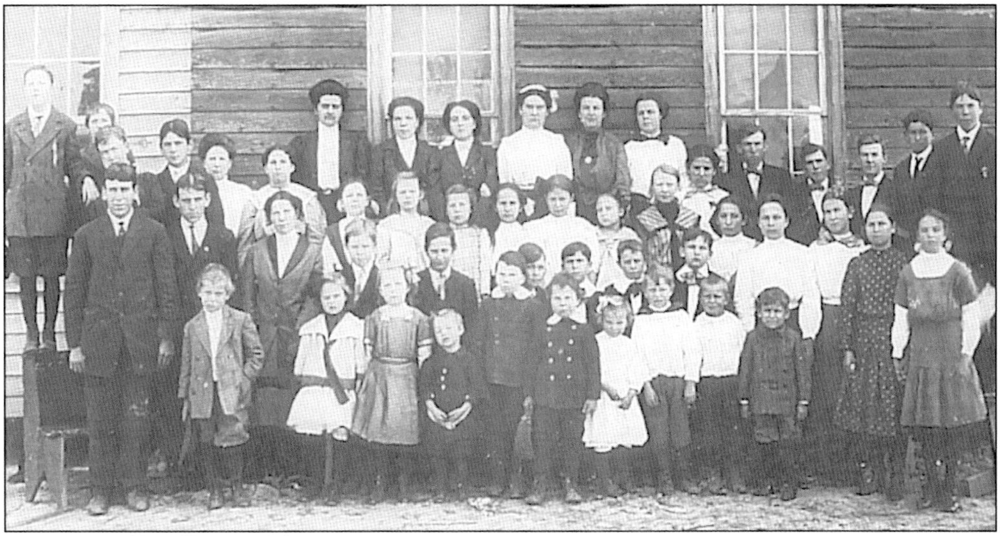

[Boiling Springs School, c. 1910.] Boiling Springs was located at the center of the county about 7 miles southeast of Gilbert near the junction of Pond Branch Road and Calk's Ferry Road. In the picture above, the 1900-era one-teacher schoolhouse, which served 50 students in a 16-week session, seems to have been expanded with the addition of a second room at the rear. This school picture taken about 1910 includes the teacher, Bertha Kleckley (Smith), standing at the far left in the fourth row.

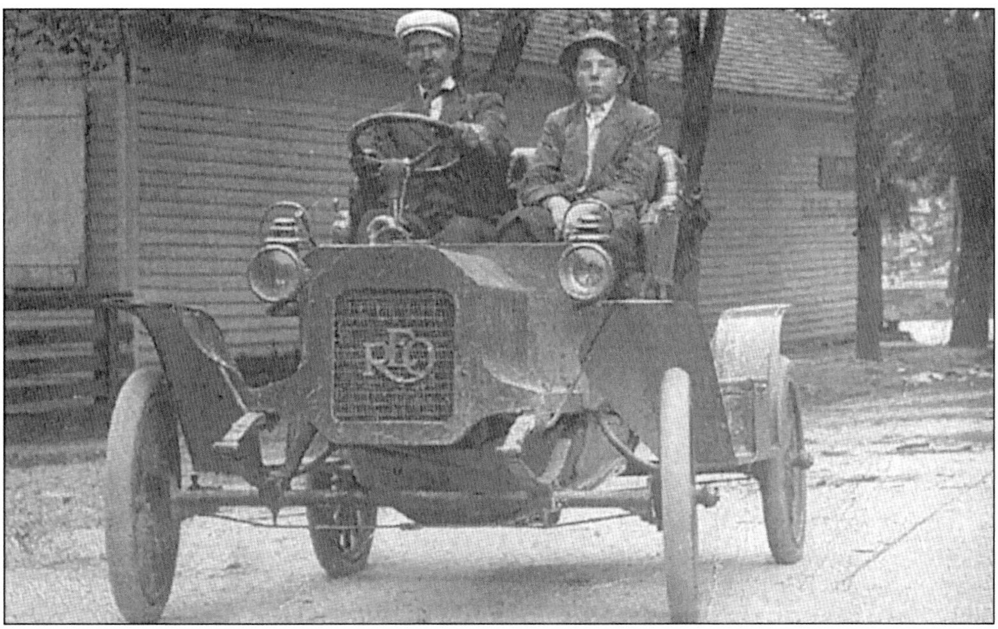

[Roswell Barr in His Reo, Gilbert, c. 1910.] The picture above shows Roswell A. Barr, left, on Lewie Street at the wheel of his Reo. Milas Sease is seated on the right. According to D.S. Shull in *Lexington County: Economic and Social* (1923), Lexington County had 2,530 automobiles in 1921. Only four other counties in South Carolina had more automobiles in proportion to its population than Lexington, which ranked fifth with 1 automobile for each 14.1 inhabitants. Greenville, Richland, Anderson, and Darlington Counties outranked her in the order named.

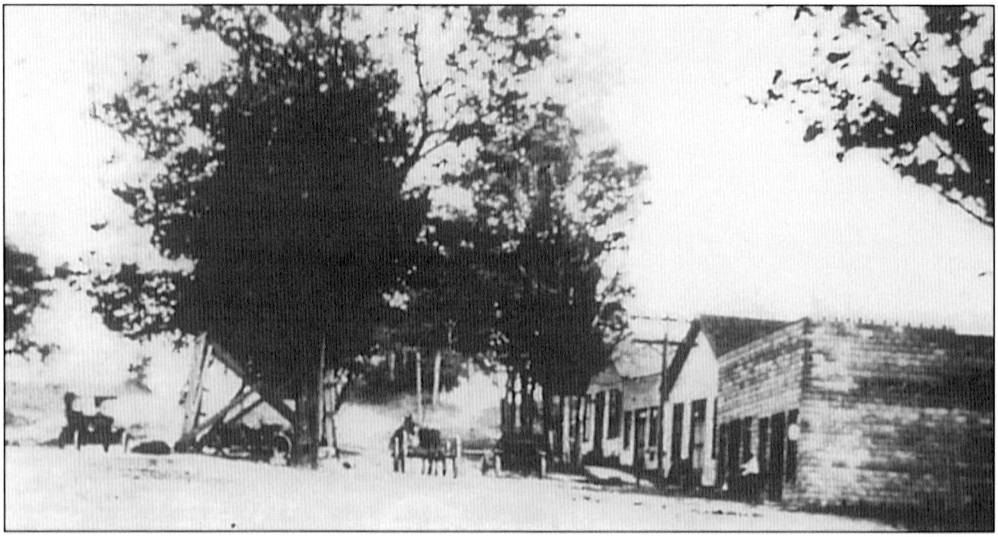

[Main Street, Gilbert, *c.* 1910.] In 1910 Gilbert was a rural railroad community with a population of 550 that had a small business district, seen above in this view looking south. In 1917, the frame stores—probably belonging to merchants Will Keisler, D.E. Hammond, and K.B. Price—were destroyed by fire. Afterwards the brick Bank of Gilbert was built on the corner of this block, along with a row of other brick structures housing the office of Dr. Smith and the establishments of the above-mentioned merchants. These buildings were still standing in 2000.

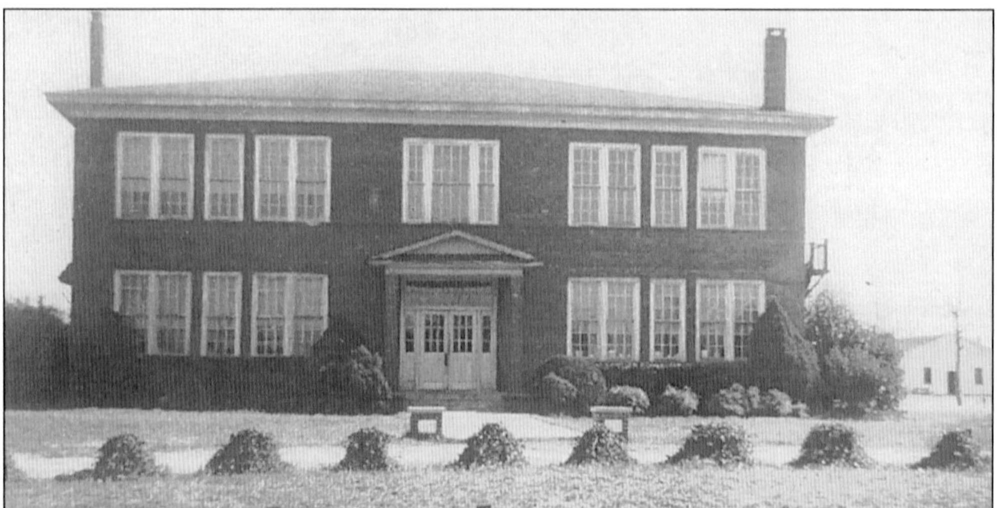

[High School, Gilbert, *c.* 1923.] The 1915 report by Gunter suggested that the growth of this two-teacher school, with an enrollment of 77 students and a session of 120 days, called for a modern three-teacher building. In 1919 Ozelia Harmon, a principal in her second year, began suggesting the need for a new building, which resulted in the 1923 facility. The brick school followed the then-current architectural guidelines prescribing three classrooms on the first floor and an auditorium and a classroom on the second. Gilbert became a hub school for over 15 nearby communities. It has been replaced by a contemporary campus complex.

[CAPTAIN JAMES HENRY LEWIE, GILBERT, *C.* 1905.] In 1886 the village was incorporated as Lewiedale, named after Gilbert Hollow native James Henry Lewie (1838–1889), shown in this early-20th-century reprint of a 19th-century picture. One of the most prominent merchants in the county, Lewie had earlier served in the Civil War as captain of Company "C," 15th Regiment, South Carolina Voluntary Infantry. He was married to Martha Ann Leaphart (1840–1911). His daughter, Alice Virginia (1867–1946) married Talton Semm Sease (1860–1940). In 1899, the town officially took the name Gilbert, which the post office did not recognize until 1904.

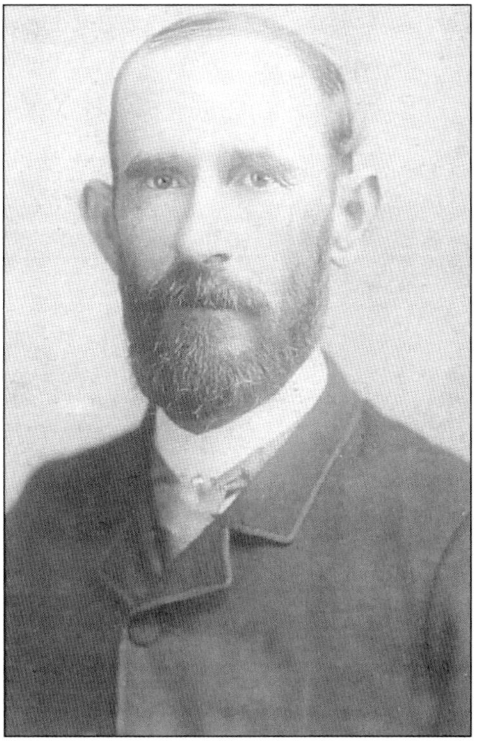

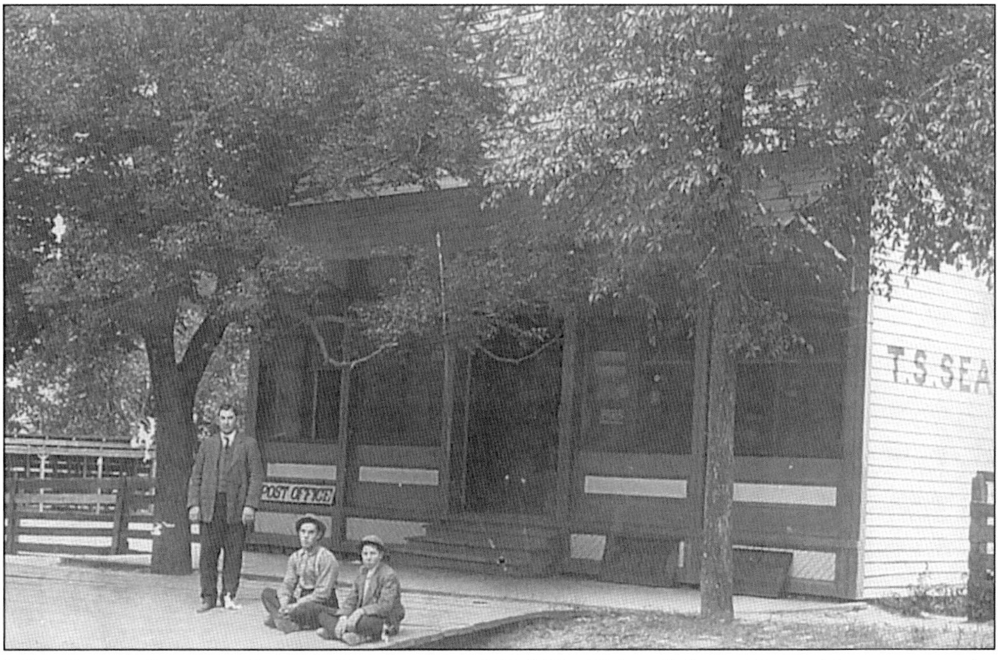

[T.S. SEASE GENERAL STORE, GILBERT, *C.* 1910.] The Talton S. Sease General Store was on the left side of Main and Lewie Streets and contained Gilbert's post office. Pictured above are Semm Sease (standing), Lewie Sease (middle), and Milas Sease (right). T.S. Sease was postmaster from 1899 to 1914 and mayor in 1899 and 1918. This building no longer stands.

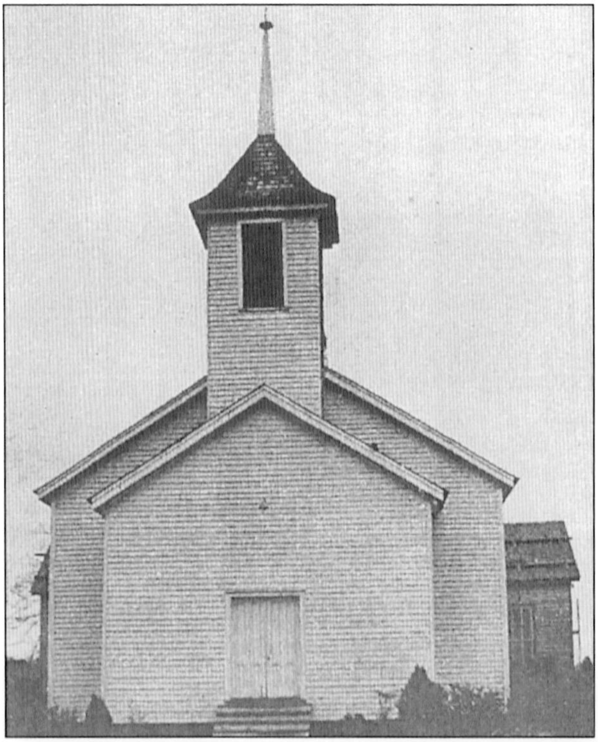

[LUTHERAN CHURCH, GILBERT, *c.* 1930.] In 1893, Grace Lutheran Church was organized and the sanctuary pictured at left was built on the corner of Main and Church Streets. On April 16, 1950, a fire destroyed the frame building in 45 minutes. A new brick church was built on the same site.

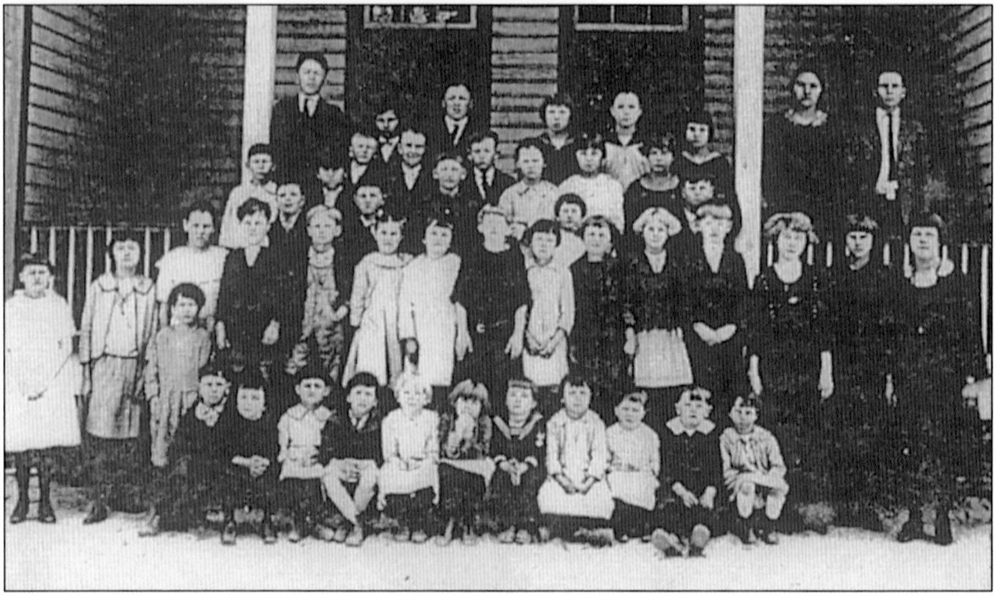

[CENTERVILLE SCHOOL, *c.* 1920.] In 1916 Lueco Gunter described Centerville as a one-teacher school in a badly arranged building with 48 students enrolled for a 100-day term. By 1919 the district had hired B.W. Harmon as the principal and had built a modern two-teacher school. The picture above, taken about 1920, shows the students and teachers standing at the entrance to the schoolhouse. Located off US 1 north of Gilbert, the building still stood in 2000 and was being used as a residence beside the dirt Centerville Road.

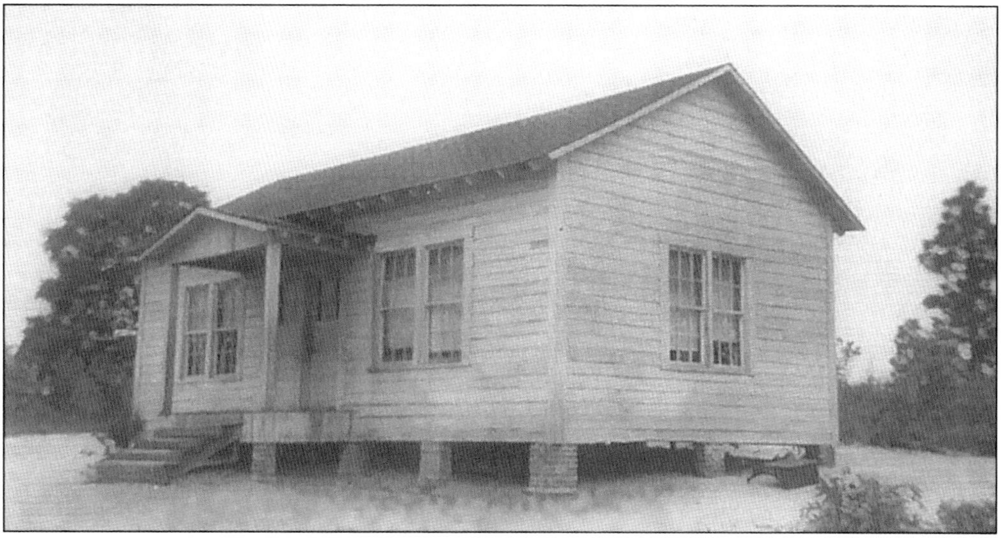

[Zion Hopewell School, Gilbert, c. 1930s.] The Zion Hopewell School and Church were on Zion Hopewell Road. The Zion school was initially supported by its founding church. By 1915 Gilbert, like the other small towns across the county, began supporting small one-room frame black schools. Gilbert's school was larger than others and was a neat, well-constructed building with a covered entrance. The average number of black students in these schools was 50 and the average length of a term was 63 days.

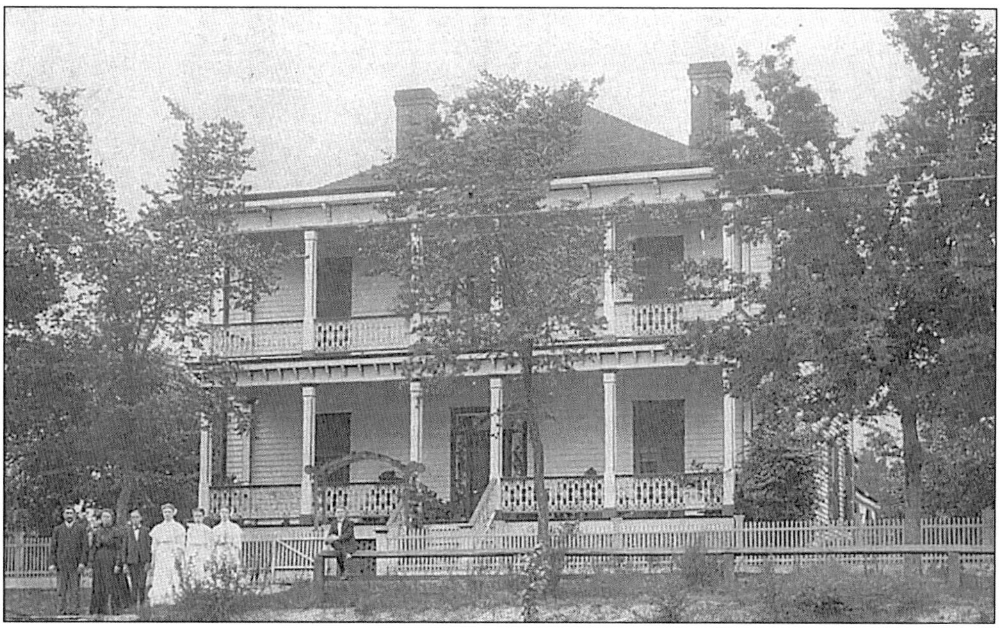

[T.S. Sease Residence, Gilbert, c. 1910.] The Talton S. Sease residence faced Washington Street. Pictured in front of the home shown above, from left to right, are the following: T.S. Sease, Alice Virginia Sease, Semm Lewie Sease, Ethel Sease Crout, Mertie Sease Barr, Lily Sease Eleazer, and 12-year-old Milas Y. Sease. The residence no longer stands.

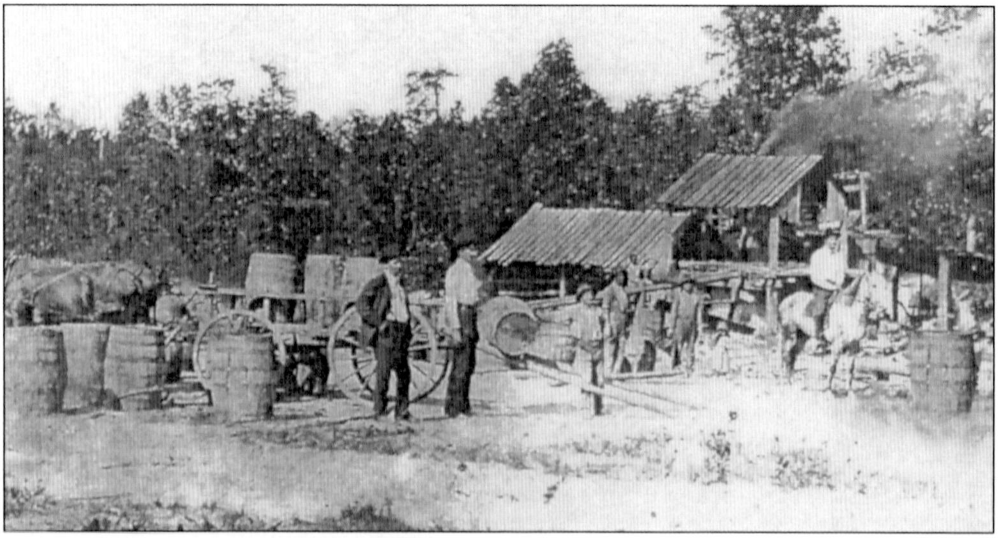

[Hartley Brothers' Turpentine Still, Summit, c. 1905.] Fred and Hamp Hartley ran this Summit still, which opened in 1896, and in 1925 they moved to Pelion to start a new one. Large turpentine stills like Hartley's were virtual factories employing small work forces that were essential to the local economy. However, many stills were small operations that an individual farmer could also use as an extra source of income. Workers made V-shaped cuts through the bark of pine trees so that the sap could run into small cups that held up to a quart of tar. The collected tar was taken to the still in 55-gallon barrels where it was put in vats and heated. This process turned the tar into turpentine, which was used in paints and varnishes.

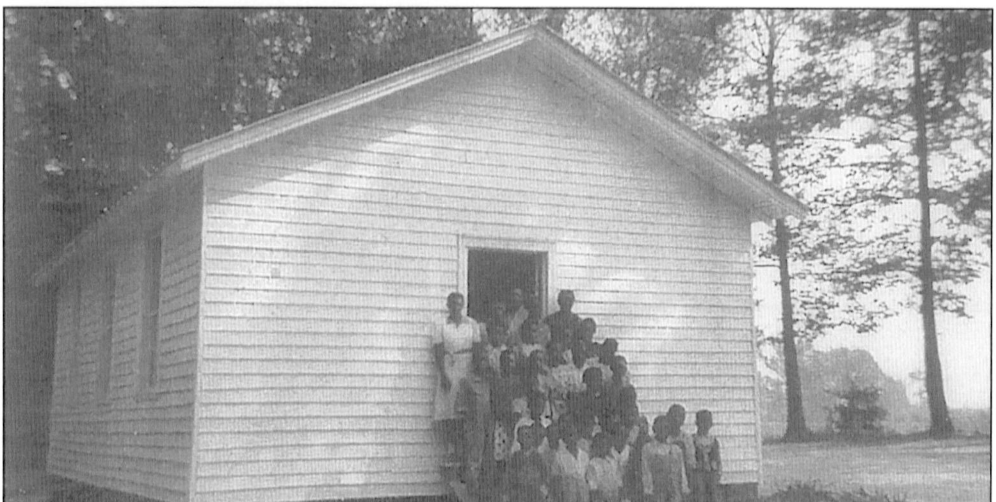

[Hollow Creek School, c. 1930s.] Hollow Creek Community had a one-teacher schoolhouse for black children that appears to have been built in the early 1930s. This rural school was located between Spring Hill Road and Calk's Ferry Road, 7 miles west of Lexington. The community had a history of supporting a school for African-American children since 1900. They likely employed one of the 38 black first-grade teachers. The state superintendent of education in his 1931 report stated that during the previous 10 or 12 years around 599 Negro schoolhouses had been created in South Carolina.

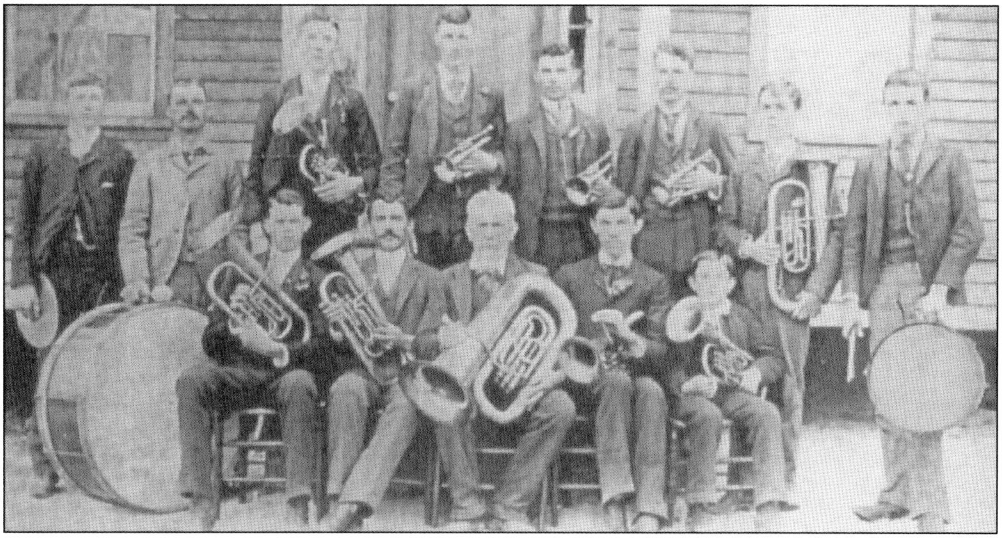

[Palmetto Brass Band, Summit, 1890s.] The Palmetto Brass Band was organized by Ida Wessinger with Rev. E.L. Lybrand of the Summit Academy (1883-1895) as director. The traveling troupe entertained audiences across Lexington and adjoining counties at various events. The musicians, from left to right, are as follows: (first row) Arthur H. Hallman, Ellicotte Shealy, Joseph F. Harmon, Fred G. Hartley, John A. Harman; (second row) Senn L. Steele, Jason S. Shealy, Rev. Cally T. Morgan, Frank W. Shealy, Elzie Long, M. Curtis Hallman, William F. Taylor, and William A. Hare. (Data researced by Raymond Taylor, Summit.)

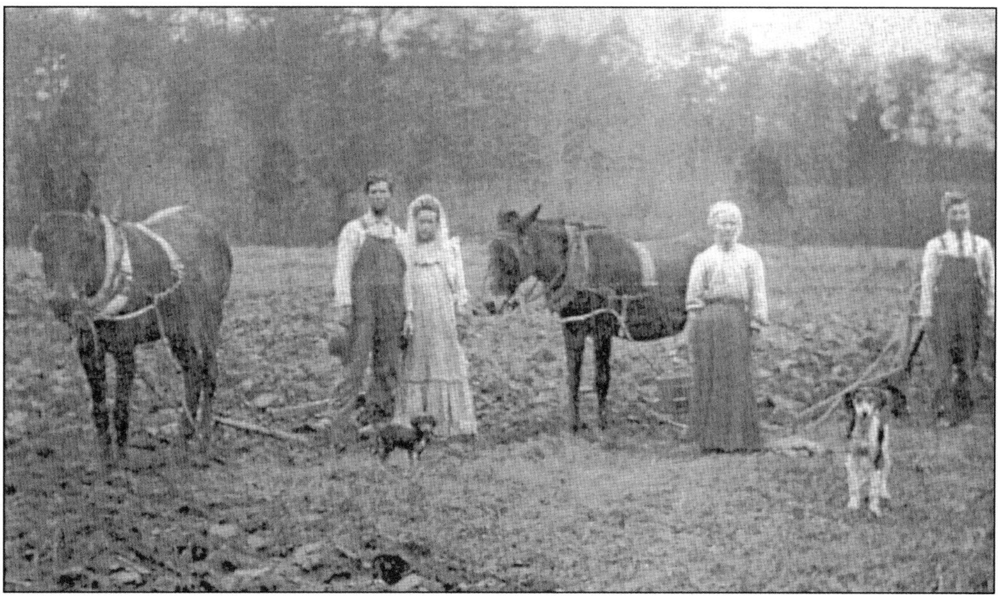

[Taylor Farm, Summit, *c.* 1910.] This farm, located off Cedar Grove Road north of Summit, was the property of Sibbie Kizziah (Anderson) Taylor (1858–1939), daughter of Henry and Mahaly (Alewine) Anderson, who married Jacob David Taylor (1862–1917), son of J.R. and Matilda E. Taylor. Jacob became a preacher at Pleasant Hill Baptist Church in 1893. Shown here, giving themselves and their mules a break from the day's work in the fields, are Jim and Jacob Taylor along with Elizabeth and Sibbie—and the family dogs.

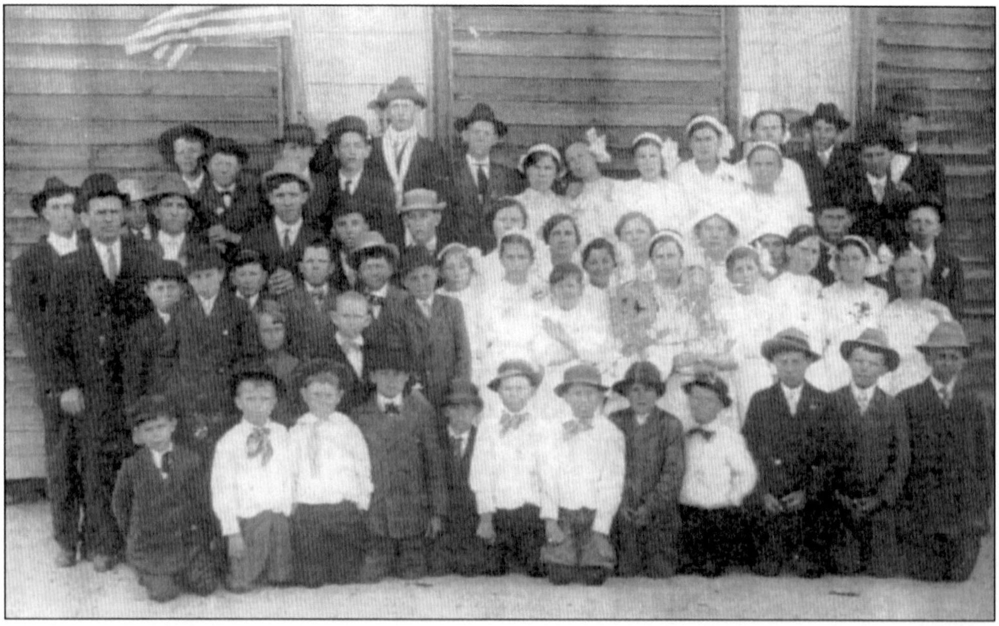

[Ridge Road School, c. 1905.] In 1900, the Ridge Road School, located on LC 46 about 8 miles north of Leesville, had 1 teacher and 55 students in a 16-week session. This photograph, taken in front of the frame schoolhouse, is possibly a 1905 graduation picture. The boys are dressed in suits, white shirts, ties, and hats, while the girls don white dresses and hair ribbons, with some holding flowers. This and successive buildings have been replaced on the site by a community center.

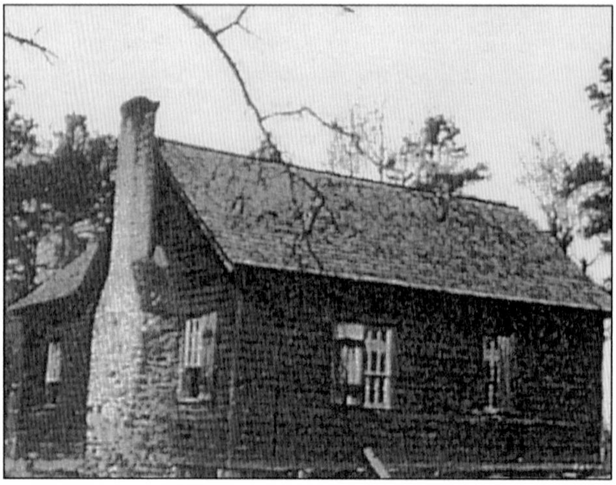

[Pineville School, c. 1910.] In 1915, when Lueco Gunter visited the pre-1900 one-room Pineville school (which in 1900 had an enrollment of 67 pupils), he found 1 teacher attempting to manage 54 students in nine grades—a situation that he thought could only result in neglect of the lower-grade pupils. The traditional style of the building could not be modified for effective teaching, and Gunter recommended construction of a new two-teacher schoolhouse. The school apparently was located in the area near Ella and Savilla, situated between Hollow Creek and Little Hollow Creek on the old Clark Ferry Road. Its name appears for the last time in the 1929–1930 issue of the *School Directory of South Carolina.*

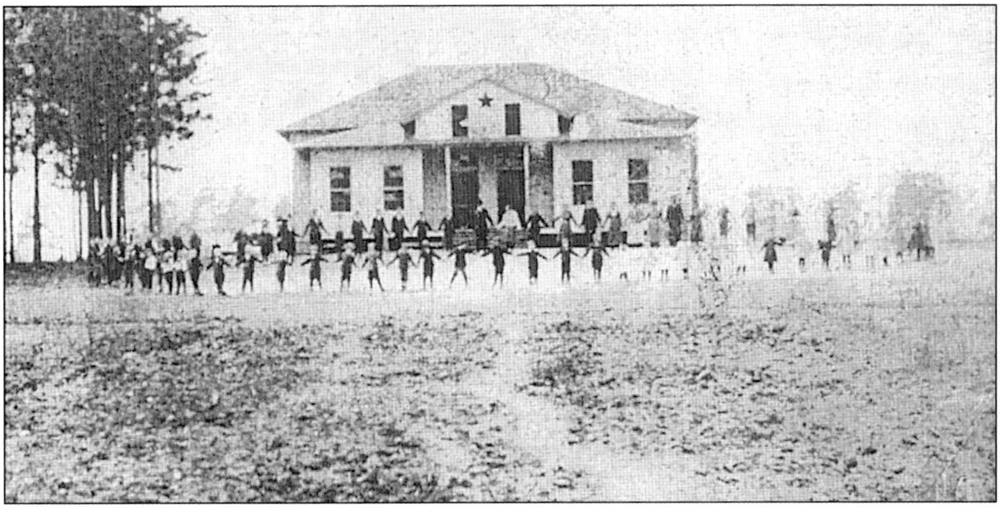

[RED STAR SCHOOL, C. 1925.] The students and teachers seen here holding hands are gathered outside their school, Red Star, located on Old Lexington Road (LC 157) near US 378, 15 miles west of Lexington and 8 miles north of Leesville. Erected in the early 1920s, the building was a frame two-teacher structure built to one of the school designs created by Clemson's School of Architecture. While rural Red Star would have been closed during the major period of school consolidation in the county, the late 1940s and early 1950s, the building still survived in 2000 as a residence in an unimproved condition on a dirt road cut through the woods.

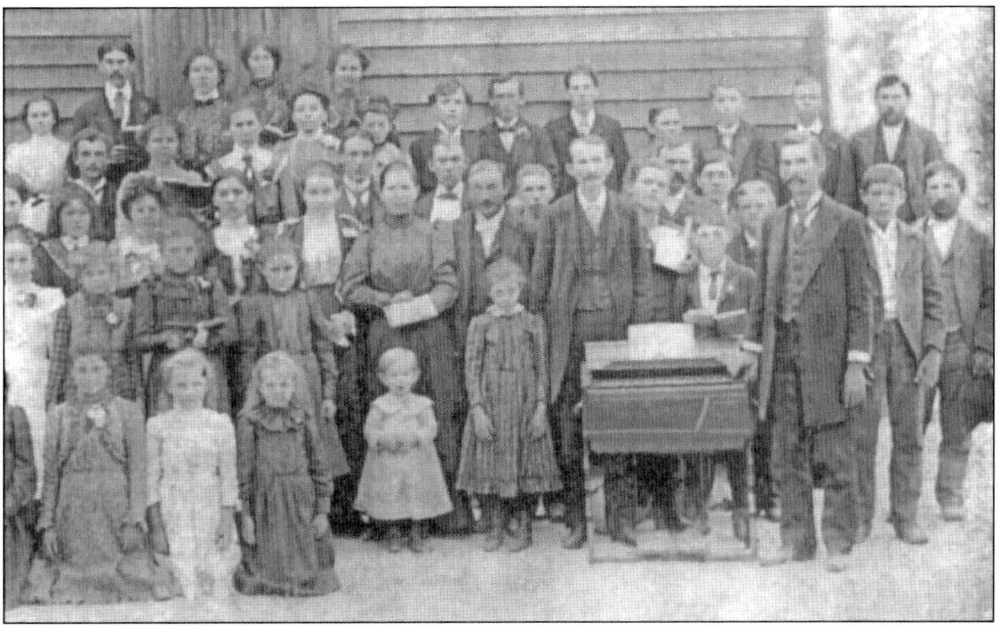

[PLEASANT HILL BAPTIST CHURCH, C. 1901.] Among the earliest images in the volume is this 1901 photograph showing the minister, congregation, and presumably a portable organ of the then newly built Pleasant Hill Baptist Church (now First Calvary), at 2320 Cedar Grove Road, north of US 1 and the community of Summit. This sanctuary, with a seating capacity of 200 and valued at $500, replaced an earlier one that had been erected in 1886 by the 48-member congregation and valued at $150.

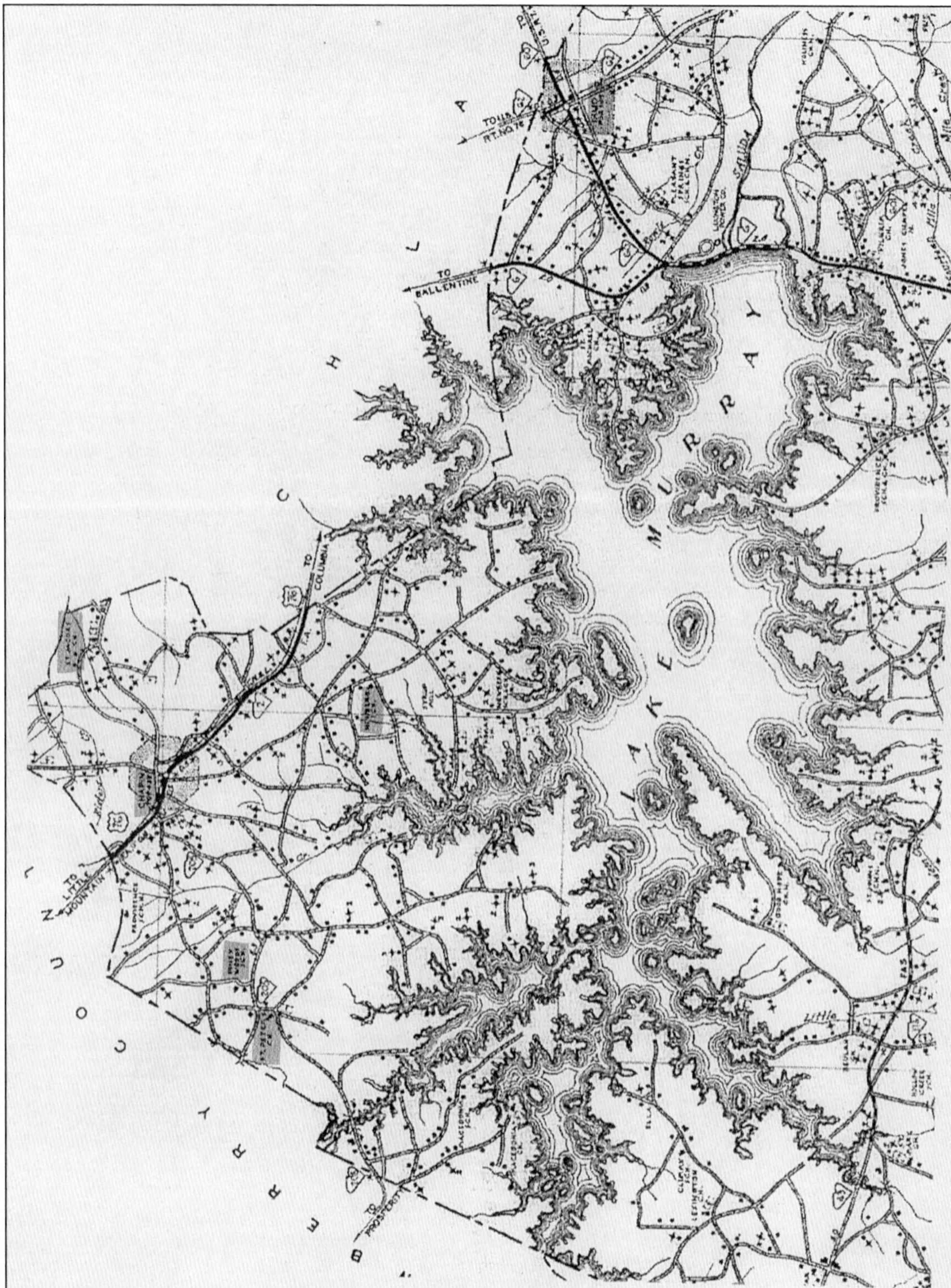

[Map of Northern Lexington County and Lake Murray, 1940.] This enlarged regional section of a 1940 highway map of Lexington County shows the area covered in chapter four. The small dark strips indicate the location of school sites. Highway jurisdictional abbreviations used in the captions are designated as follows: LC (Lexington County), SC (South Carolina), and US (United States). Other map sections are found on pages 8, 11, and 52.

Four

Northern Region

Postcards from the northern reaches of Lexington County, those of the Dutch Fork and of Lake Murray, reflect the experience of a region established in large part by folk of German-Swiss origin. The pictures reveal the impact of the railroad in the creation of the depot towns along the northern border, the proliferation of Lutheran churches, an insistence upon providing schools, and the determinative influence of the area's water resources on its economic and social life.

Some 5,000 area inhabitants were affected drastically by the damming of the Saluda River and the creation of Lake Murray in what was at the time (1927 to 1930) the largest project of its kind in the world. The effects were felt in terms of loss: acres and acres of woodland, some farms and homes—even a steel bridge. The gains have been measured in terms of hydroelectric power, premier recreational development, and land values that have since become some of the highest in South Carolina.

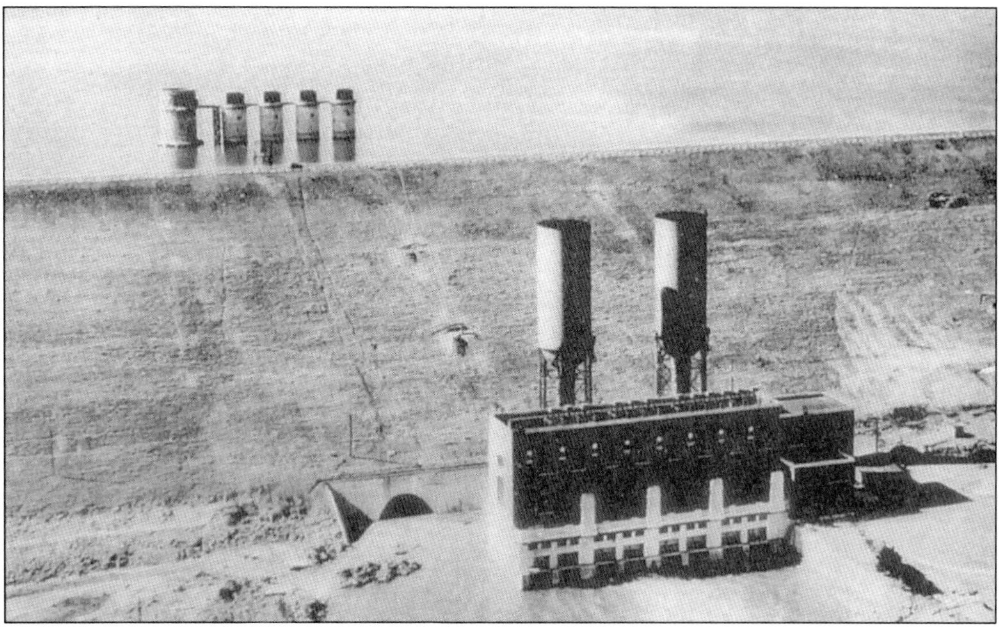

Saluda (Dreher Shoals) Dam, Showing Power Plant and Intake Towers Beyond, Columbia, SC [c. 1930]. The single large dam at Dreher Shoals was 1.5 miles wide and 208 feet high, at the time of its construction the largest earthen dam in cubical content for power purposes in the world. The water intake towers shown here rise 223 feet high out of Lake Murray. The lake, created by flooding some 50,000 acres of land covering 78 square miles, was 41 miles long and 14 miles wide. The project purchased 1,100 parcels of land and displaced 5,000 people, 3 churches, and 6 schools. It was named for William Spencer Murray of the New York firm of Murray and Flood that designed the project.

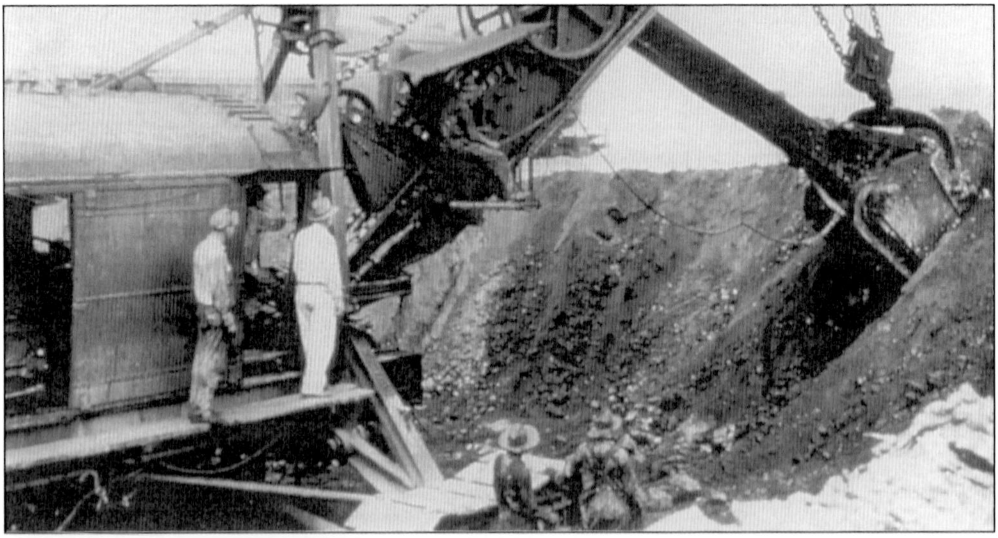

[STEAM SHOVEL, LAKE MURRAY DAM, *c.* 1930.] In his 1990 book *Irmo and the Dutch Fork Legacy*, Gene Able provides a succinct history of this second-most important development in the area (after the railroad). In the chapter entitled "Lake Murray and the Dam," he reports that the first load of dirt was dumped on the site on September 21, 1927; the final load, on June 28, 1930. More than 4,000 people were employed by the project during the three-year period of the construction of the dam on the Saluda River, which constituted the most ambitious engineering project in the state to that time.

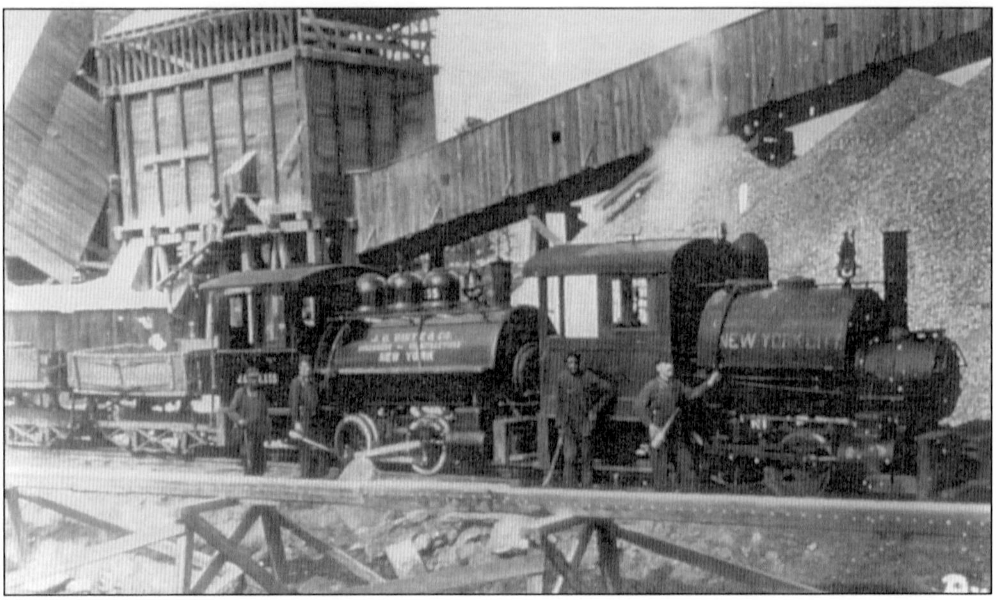

[LOCOMOTIVE ENGINES, LAKE MURRAY DAM, *c.* 1930S.] Before its completion in 1930, Lake Murray consisted of many acres of woodland. Anywhere from 500 to 1,800 men were employed in the various lumber camps that were responsible for clearing some 100,000,000 board-foot of lumber from the land. Some of it was used to build the mile-long spur line in Irmo that connected with the Columbia, Newberry & Laurens Railroad at the St. Andrews Road crossing. Construction equipment for the project could then be shipped in by rail.

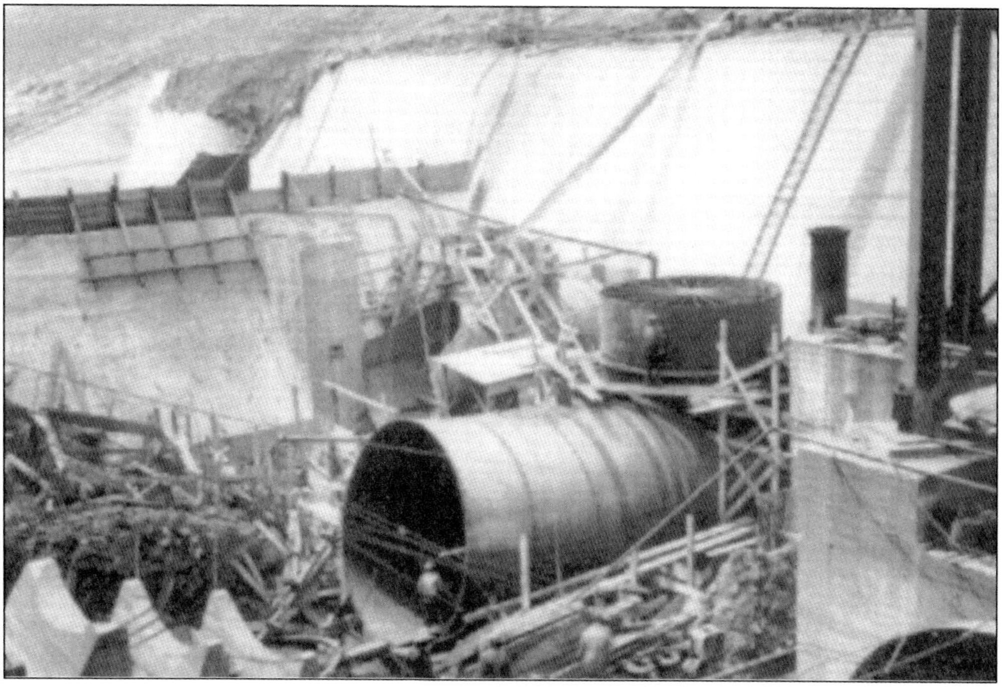

[Riveting Penstocks, Lake Murray Dam.] Shown here in the riveting stage of its construction is one of the gigantic 16-foot-wide penstocks, or long pipes, that were placed at the foot of each of the smaller towers to convey water from them under the dam to the turbines—at 15 feet per second—to produce electricity. The 986-foot-long pipes consisted of 129 rings of 11/16-inch plate, each 7 by 11 3/8 feet long, that were encased in concrete. During their construction on the north side of the Saluda River, a 3,500-foot dike was required to keep the water out.

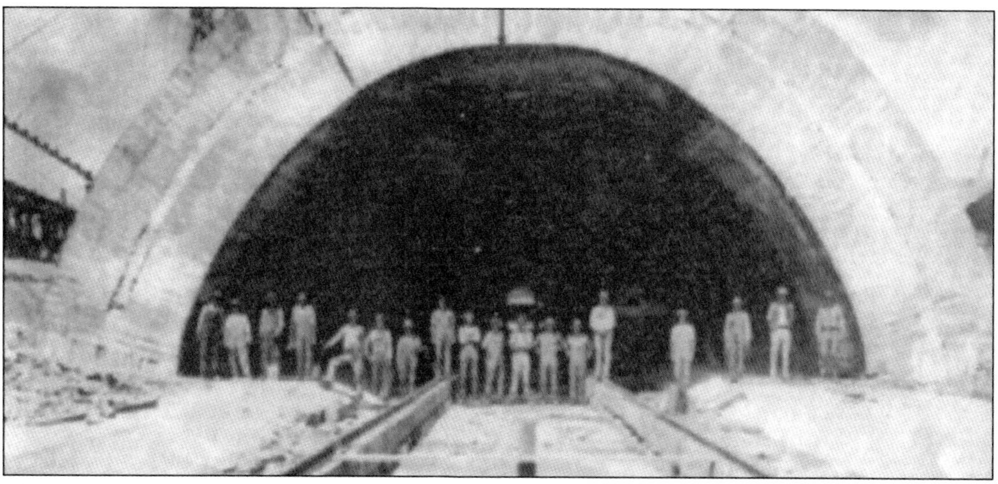

[Construction of the Arch Tunnel, Lake Murray Dam, c. 1929.] This picture illustrates as well as any other the magnitude of the structures that had to be built in the course of creating the Saluda River Dam and Lake Murray. The 48-foot-wide arch tunnel, with walls from 5 to 9 feet thick, was designed to carry the water through the dam during construction and to provide a location for a future penstock. In the 1950s a fifth penstock was added to increase the electrical output.

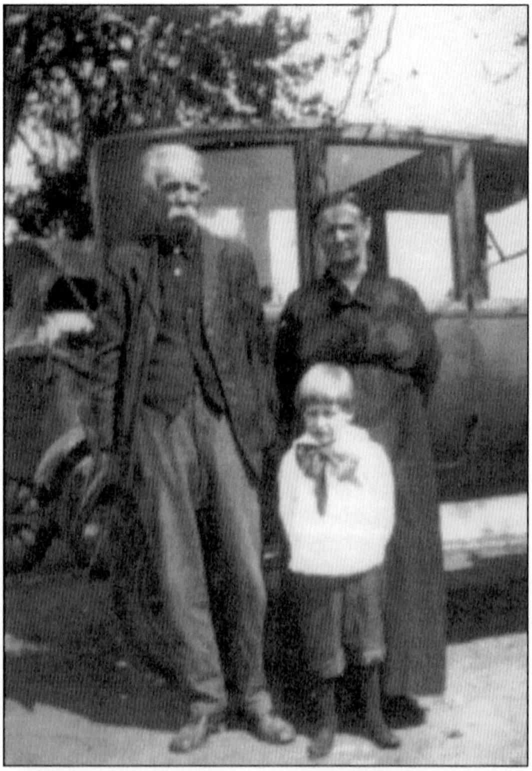

[Portrait of the H. Luther Shealys and Grandson, Holley Ferry, *c.* 1915.] H. Luther Shealy and Elizabeth Holley Shealy, along with their grandson William, are posed here next to the family automobile in front of their home on the Saluda River. Around 1900 Shealy operated the Holley Ferry, one of ten such enterprises whose river-traffic services were eliminated with the creation of Lake Murray.

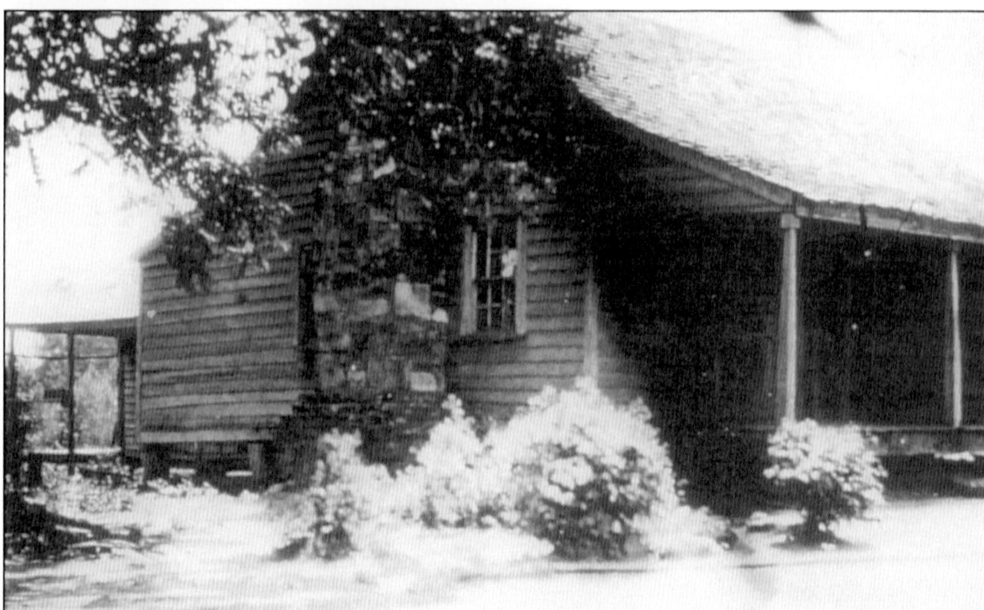

[Home of H. Luther Shealys, Holley Ferry, *c.* 1915.] The home of H. Luther Shealy, the Holley Ferry operator, stood on the south side of the Saluda River near the borderline between Lexington and Saluda Counties. The house was disassembled and removed from the site, which is now beneath the waters at the western end of Lake Murray.

[Red Knoll School, c. 1905.] The Red Knoll Community was located near LC 690 between the former Frey Branch and 18 Mile Creek, Saluda River tributaries that were inundated by Lake Murray on its south side. Existing as early as 1900, when it served 14 students in a 20-week session, the school by 1905 had 20 students, shown here with their teacher, Professor J.E. Rawls (back row, far left). This schoolhouse burned, and a new one built in 1915 was used until 1927–1928, when its name appeared for the last time in the *School Directory of South Carolina.*

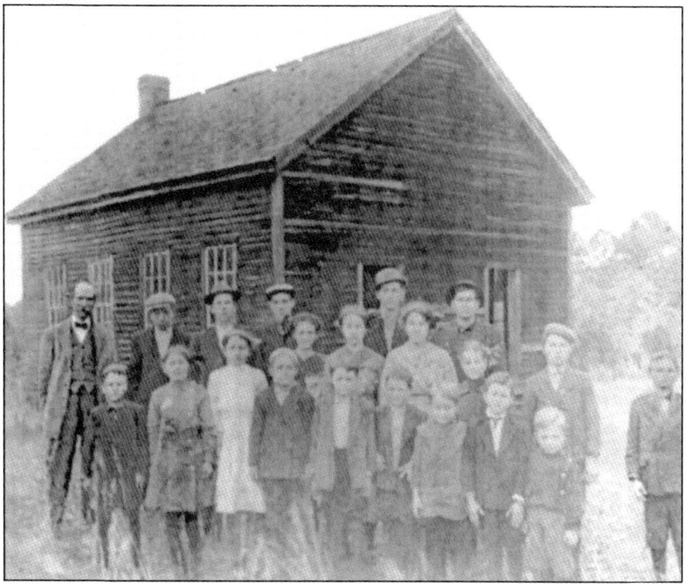

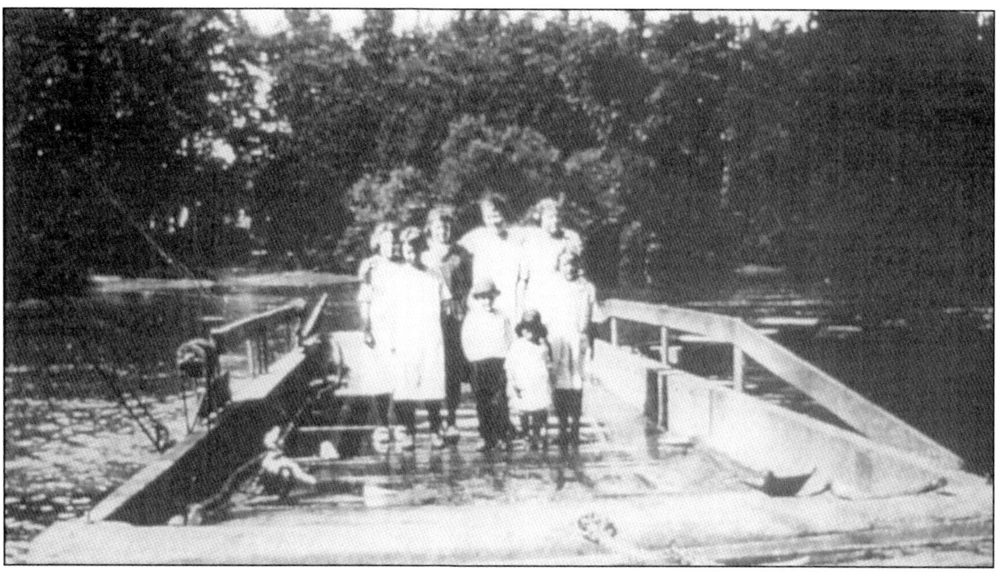

[Holley Ferry, Saluda River, c. 1926.] The Holley Ferry crossing of the Saluda River connected Bethel Church Road in Newberry County with the Holley Ferry Road at the point along the Lexington and Saluda County line where it led near the old Lexington Baptist Church (1813) and continued to the present US 378. The ferry, shown in the close-up view above, was operated by being pulled manually across the water on ropes secured to trees on each side of the river. Seen standing on the ferry are children and relatives of Minick Shealy, son of Luther Shealy, the last operator of the Holley Ferry.

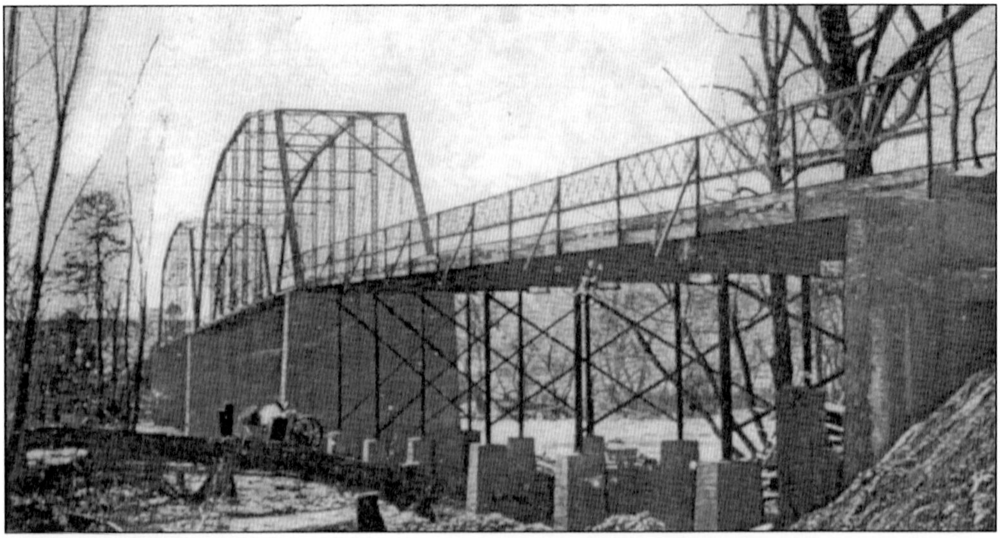

STEEL BRIDGE OVER SALUDA RIVER, WYSES FERRY NEAR LEXINGTON, SC [C. 1923]. On Sunday, February 26, 1911—"the greatest day in the history of the county"—some 500 men, women, and children gathered at the site of Wyse's Ferry on the Saluda River for an old fashioned country picnic to celebrate the completion of "the greatest piece of public work that has ever been accomplished by her citizenship" *(The State*, February 27). Built by the Carolina Engineering Company of Burlington, North Carolina, for $11,980, the 475-foot steel span connected Chapin and the north side (Old Lexington Road) and the county seat on the south side (Old Chapin Road). Within two decades the floor of the bridge would be 150 feet below the waters of the new Lake Murray.

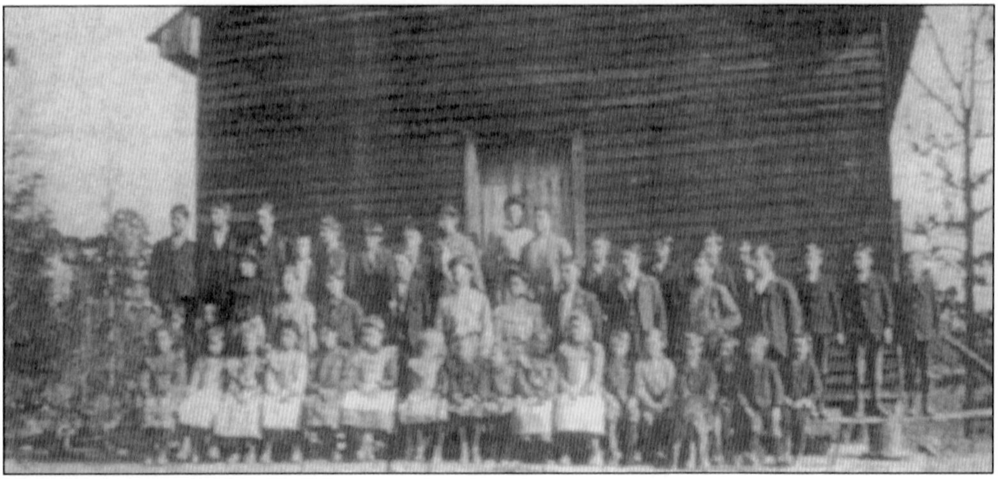

[MAGNOLIA SCHOOL, NEAR IRMO, C. 1900.] Located near the High Hill Creek Community, the old Magnolia School was a traditional one-room structure in which 1 teacher (who lived in Countsville) taught 35 students for a 12-week session in 1900. It remained a one-teacher school through 1915, although a wing was added at the rear to make an L-shaped building. Students were divided into nine grades for a 120-day session. Since it was situated within the Lake Murray flood plain (on the north side), the schoolhouse was disassembled before the waters covered the site (about 1930). Its name appears for the last time in the 1929–1930 issue of the *School Directory of South Carolina.*

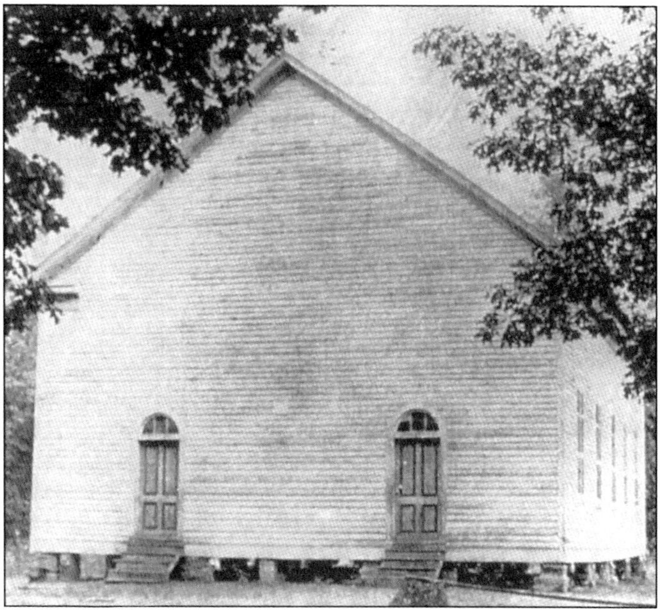

[Bethel (Hill High) Lutheran Church, near Irmo, c. 1925.] Bethel, claimed as the oldest active congregation in the lower Dutch Fork, was organized about 1762 by German settlers whose first sanctuary was a log structure built on High Hill Creek, at a site near Wise Key, now under the waters of Lake Murray. A second building erected on a different site, south of the present Susie Ebert Island, was built with subscriptions of $775.15. The sanctuary pictured here (the church's fourth) was dedicated in 1882. In 1929, because of the Lake Murray project, the congregation moved about 3 miles to White Rock and constructed its present brick sanctuary.

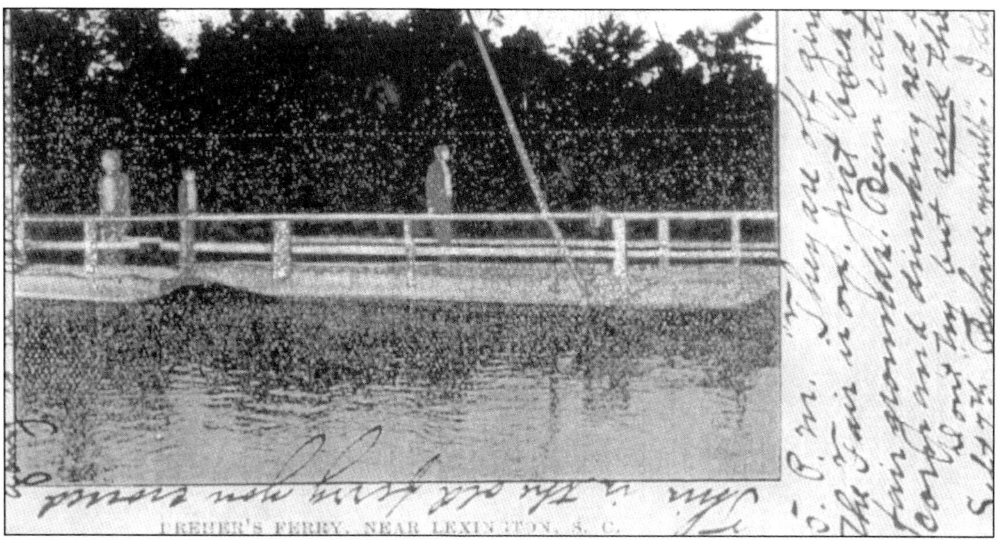

Dreher's Ferry, near Lexington, SC. The old Dreher's Ferry is shown on this postcard mailed on October 16, 1906, from Lexington to Fredericksburg, Virginia. A portion of the note written on it reads as follows: "This is the old ferry you crossed going to the Blue Church over in the Dutch Fork." The "Blue Church" was what St. Michael's Lutheran Church came to be called because its ceiling was painted blue. This ferry site on the Saluda River, now under Lake Murray, is about a mile west of the dam and was on the main road from Lexington to Irmo.

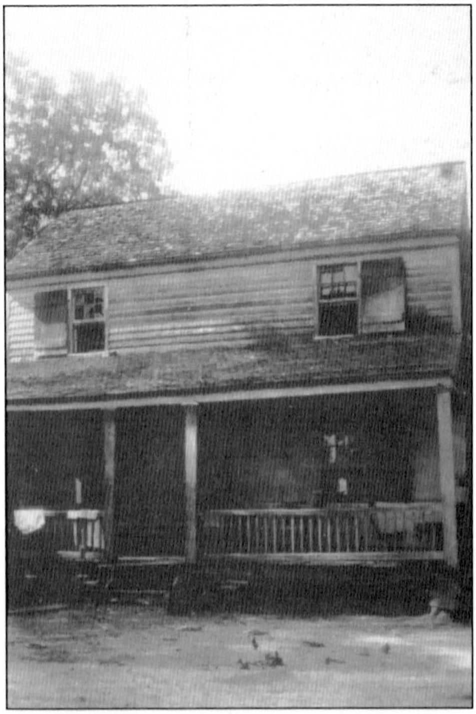

The sturdy people who made their way up the Broad and Saluda Rivers into the Dutch Fork ("Dutch" being the vernacular corruption of "Deutsch")—that territorial V formed by the confluence of these rivers at Columbia—brought with them a penchant for hard work and good order, a respect for discipline and authority, a deep loyalty to family and church, a commitment to education, and community spirit coupled with a fierce sense of independence.

Above: **[Home of John S. Smith, High Hill Creek near Irmo, c. 1930.]** This early two-story heart-of-pine residence, built on the land-grant farm of John S. Smith located at High Hill Creek near the Saluda River, was spared by Sherman on his raid through the Dutch Fork because of proof shown that its owner had a Masonic affiliation. Condemned for purchase under the right of eminent domain during the development of the reservoir in the late 1920s, the house now lies under Lake Murray.

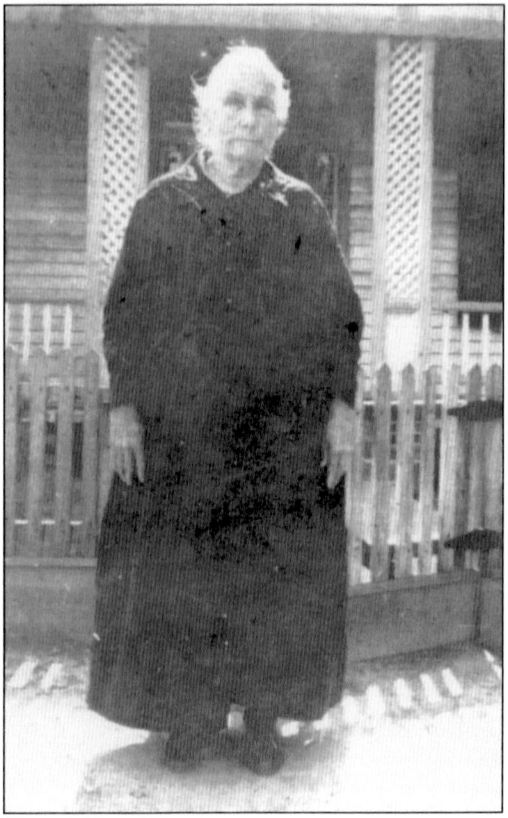

Right: **[Portrait of Carrie Smith Mathias, Irmo, c. 1930.]** Martha Caroline ("Carrie") Theora Smith Mathias (1848–1945) was the youngest of the children (four daughters and a son) born and reared in the farmhouse above. She attended nearby Magnolia School and High Hill Lutheran Church. Luther Sharred Mathias (1844–1922), whom she married in 1865, managed Carrie's farm and became Irmo's first mayor.

[Buggy House, Smith/Mathias Farm near Irmo, c. 1930.] Louise O' Sheal Younginer remembers the occasion in 1930 when her grandfather, Luther Mathias, took her as a child to the farm for their last look at the home, the buggy house (shown here), and 700 acres of land, which were soon to be inundated by the new Lake Murray. She watched as he, using his Kodak camera, took pictures of their High Hill Creek farm before the waters covered the site. The buildings are under the lake near Goat Island.

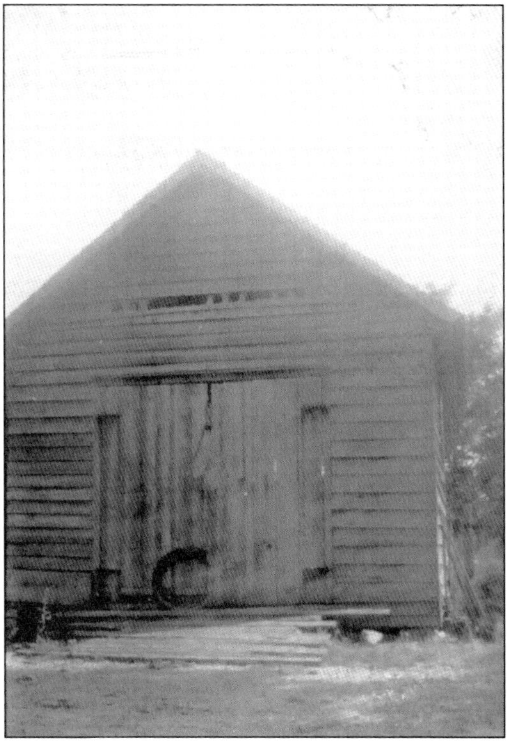

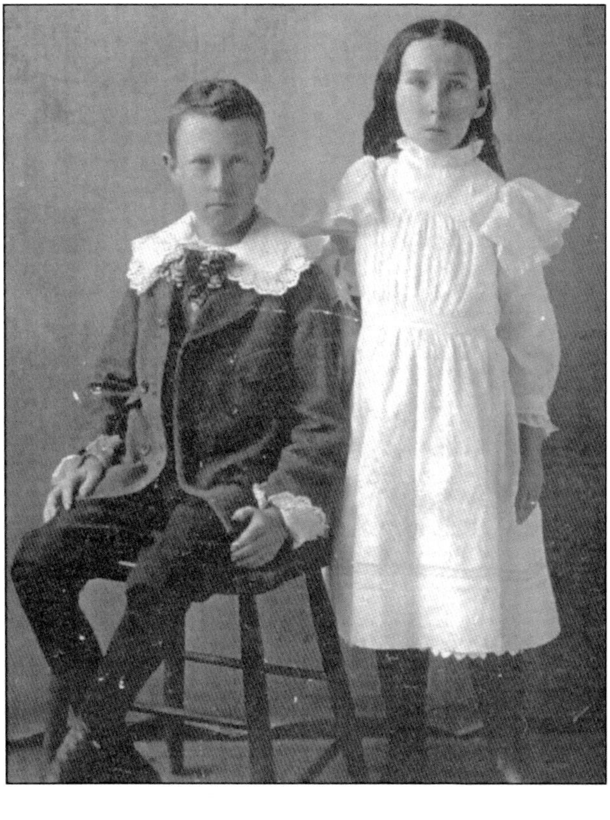

[Portrait of John Homer Mathias and Eula Mathias, Irmo, c. 1903.] Young John H. Mathias and his sister Eula, two of the children of Luther and Carrie Mathias, are portrayed here by an unidentified photographer in 1903. John became a physician in Lexington. A graduate of the Irmo Academy, where she later returned to teach, Eula first taught in the schools of Little Mountain and Abbeville County. In 1924 she married J. Frank O'Sheal of Pickens. The two lived with Carrie in the home that Eula later inherited. The face of Eula Mathias here is one of the most haunting and unforgettable in the book.

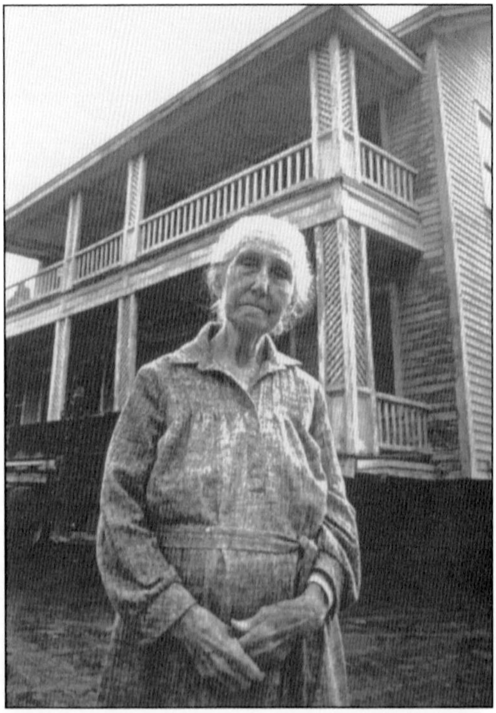

[EULA MATHIAS O'SHEAL AND THE MATHIAS HOUSE, IRMO, C. 1930S.] Eula Mathias O'Sheal (1889–1989) is portrayed here in front of her family home as it looked when it was located in Irmo at the corner of St. Andrews Road and SC 60, facing the railroad. Built about 1890, the house was moved twice: first to Irmo Drive and later to the Little Mountain area, where restoration remains incomplete.

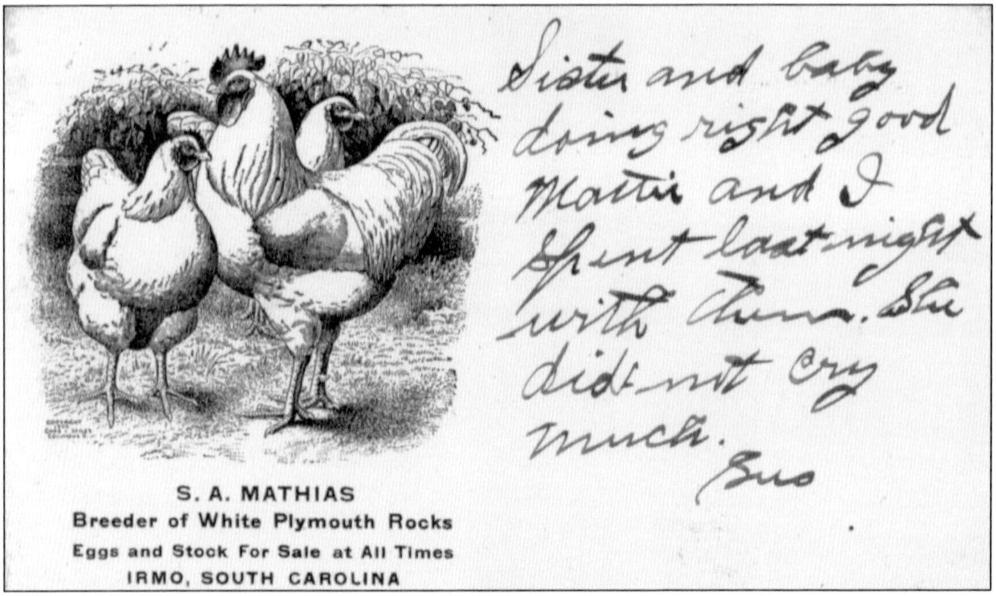

[POULTRY ADVERTISING CARD, IRMO, C. 1907.] The generic advertisement card above was utilized by Samuel Augustus ("Gus") Mathias (1872–1933) in the promotion of the poultry business, which he operated as a sideline. The oldest son of Luther and Carrie Smith, Gus assisted his father in running the country store, which the Mathias family had opened in Irmo when a depot was established there in 1890. After Luther's death in 1922, Gus ran the store until he died in 1933.

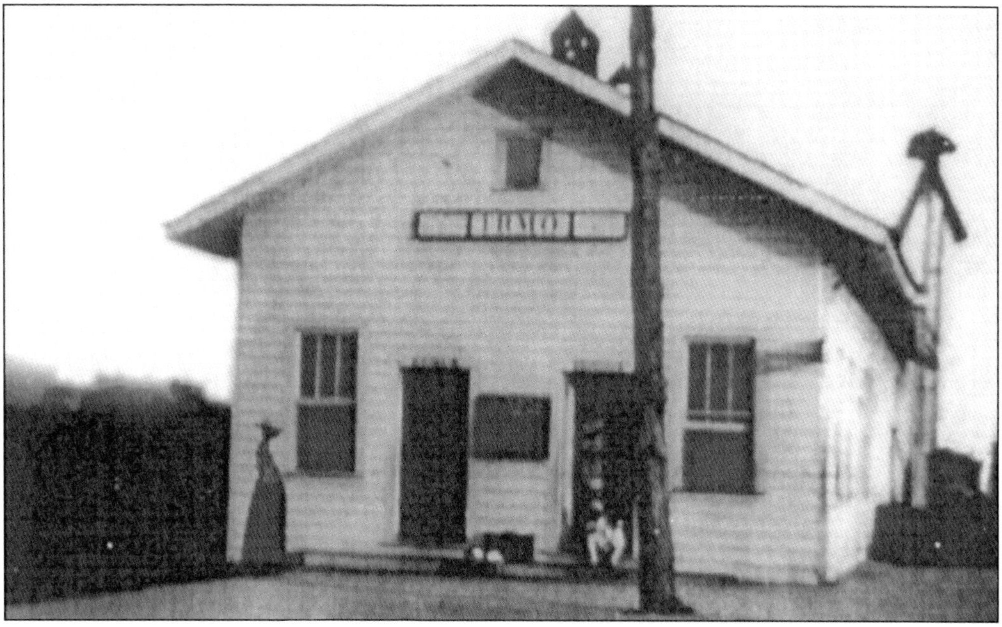

[Irmo Depot, c. 1910.] In *Irmo and the Dutch Fork Legacy* (1990) Furman R. Younginer states that Irmo was the name given to the site about 10 miles from Columbia that was needed for water and refueling the wood-burning locomotives on the new Columbia, Newberry & Laurens Railroad, which began service through the 1-square-mile town in July 1890—the same year in which the town was incorporated. The name was created by combining the first two letters from the last names of Iredell and Moseley, executives with the railroad and the Piedmont Investment Company, which laid out the town. By 1910 (about the time this picture was taken) Irmo had a population of 300. The depot, the first one to be completed on the CN&L line, was closed and demolished in 1965.

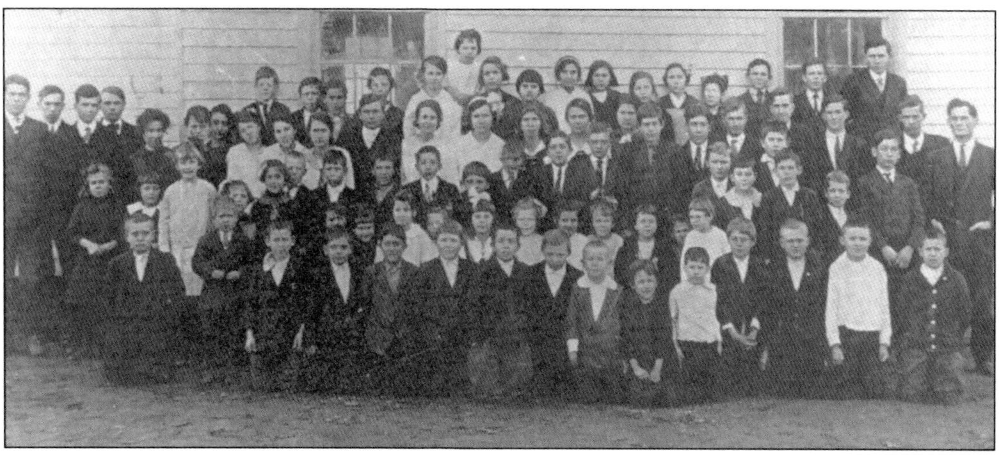

[Irmo Academy School Picture, c. 1915.] Established in 1890, the Irmo Academy was housed in a 35-by-20-foot frame building surmounted by a belfry and situated on the corner of Newberry Avenue and Third Street. In 1900, the private one-teacher school had 55 students for a 20-week session. Eula Mathias is included in the 1915 group portrait above, which provides graphic evidence for the fact that at this time all grades attended classes in the same building. In 1925 the Irmo Academy was replaced by the Irmo Grammar School located on Woodrow Street.

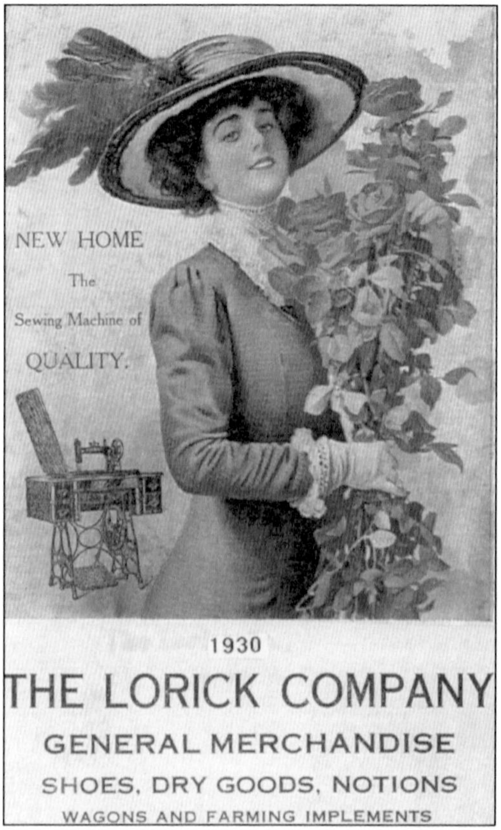

[The Lorick Company, Irmo, *c.* 1930.] This generic ad card with its stylized image of a handsome, neatly dressed woman of an earlier era was imprinted with the name of the Lorick Company and circulated to promote the various lines of general merchandise—shoes, dry goods, notions, sewing machines, wagons, and farming implements—offered by this Irmo store.

[Portrait of the Lorick Family, Irmo, *c.* 1907.] The Loricks pose for a portrait in front of their family home, which was built in 1890 on Woodrow Street, two blocks south of the store. They are shown here from left to right, as follows: Hampton Alexander Lorick (1867–1930) and his wife, Lillian Maude Lorick (1869–1964); (in front of her mother) seven-year-old Daisy Aline Lorick (1900–1984), William Wade Lorick (1896–1969), Olive Maude Lorick (1892–1980), Lillian Viola Lorick (1893–1970), and Wilhelmina Bookman Lorick (1886–1941). The house was sold to David F. Lorick in 1912 and was demolished in 1974.

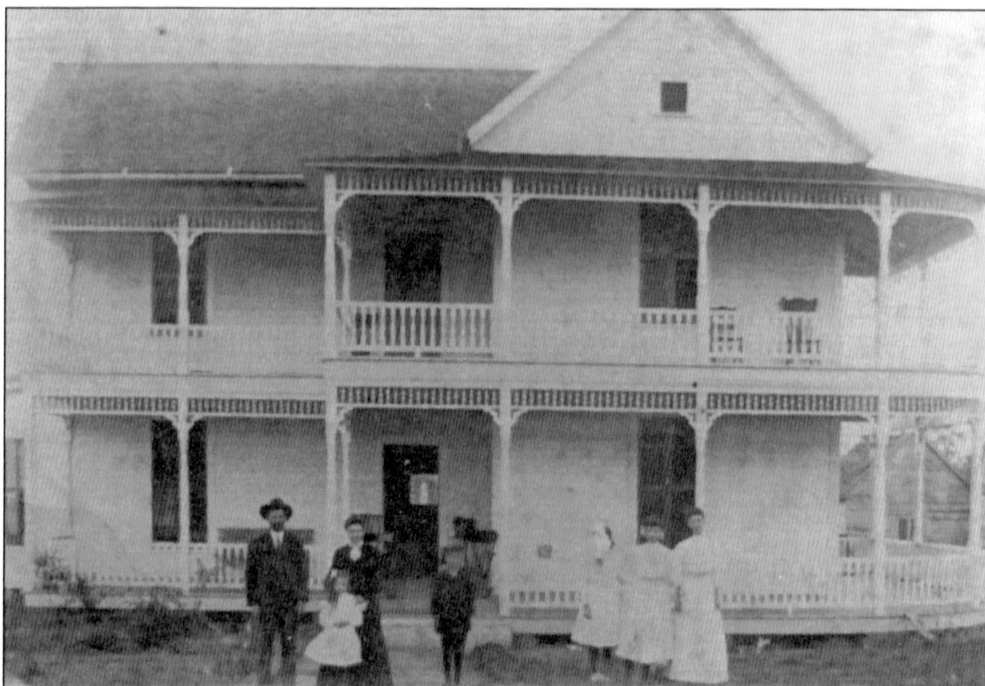

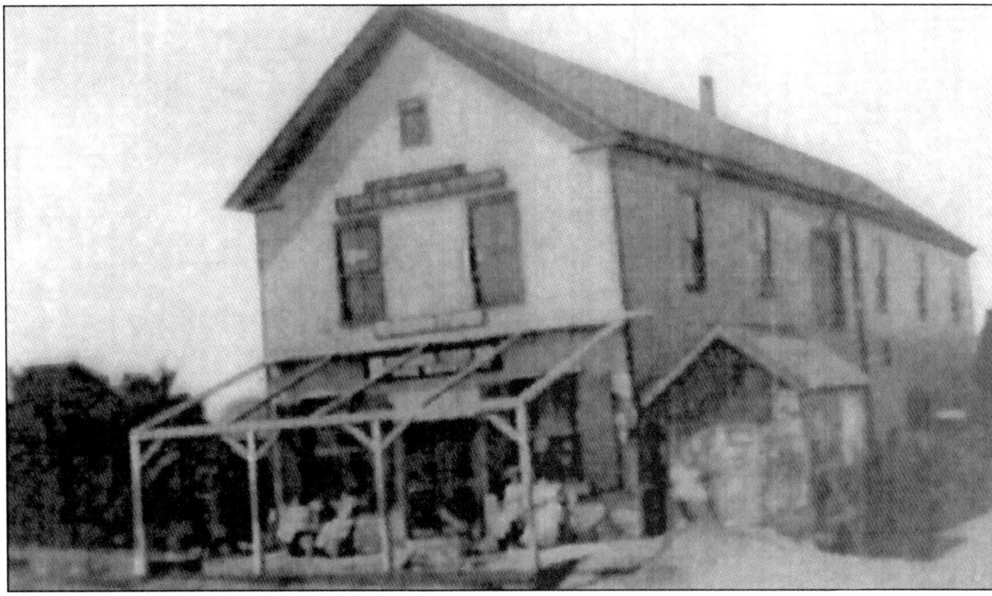

[The Lorick Company, Irmo, c. 1920.] Established by Hampton A. Lorick in the 1890s, the Lorick Company was located on Woodrow Street (now St. Andrews Road extension) on the west side of the Columbia, Newberry & Laurens Railroad tracks and sold general merchandise ranging from dry goods and caskets to farming implements. The store was later sold to David F. Lorick (1871–1942), Jacob E. Lorick (1876–1962), and William H. Lorick (1883–1964). In 1946, the Loricks sold it to James A. Leitner, who owned it until it was destroyed by fire in 1976. In 2000, the site was occupied by Blockbuster Video at 7249 St. Andrews Road.

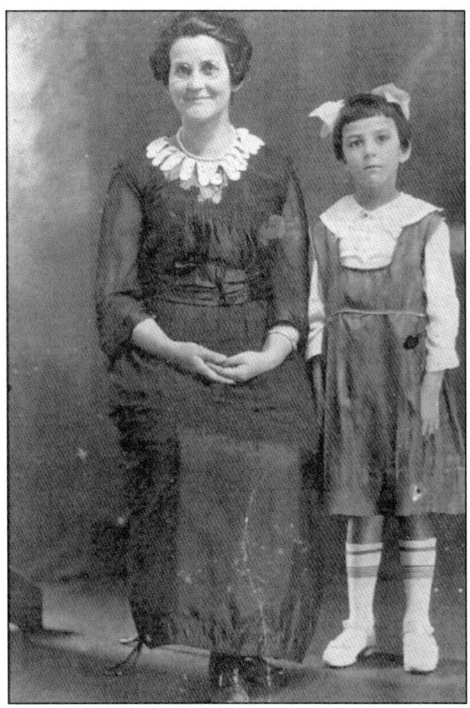

[Portrait of Alice and Cora Lorick, Irmo, c. 1919.] This portrait of Irmo residents Alice Isabel Leitner Lorick (1876–1960) and her daughter Cora (1912–1985) was made sometime between 1919 and 1923 by an unidentified studio photographer.

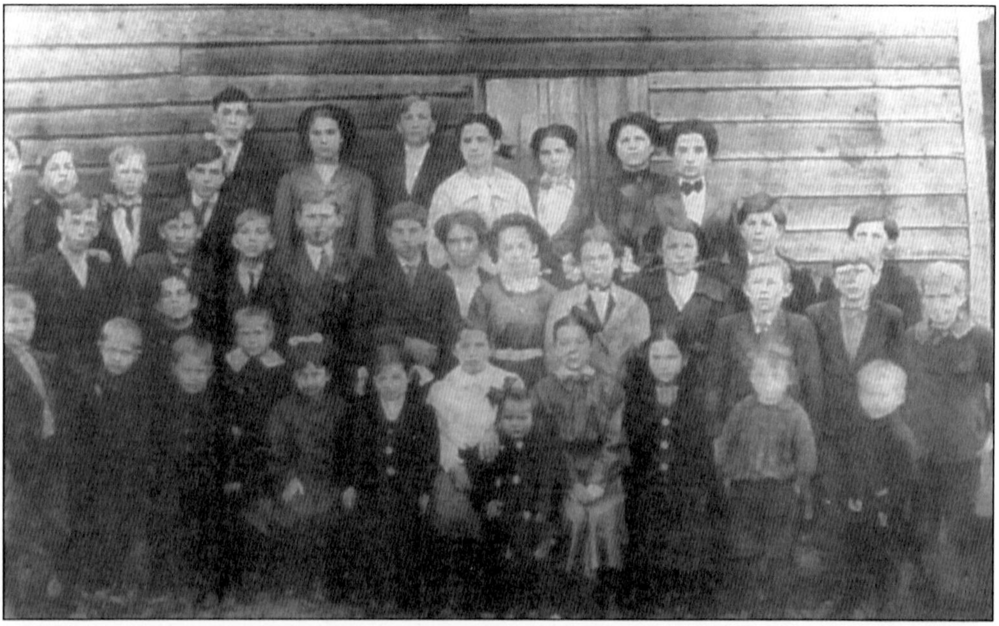

[Forkville School, Dutch Fork, *c.* 1910.] The Forkville School once stood near 526 St. Andrews Road across from the initial site of St. Andrew's Lutheran Church and its remaining cemetery on residential property near Redeemer Lutheran Church in the Seven Oaks School area. In 1916, it was a one-teacher school of 7 girls and 20 boys.

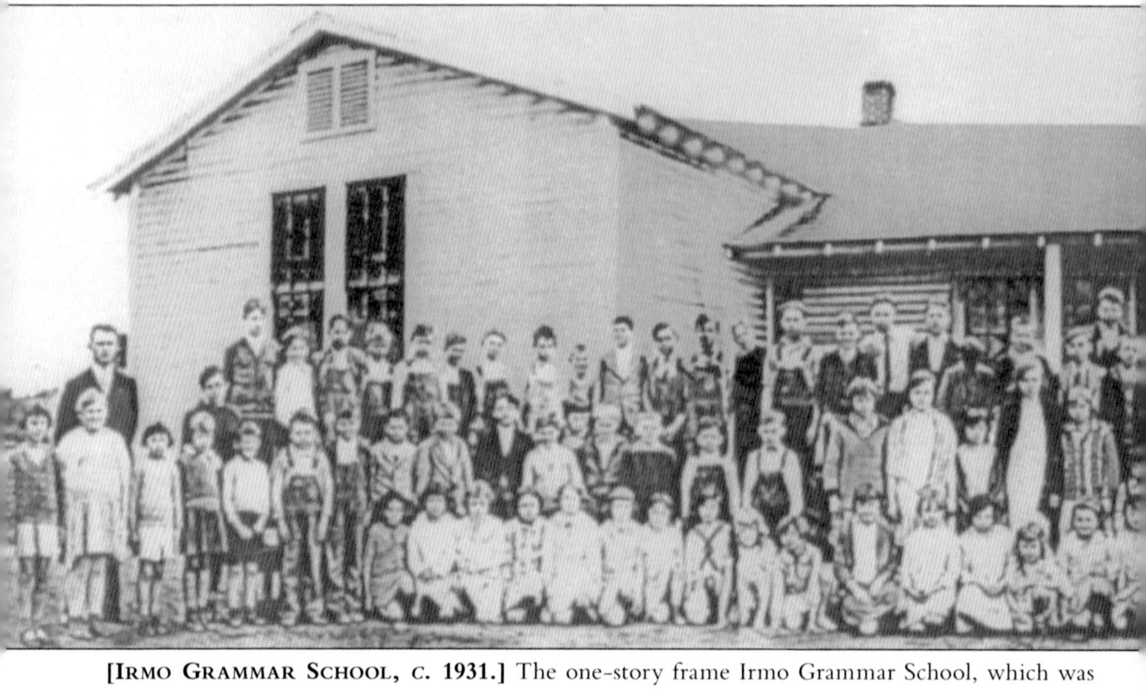

[Irmo Grammar School, *c.* 1931.] The one-story frame Irmo Grammar School, which was built on Woodrow Street about 1925 and served grades one through seven for a decade or so, consisted of seven rooms and a porch. A large cast-iron stove in each room was the only source

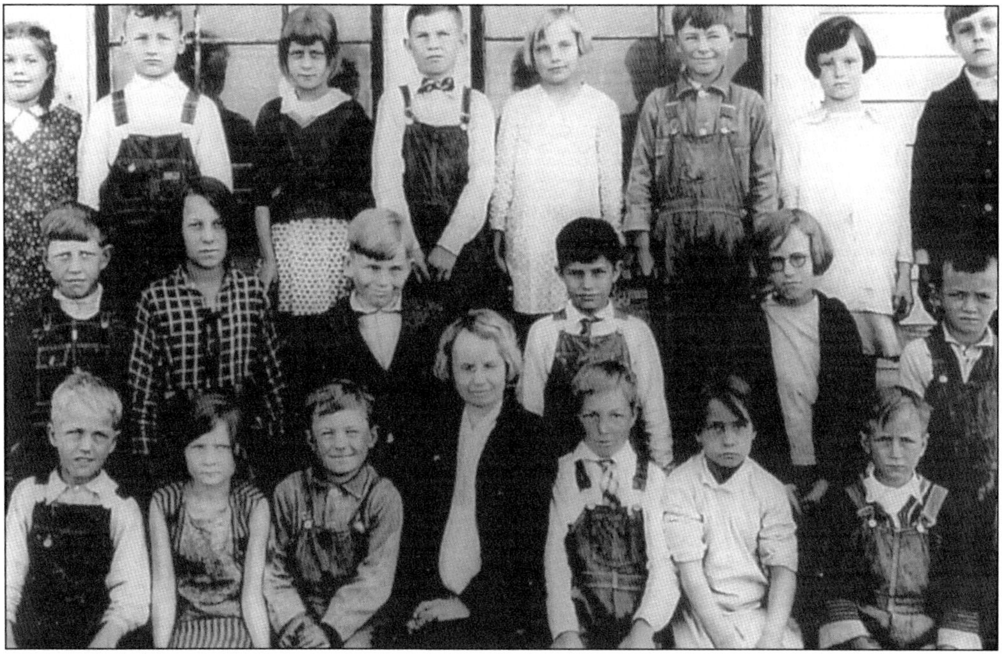

[IRMO SCHOOL, THIRD GRADE CLASS.] This 1931 class portrait of the third grade of the Irmo School was taken outside the seven-room frame schoolhouse built across the railroad tracks in the 1920s to replace the old one-room school. After the first Irmo High School was built in 1928, this frame building continued to house classes for grades one through seven.

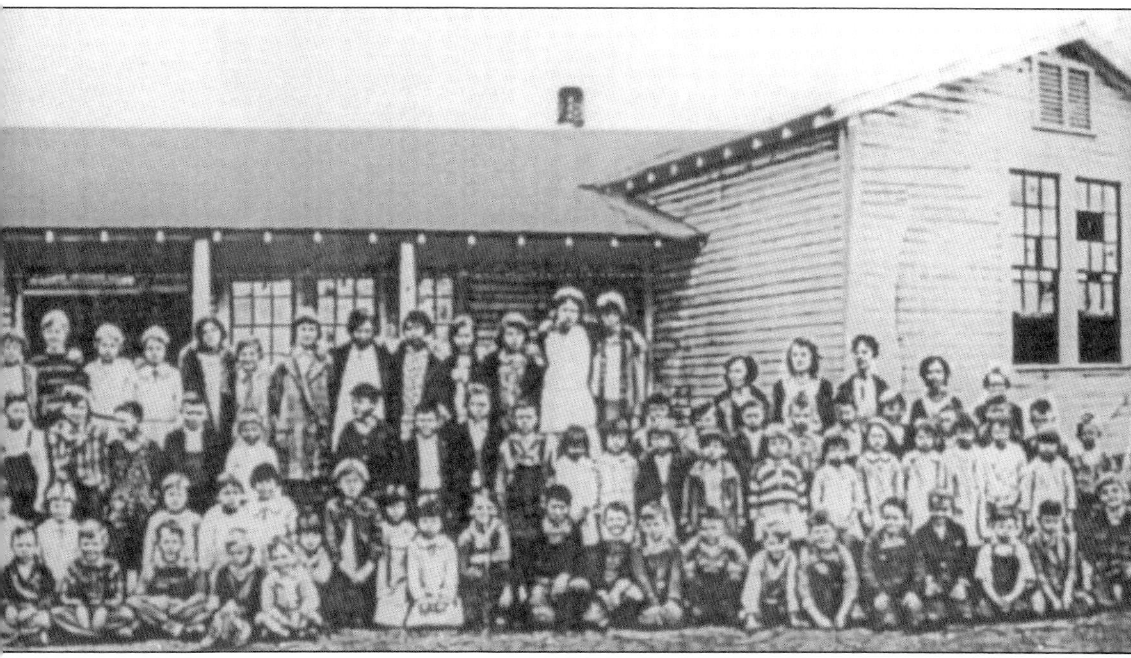

of heat, and two outdoor privies provided the sanitary facilities. In 1930 F.L. Lineberger was the principal. The Irmo district had 10 teachers and 267 pupils.

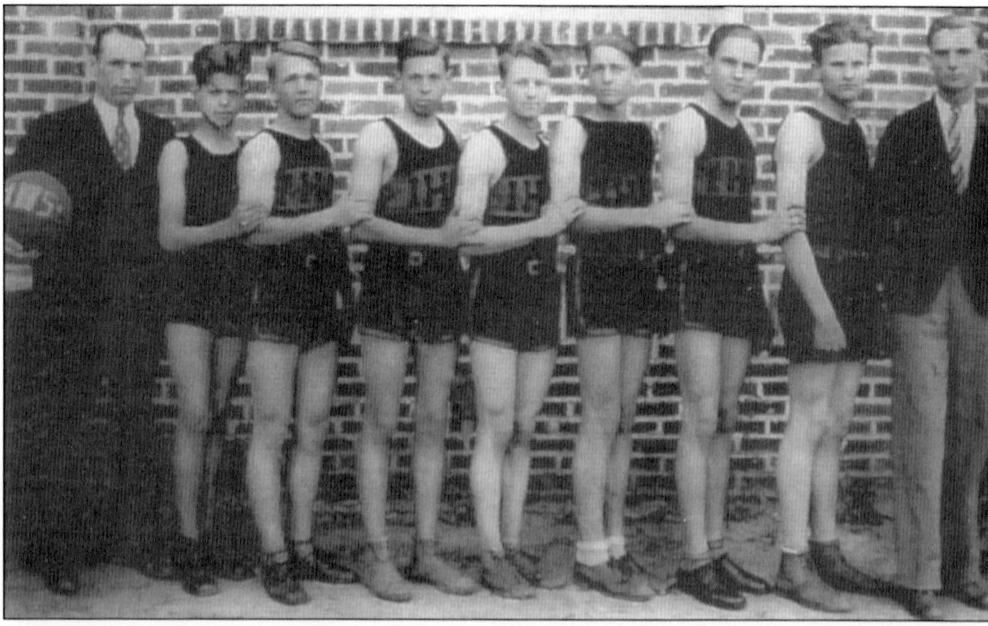

[Basketball Team, Irmo High School, c. 1931.] Pictured at the far left in this picture taken outside the new brick Irmo High School (1928) is Irmo native Karl S. Lowman (1906–1990), who in 1930 had been persuaded to come back to take over as principal and to organize an athletic program. "He rounded up his ballplayers and a few of their fathers, utilized some good mules and wagons and cleared the field across the tracks from where Irmo Village Shopping Center is now for Irmo's first football field" (*Irmo and the Dutch Fork Legacy*). During his 11 years here he coached the football, basketball, and baseball teams—and gave them the name of Yellow Jackets.

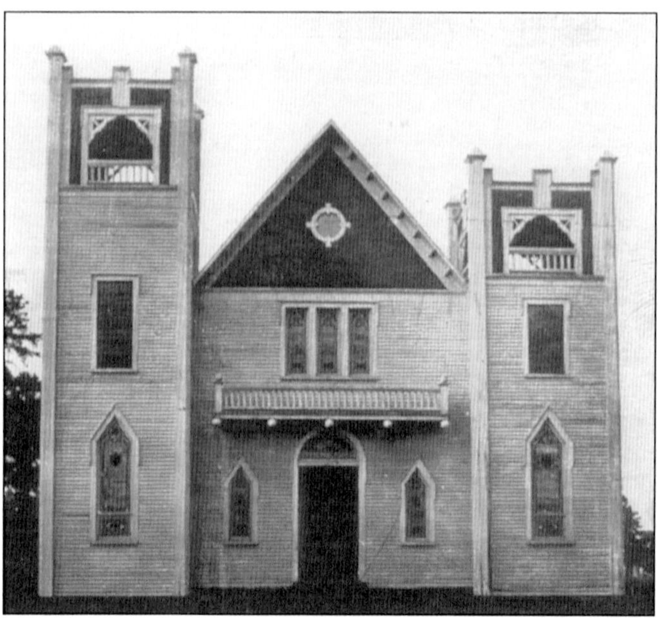

[St. Michael's Lutheran Church, Irmo, c. 1930s.] Formed by Bethel-High Hill dissenters who wished to have their worship services conducted in English rather than in German, the congregation that became St. Michael's Lutheran Church began meeting officially in 1814 in a schoolhouse on River Road. The Southern Country Gothic–style sanctuary shown here, built in 1921 on 6 acres that had been donated by John Dreher in 1877, replaced an earlier edifice of unknown date.

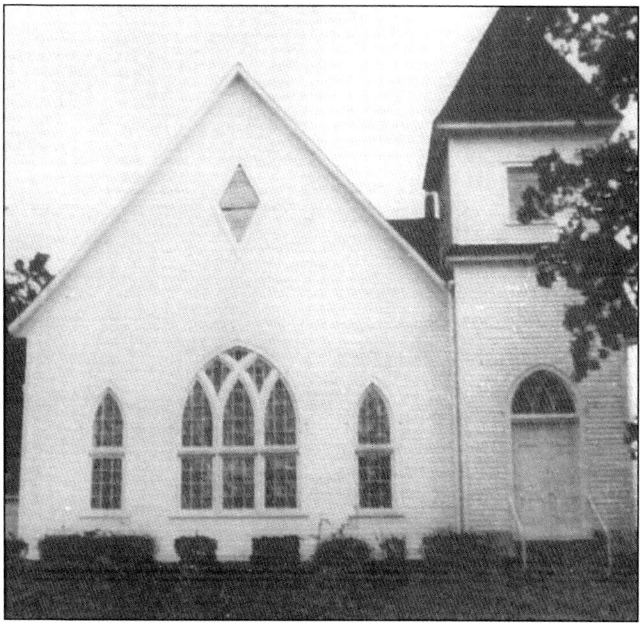

[UNION CHAPEL METHODIST, IRMO CHARGE, *c.* 1923.] The beginnings of this Methodist congregation go back to 1857, when it was called Kennerly Chapel or Kennerly Meeting House. The Country Gothic sanctuary shown here was built in the 1890s, replacing a small one that had been erected on the 3-acre plot donated by Preston C. Lorick in 1889 and located on what is now Woodrow Street. The building seen here was removed in 1964 and replaced by a new facility. This picture was probably made between 1920 and 1924 when, after lightning had struck the steeple in 1920, a new vestibule was created and stained-glass windows were installed.

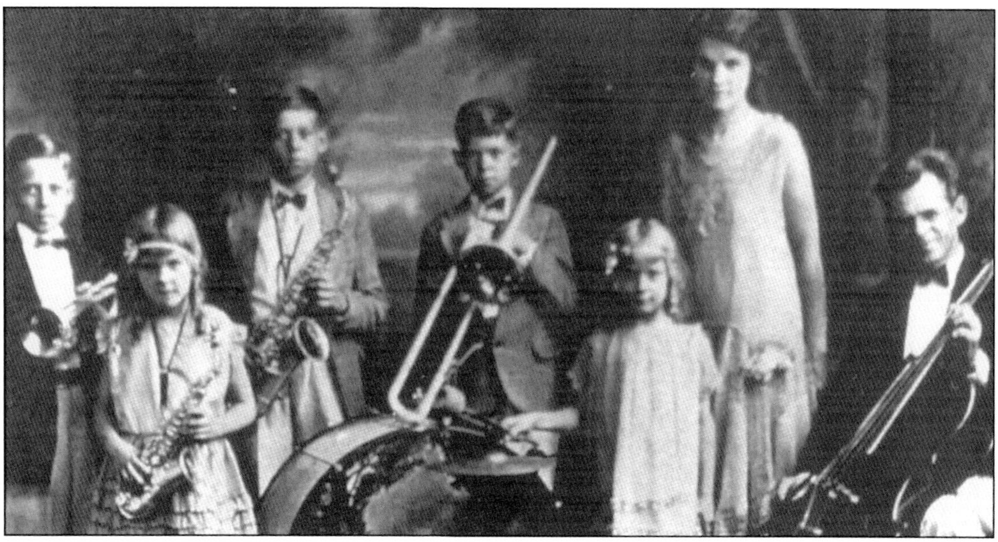

[PARSON'S BAND, IRMO, *c.* 1929.] The Parson's Band was the musical brainchild of the Reverend Fred Louis Lineberger (1886–1962), who during the period from 1928 to 1932 accepted the call to the ministry to St. Michael's and St. Andrews Lutheran Churches, Irmo, and Holy Trinity, West Columbia. Made up of Lineberger; his wife, Mana Corley (who taught piano in the Irmo schools); and children (shown left to right as follows: Corley, Sarah L. Rast, Ted, Henry, and Betty L. Brissey), the band gave church-sponsored public programs at various area venues. Admission was "only 15 and 25 cents" (*Dispatch-News,* December 10, 1930).

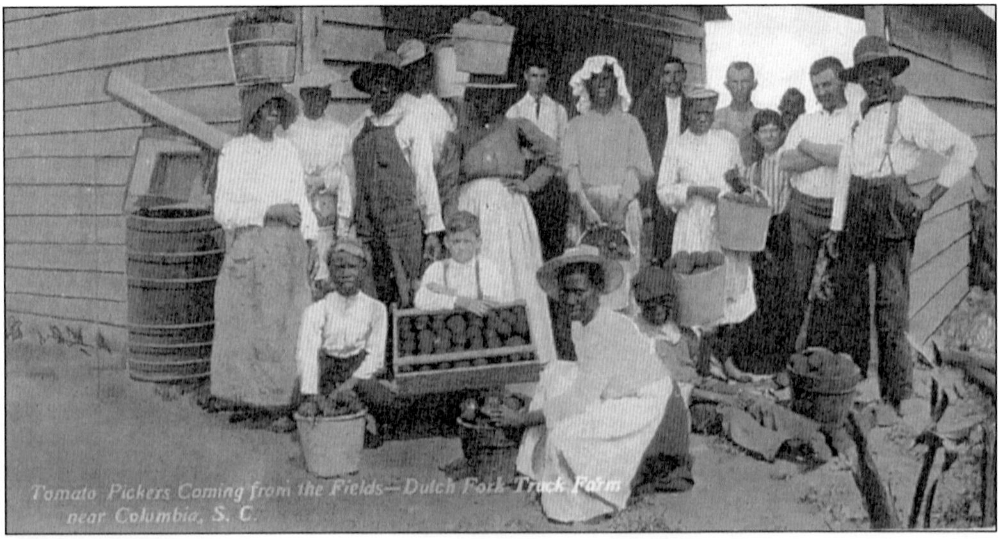

Tomato Pickers Coming from the Fields, Dutch Fork Truck Farm near Columbia, SC [c. 1909]. "Laboring together in the fields," late *Columbia Record* editor Harrison Jenkins once wrote, "the men and women [of the Dutch Fork] lived cheaply, buying nothing but absolute necessities, except whiskey and tobacco for the men and perhaps ribbon and calico for the women." The work force portrayed outside a packing shed on this Dutch Fork truck farm of undetermined location is seen to be made up not only of men and women, but also of black and white persons.

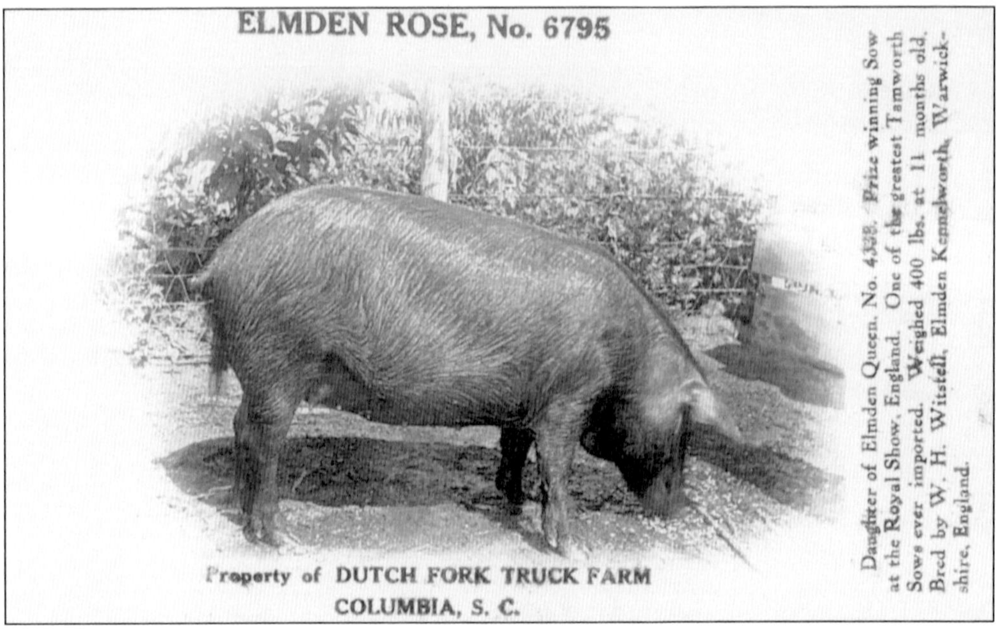

Elmden Rose, No. 6795, Dutch Fork Truck Farm, Columbia, SC [c. 1910]. Elmden Rose, with her registration number and pedigree recorded on the card, means business—her presentation here indicative of the seriousness with which Dutch Fork countrymen took their livestock investments. Brady Lee Frick, as reported in *Chapin . . . The First 100 Years*, remembered that his family had a good many hogs, that beef and pig clubs were "the thing," and that his father would kill 20 to 21 hogs for local barbecues.

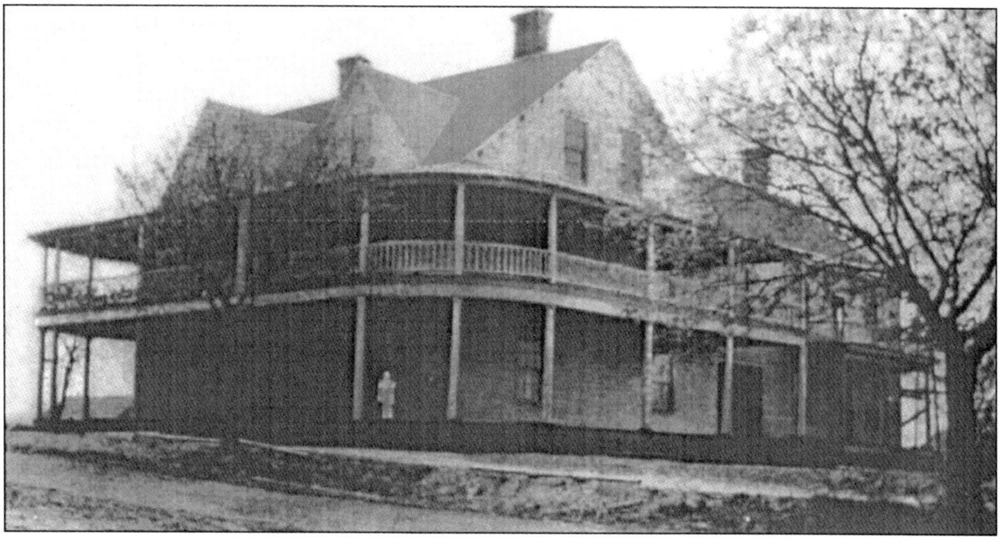

[CHAPIN HOTEL, C. 1910.] The Chapin Hotel catered largely to the drummers (salesmen) who arrived by train to do business in town or in the surrounding countryside. It was the only place to get lodging and meals between Newberry and Columbia. The hotel was operated at different times by the Arthur Sease Williams family, by Gus Howard, and by P.M. Frick and his wife, "Miss Minnie." Catherine Eleazer Gates recalls that when her husband, Lewis Taylor Gates (1910–1966), came to teach in the Chapin School in 1931, he lived in "Mrs. Frick's boarding house [which] was known as the Chapin Hotel" (see *Completion of Appointed Rounds*).

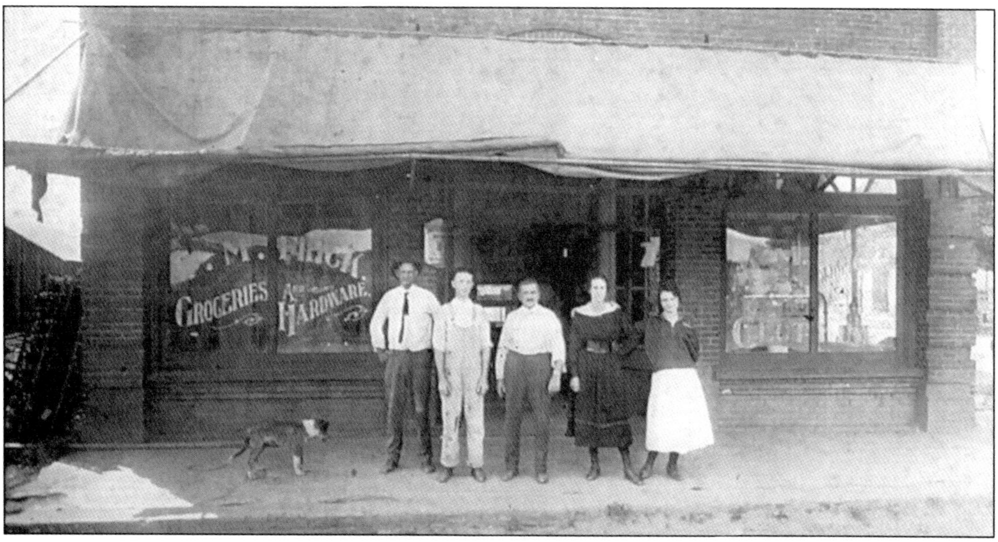

[P.M. FRICK'S GROCERY AND HARDWARE STORE, CHAPIN, C. 1910.] Distinguished by its three Romanesque arches, P.M. Frick's two-story grocery and hardware store, which faced Clark Street on the corner of Beaufort and Clark, was one of several buildings erected in Chapin in 1908 by the John W. Fry Construction Company using brick manufactured locally at C.P. Robinson's Brick Company (which moved to Columbia *c.* 1916). Located near the railroad tracks, the store was later used for various commercial enterprises (a gun shop and a thrift shop) before being torn down in the fall of 1999. Shown here in front of the store, from left to right, are Cork Harmon, R. Alvin Frick, P.M. Frick, Bessie Daily, and Rosalie Stockman.

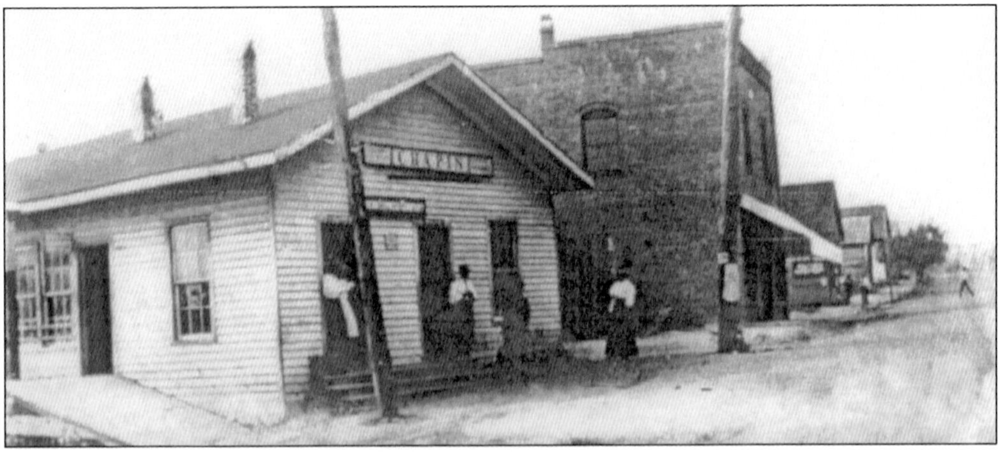

[Columbia, Newberry, and Laurens Railroad Depot, Chapin, *c.* 1910.] Chapin, another stop on the Columbia, Newberry & Laurens Rail Road, was incorporated in 1889 and named for Martin Chapin, who about 1850 settled in the "piney-woods" area some 10 miles from Irmo, established a sawmill business, and eventually gave the land to lay out the streets of the new town. By 1910 Chapin had a population of 600. Sometime between 1953 and 1955 Clarence ("Jack") O'Brien Comalander reportedly paid $1,500 to have the depot moved to his property on Lazy Brook Drive west of Chapin for use as a farm storage unit.

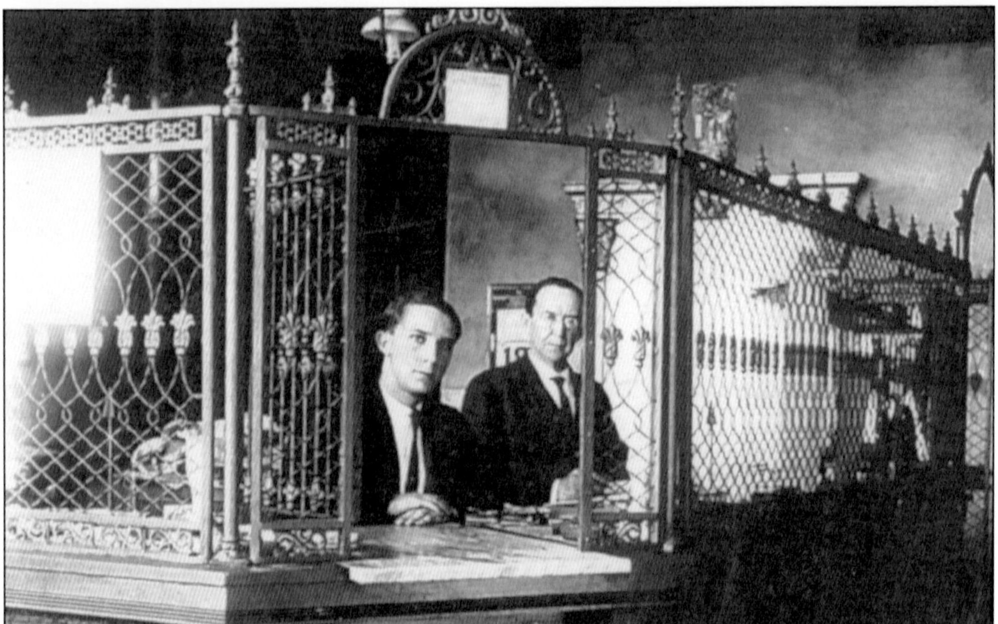

[Bank of Chapin, Interior, *c.* 1910.] The Bank of Chapin was organized by Job S. Wessinger, P.M. Frick, and J.S. Honeycutt in 1907. The next year, they began doing business in their new building on Beaufort Street. Built by John W. Fry Construction Company, using brick made at a local kiln owned by C.P. Robinson, the bank still stands. Its prosperity probably peaked in 1919, when deposits tripled what they had been three years earlier. Twelve years later it failed. Cashier Harry D. Wessinger, shown at left here with President J.S. Wessinger, worked in the bank until 1920.

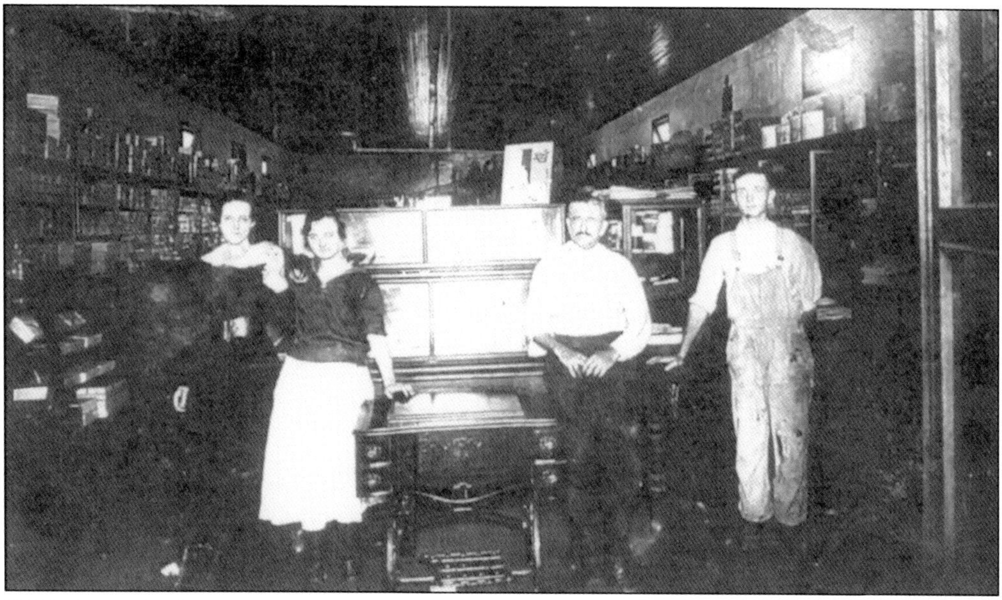

[P.M. FRICK'S STORE, INTERIOR, CHAPIN, C. 1910.] This photograph of the interior of P.M. Frick's store was probably taken the same day as the exterior one on page 99. Here, from left to right, are Bessie Daily, Rosalie Stockman, P.M. Frick, and R. Alvin Frick. P.M. Frick, one of the organizers of the Bank of Chapin in 1907, had by 1915 been characterized by the *Lexington Dispatch* as "the prince merchant" of Chapin.

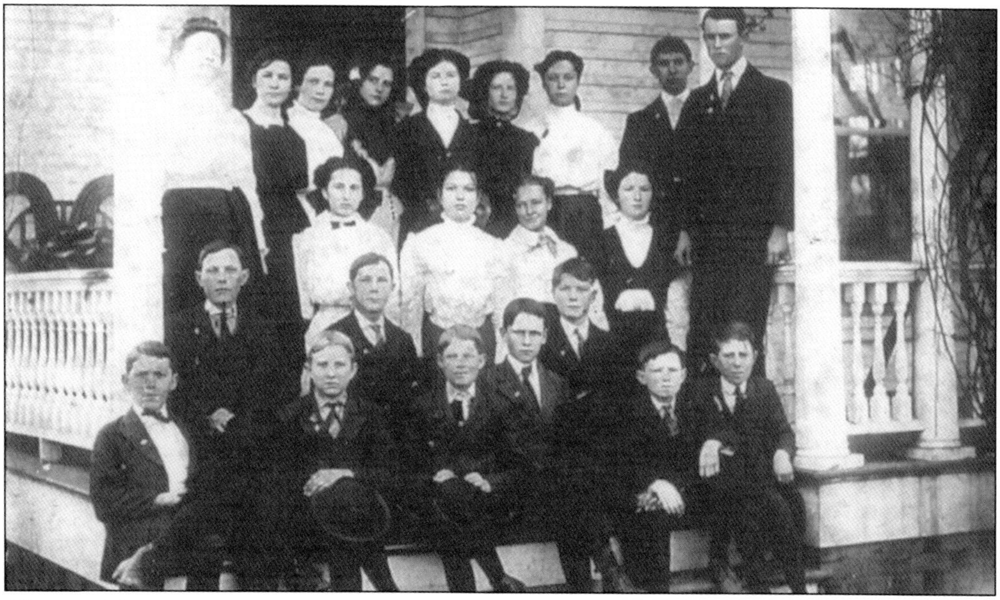

[CHAPIN TEMPERANCE LEGION, CHAPIN, C. 1909.] Temperance literally went with the territory in Chapin. A provision in the town's articles of incorporation in 1889 prohibited municipal authorities from granting licenses to sell liquor. Local "temperance legions" such as the group of young people pictured here were organized as early as 1908, perhaps by Mrs. E.P. Robinson (wife of prominent Chapin businessman Charlie Robinson), who became a state official in the Women's Christian Temperance Union and on the front steps of whose home this picture was made.

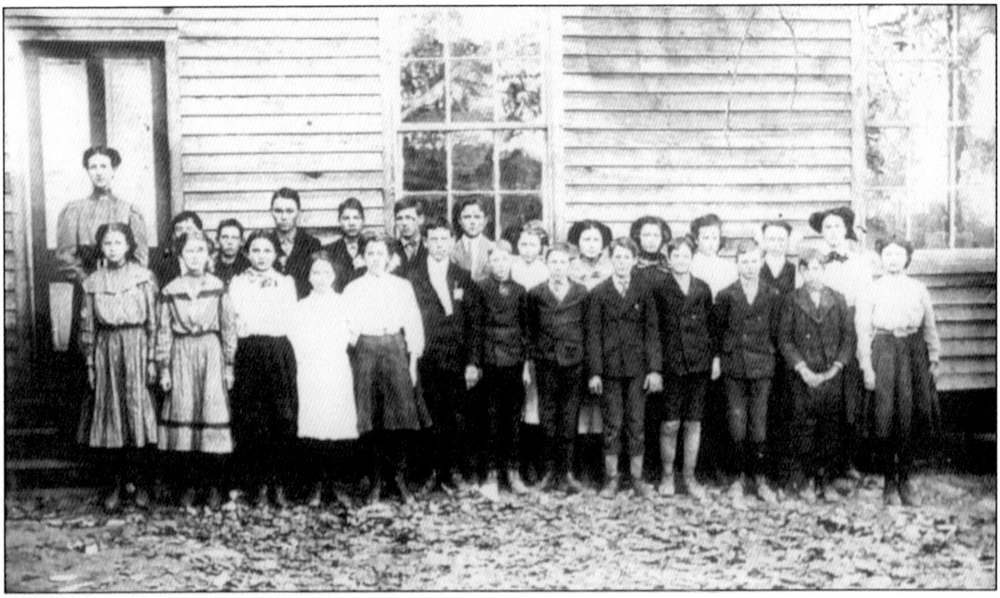

[Chapin School Class Picture, c. 1905.] In October 1890, the *Lexington Dispatch* mentioned that "a large school building will soon be started [in Chapin], which when completed, will add much to the appearance of the place." The frame building shown here must have been the one in place on Peak Street by 1893, which in 1900 was a one-teacher school with 87 students in a 20-week session. The teacher at left in this picture has been identified as a Mrs. M. Henry. Five years later, this structure was replaced by the brick one seen on page 103.

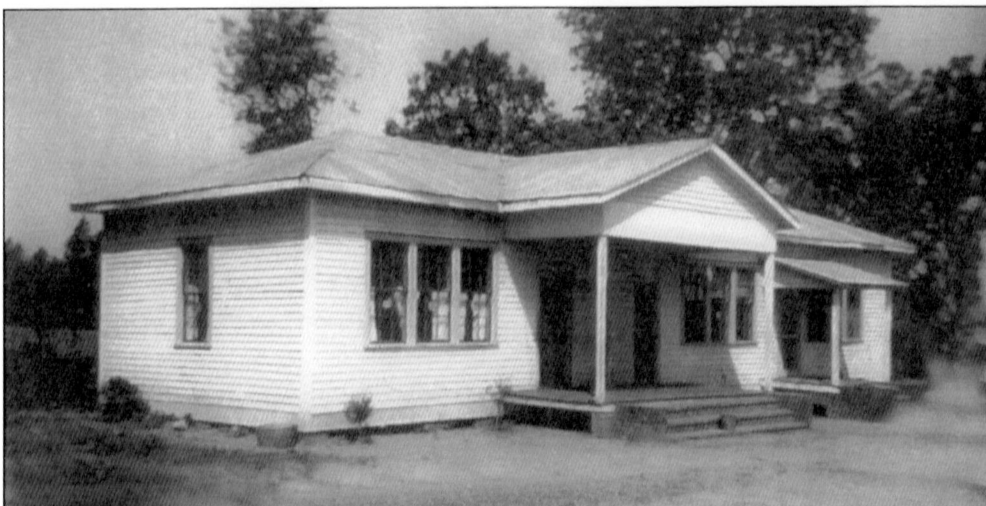

[Chapin School, c. 1930s.] The schoolhouse pictured above, which is remembered as having consisted of three classrooms, once served the Chapin area's African-American children during the decades in South Carolina when educational facilities were racially segregated. It reportedly stood on the still-unpaved Broomstraw Road not far from St. John A.M.E. Church and on the same side of the road. When it closed in the early 1950s, students were then transported to the Rosenwald School in Lexington. In its later years, Chapin's reputedly excellent basketball teams played their games outside on a court in front of the school.

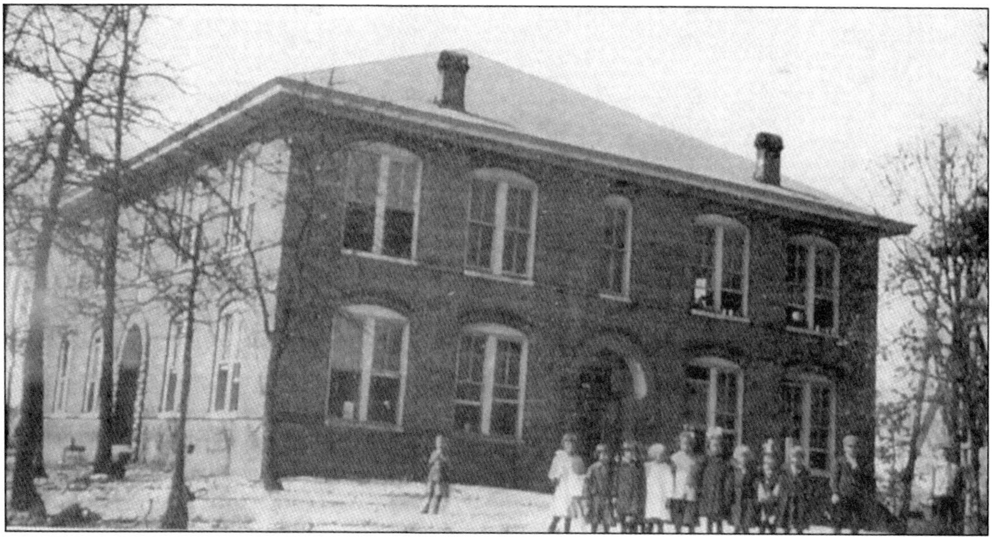

[**Chapin High School, c. 1912.**] Built in 1910 by the John W. Fry Construction Company, the new brick Chapin High School on Peak Street consisted of four large classrooms with a central hallway downstairs, and an auditorium and two large classrooms upstairs—one for 8th and 9th grades, the other for 10th and 11th. By 1919–1920, Chapin had achieved classification as a third-class school; it employed two full-time teachers and offered a three-year curriculum with 32 to 36 weeks of classes of 40 minutes each. On the cornerstone of the building, which has since been torn down, were the names of the school trustees: J.S. Wessinger, T.O. Stoudemire, and P.S. Fulmer.

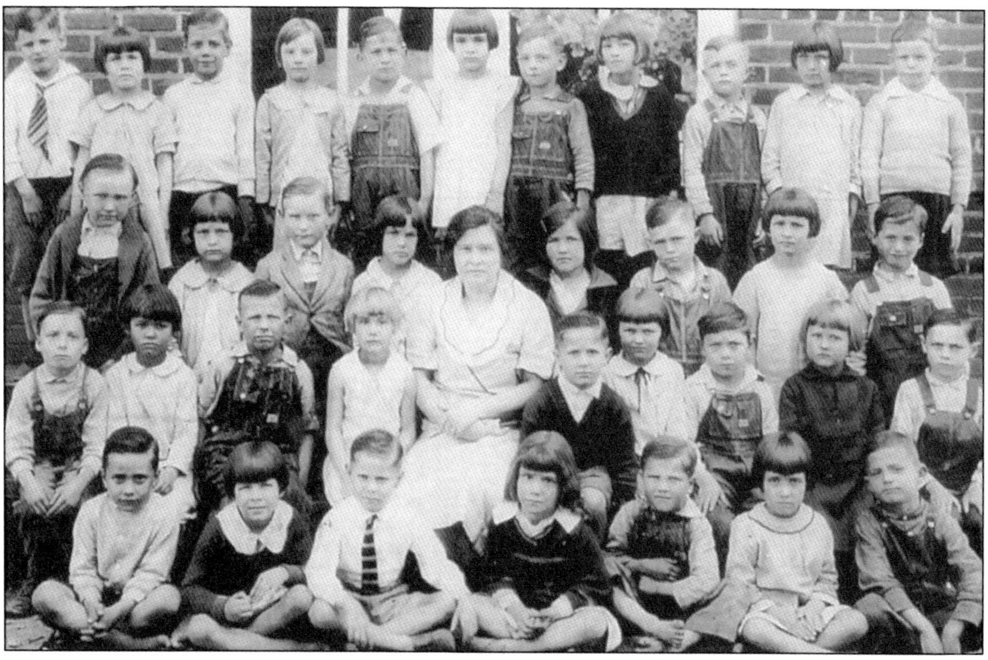

[**Chapin Elementary Class, c. 1931.**] An unidentified local photographer made this outdoor portrait at Chapin Elementary School of grades one through four with their teacher sitting in the middle. R.W. Frick was the principal of the grammar school and J.D. Brown was superintendent of the Chapin School District at the time this picture was taken.

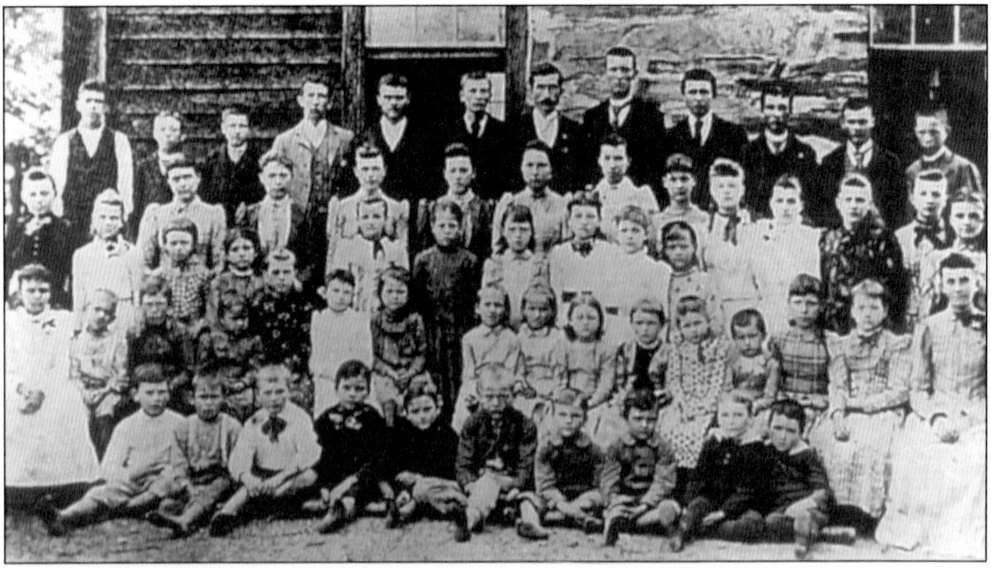

[Piney Woods School, c. 1900.] In 1900, the Piney Woods District supported both white and black schools. The white student body numbered 45; the black, 55. The white school's term of instruction was 20 weeks; that of the black school's term, 8 weeks. By 1916 the old one-room school structure near Chapin—between St. Peter's Church Road, O.L. Ranch Road, and Paul Fulmer Road—had expanded to accommodate 2 white teachers, a man and a woman, who taught 45 girls and 48 boys.

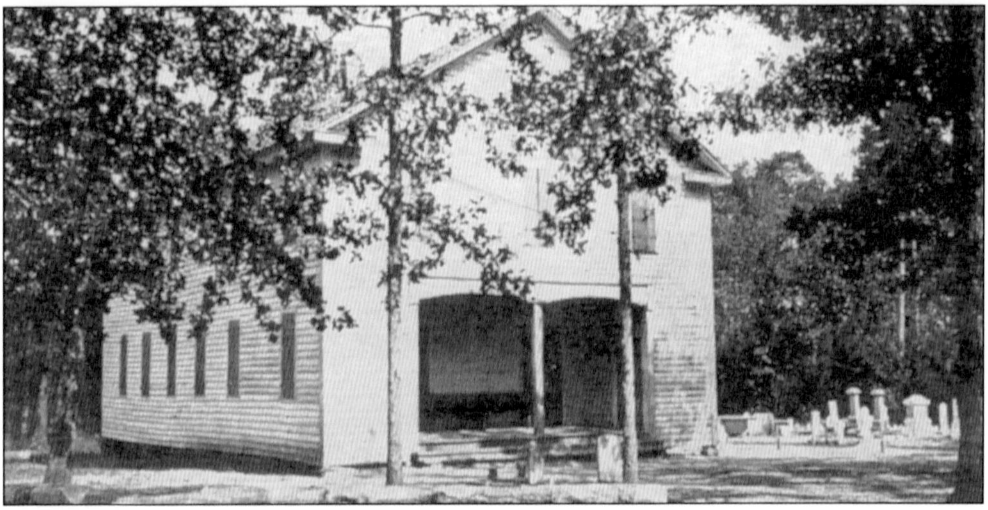

[St. Peter's Lutheran Church, near Chapin, c. 1910.] St. Peter's Lutheran Church, established in 1794, became known as the Piney Woods Church to distinguish it from a church across the river with the same name and because it stood in a dense forest of long-leaf pines. The Reverend Godfrey Dreher, 1833 to 1852, was the first Lutheran minister in the Fork to introduce the English language into the worship service. The building shown on this card is the 1888 enlargement of the church's second sanctuary, a two-story structure with three doors: one on the right for men, one on the left for women, and one at the end for the slaves who were seated in the gallery. By 1926 this sanctuary had been replaced by a $40,000 brick one, located on a bend in the present Dreher Island Road, just off St. Peter's Church Road a few miles southwest of Chapin.

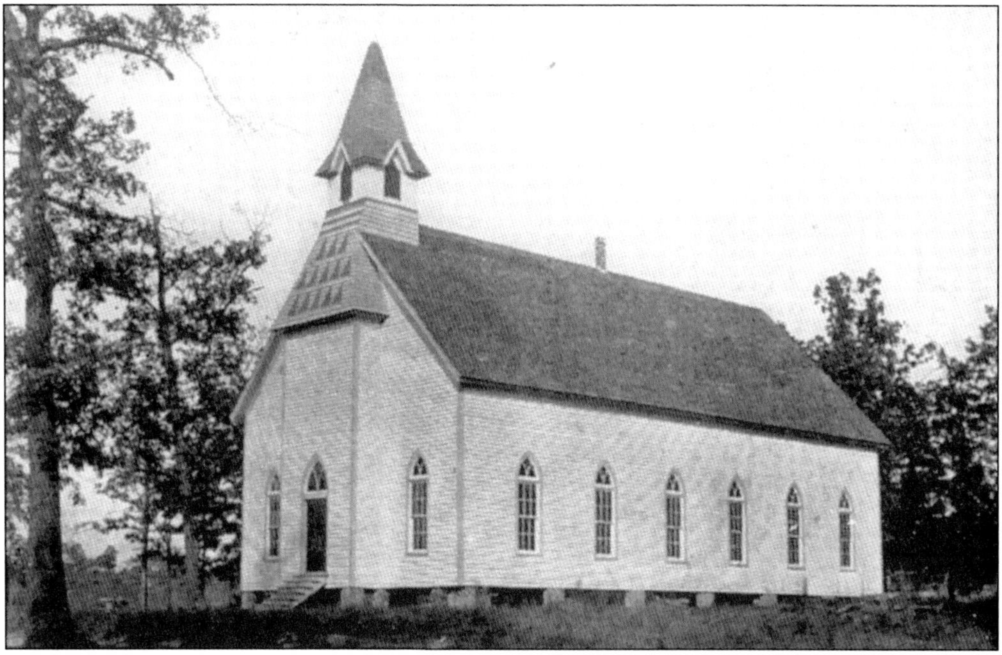

[ST. JACOB'S LUTHERAN CHURCH, NEAR CHAPIN, *c.* 1910.] St. Jacob's Church, located off I-26 northeast of Chapin on LC 689, was organized about 1760 and incorporated in 1788. Replacing an original log sanctuary, the one pictured here was built under contract in 1853 by Levi Seay of Lexington and was remodeled in 1905. It has been said that St. Jacob's Church attracted considerable local attention because it was the first church in the area that had a gallery in it.

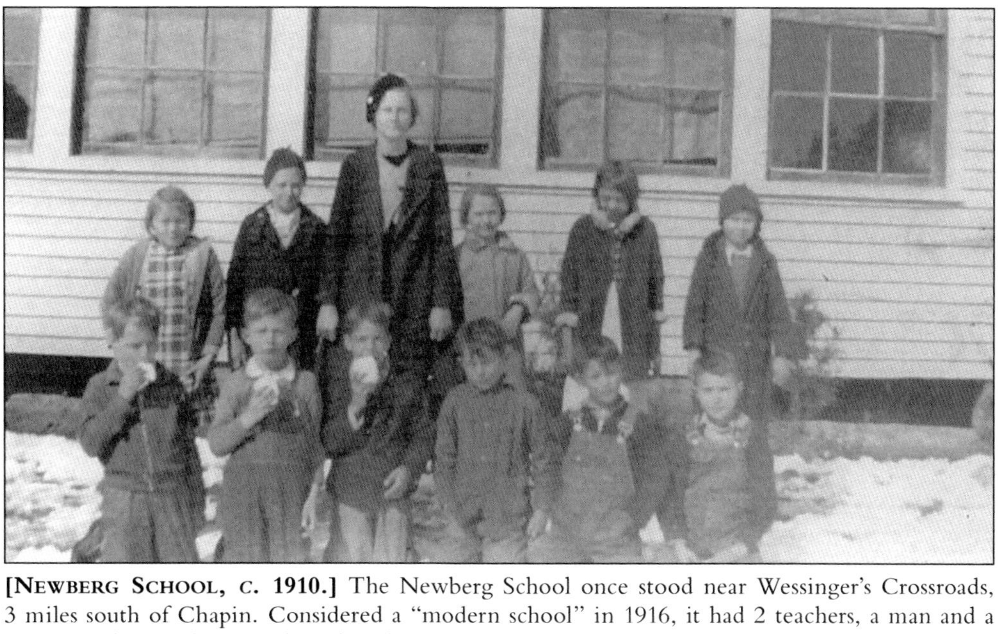

[NEWBERG SCHOOL, *c.* 1910.] The Newberg School once stood near Wessinger's Crossroads, 3 miles south of Chapin. Considered a "modern school" in 1916, it had 2 teachers, a man and a woman, who taught 53 girls and 43 boys. This unusual picture captures teacher and students—some of them holding and eating snow—reveling in the rare photo opportunity afforded by the conditions of an extraordinary winter day.

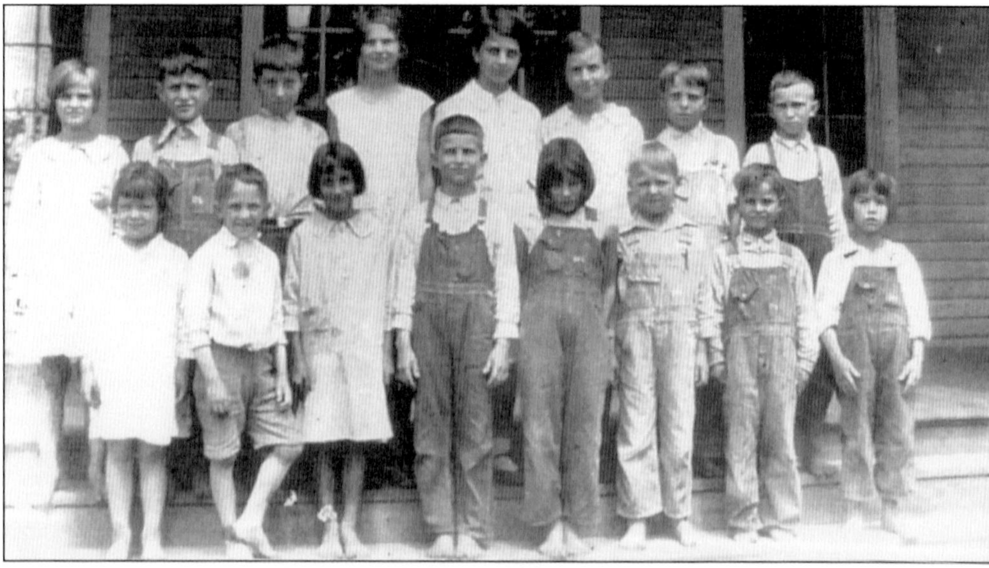

[Grammar School, Peak, *c.* 1932.] Peak, which started out as Peak's Station in 1853 when it was established as a habitation for workers on the Greenville and Columbia Railroad (it was named for railroad superintendent H.T. Peak), was not incorporated until 1880. The school picture above was taken in front of the building that replaced the two-teacher structure described by Lueco Gunter as being an old unpainted type with a partition down the middle housing 43 pupils for a 140-day term. By 1920, Peak had become a part of Newberry County.

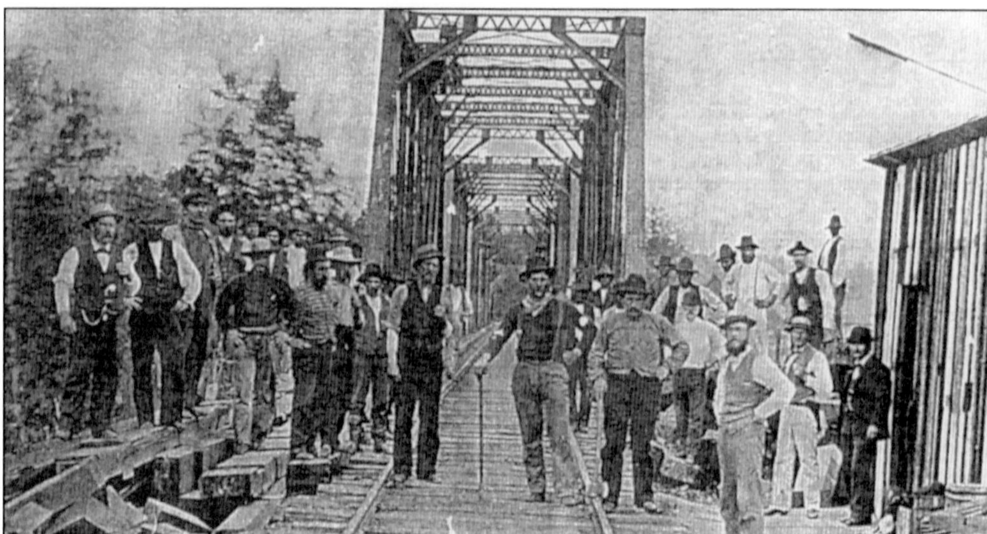

[Repair of the Railroad Trestle, Peak, *c.* 1903.] In 1865 Federal troops destroyed the trestle across the Broad River. A new Southern railway trestle was completed in 1903, providing a link with the Columbia-to-Spartanburg track on the Fairfield County side, thus connecting Peak with towns across the river and up the line—Pomaria, Prosperity, Newberry, and Clinton. Since the only crossing of the Broad River for a 40-mile stretch between Columbia and Shelton was this trestle, some residents would walk across the trestle to cars parked on the Fairfield side to get to their destinations across the river.

Five

East Central Region

In 1938, the town of New Brookland, located immediately across the Congaree (or Gervais Street) bridge from Columbia, officially changed its name to West Columbia. This was both a pragmatic and an emblematic move signifying that much of the growth and development of New Brookland—as well as of Cayce, her neighbor to the south—had long been allied to that of South Carolina's capital city. The two Lexington County towns, while retaining their own distinctive characteristics, became important commercial and residential extensions of their larger sister city to the east.

It is appropriate that the last chapter in this volume should end with views of this east central enclave of Lexington County, especially New Brookland and Cayce. For the next step to be taken is into the town and county across the Congaree.

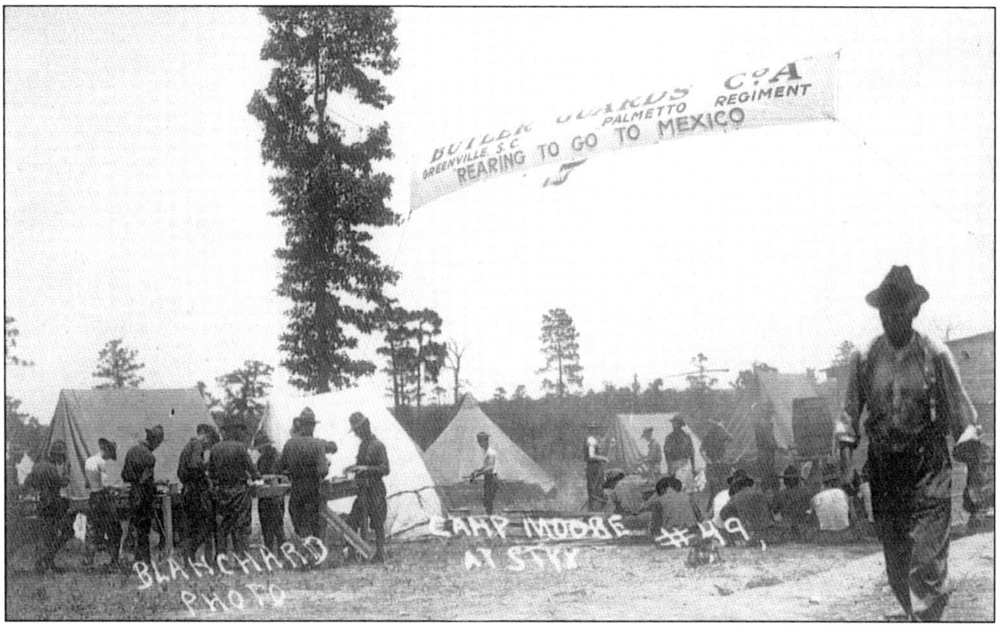

Butler Guards, Camp Moore, Styx, [Pine Ridge, 1916]. In 1913 the South Carolina National Guard obtained a 1,007-acre undeveloped site 7 miles from Columbia to utilize as an annual state encampment ground. Located on a sandy hill south of Congaree Creek 3/4 mile southeast of the Southern Railroad station at Styx, the site required improvements in every sector before it could be used: grounds, roads, rail facilities, water, and sanitation. Today the new Pine Ridge Armory on Fish Hatchery Road sits high on the hill (south of I-26 and west of US 321) near what would have been the center of Camp Moore. Shown here with their banner are the Butler Guards from Greenville, in a picture that was also printed in *The State* on July 9, 1916.

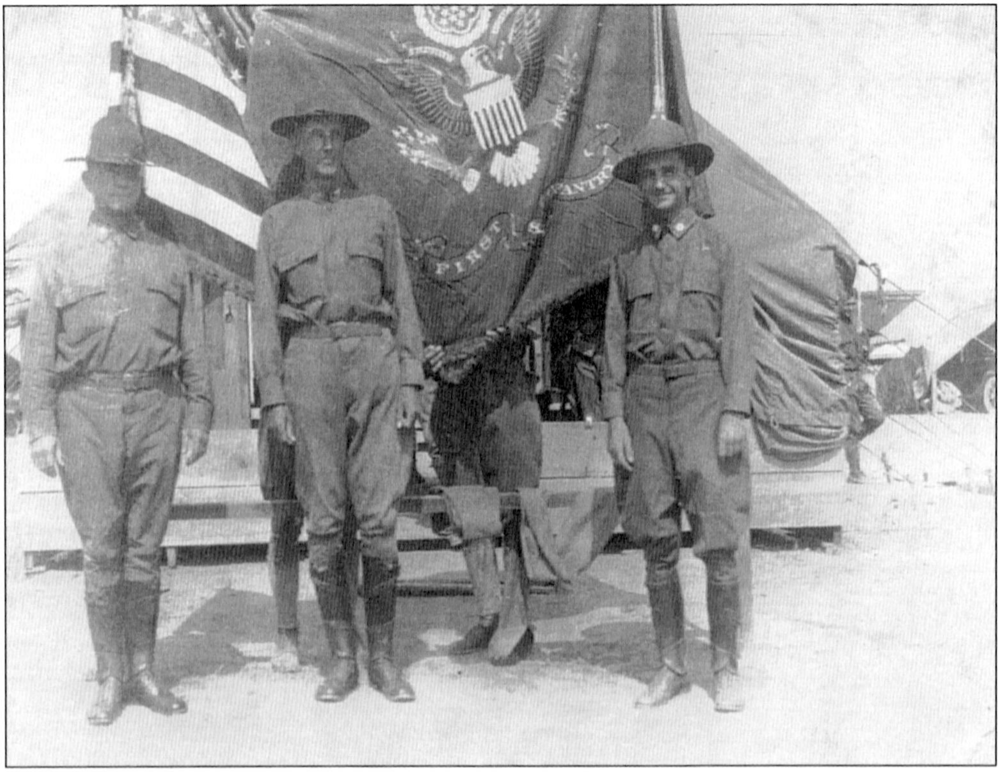

[Officers and Flags, Camp Moore, Styx, 1916.] Shown here with the national and regimental flags are the principal officers of the First Regiment, National Guard of South Carolina: (center) Col. Edgeworth Montague Blythe (1873–1945), commander, and (at right) Capt. Gabriel Heyward Mahon, adjutant. The officer at left is possibly Brig. Gen. W.W. Moore, adjutant general, for whom the camp was named. When the First Regiment left for El Paso, Texas, on August 7, 1916, it had an enrollment of 53 officers and 1,015 enlisted men. By then, all national guard units had been shifted to federal control.

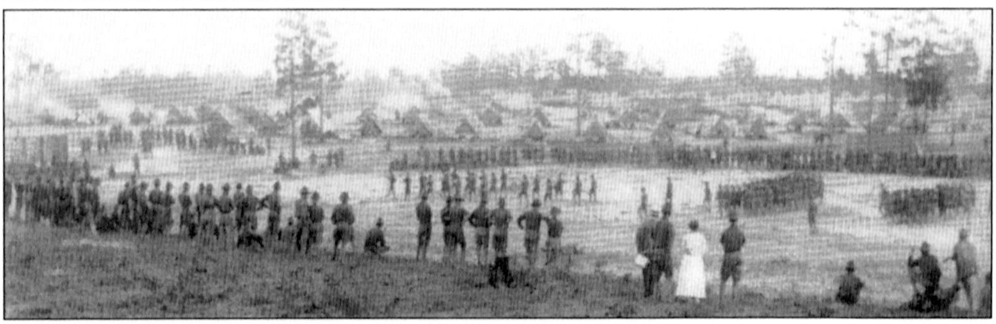

Camp Moore, Styx, 2nd Reg. [Parade Grounds, 1916]. On June 21, 1916, the first complement of soldiers—the Second Regiment's 73-man Olympia Unit (Co. "G") of the Columbia Light Infantry (organized in 1901)—arrived at Styx to begin clearing the site. The second to arrive was the 75-man Company "H" of the Brookland Light Infantry (organized in 1904), followed by the 59-member Governor's Guard, Company "F" (organized in 1843), and the Charleston Light Dragoons on June 24. On August 10 the Second Infantry, under the command of Col. Holmes B. Springs, Georgetown, left for the Mexican border, and within days all the tents had vanished from Camp Moore.

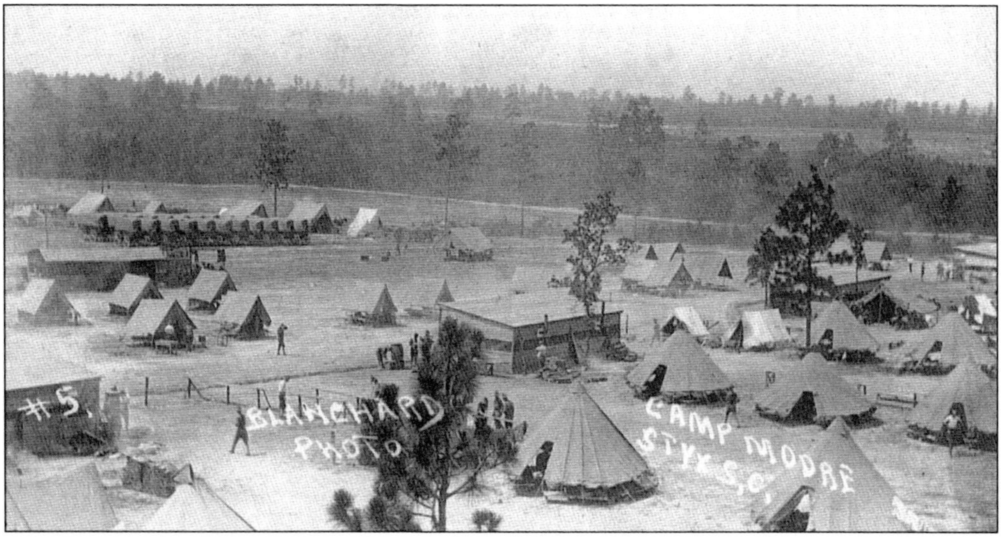

CAMP MOORE, STYX [BIRD'S-EYE VIEW, 1916]. When the order came to open Camp Moore, Company "F" of the Governor's Guard obtained tents and supplies from the state armory in Columbia and sent them to the camp site. This view, one of many made by Blanchard of Columbia, shows the tents of the First and Second Regiments—the First's at an oblique angle to the 600-yard rifle range, the Second's parallel to the range, and the Light Dragoons' on its other side. The frame buildings at center, set up by July 1, were used to house the post office, Blanchard's studio, and the telegraph and telephone exchanges. Blanchard's viewcards of Camp Moore probably went out in every mail, to show the folks back home something of army camp life.

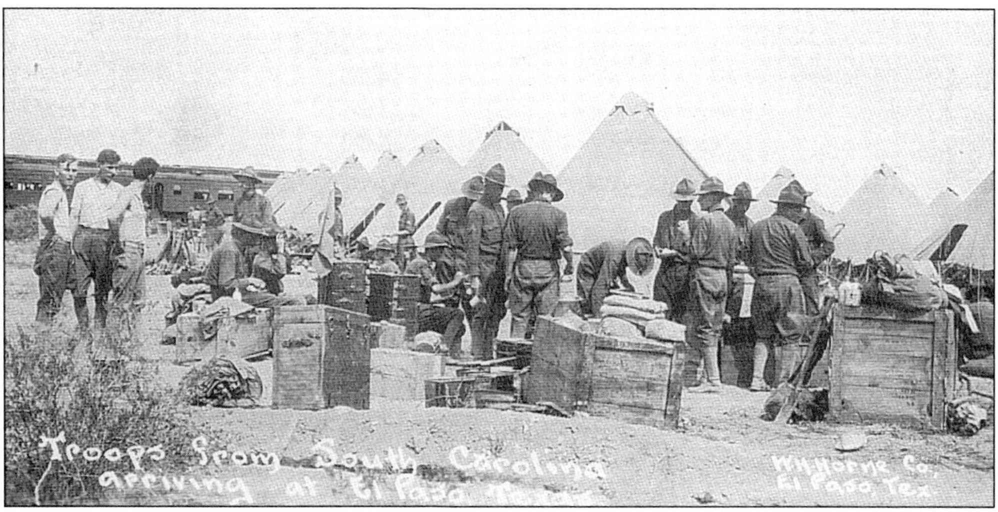

TROOPS FROM SOUTH CAROLINA ARRIVING AT EL PASO, TEXAS [1916]. South Carolina national guardsmen stayed three and a half months at Camp Owen Bierne and at sites along the border as a portion of the 20,000 guardsmen who helped to constitute a force of 175,000 men under the command of regular U.S. Army troops. The Carolina units returned to the state between November 30, 1916, and March 20, 1917, to be mustered out at Styx. The Mexican border crisis allowed troops to train with new concepts and equipment that would be put to valuable use in World War I. Camp Moore eventually closed in the 1920s.

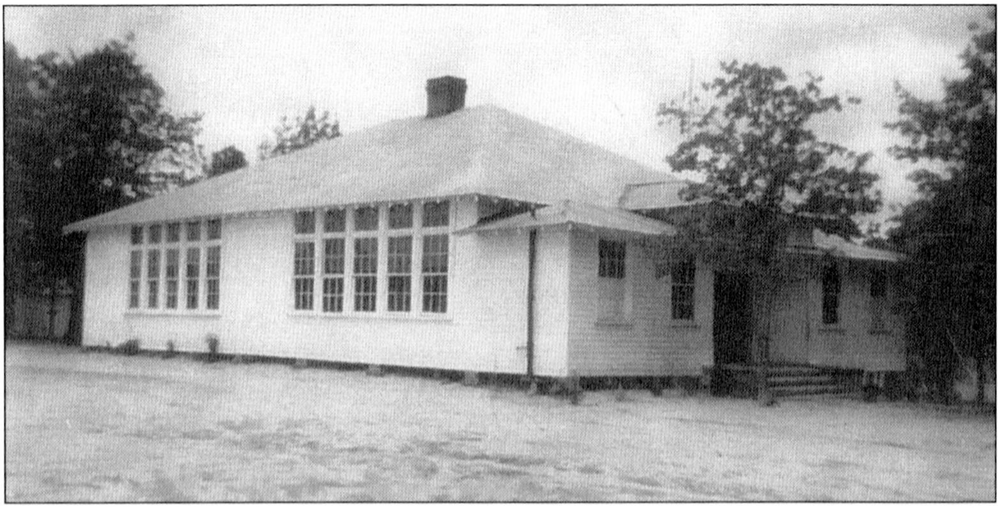

[Congaree School, c. 1930s.] In 1915 when Lueco Gunter visited the site of the Congaree School, located on Ramblin Road, he found a new, modern, two-room building with new desks and equipment—and a student body of 76 pupils dispersed through seven grades for a 120-day session. It replaced a schoolhouse, which had been destroyed by fire the previous year. The "new" one shown here was razed when the contemporary Congaree Elementary School was built at the front of the site.

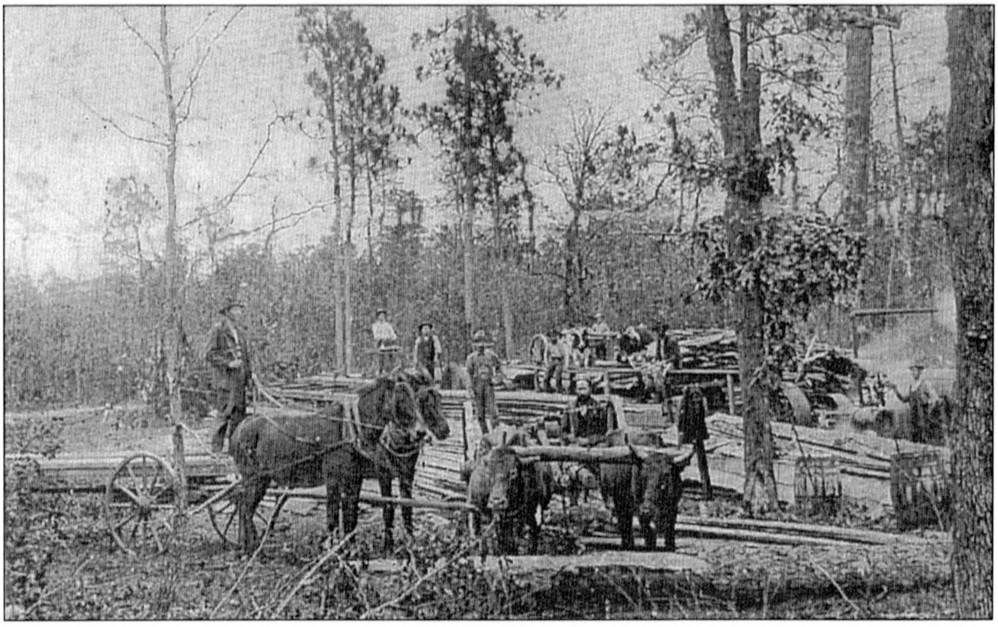

[Sim Long's Sawmill, Edmund, c. 1902.] This early view of Sim Long's sawmill in Edmund documents one of the many mill operations that moved from farm to farm harvesting the pines, which had become one of Lexington County's significant crops. The extensive slash-pine forests that covered the sandhills grew fast and tall and became the lumber of choice. The crews used oxen to drag the logs to the mill site, where other crew men employed portable steam-driven saws to cut the lumber. They then stacked it on wagons and drove it to the lumberyard. Edmund had a population of 125 in 1910.

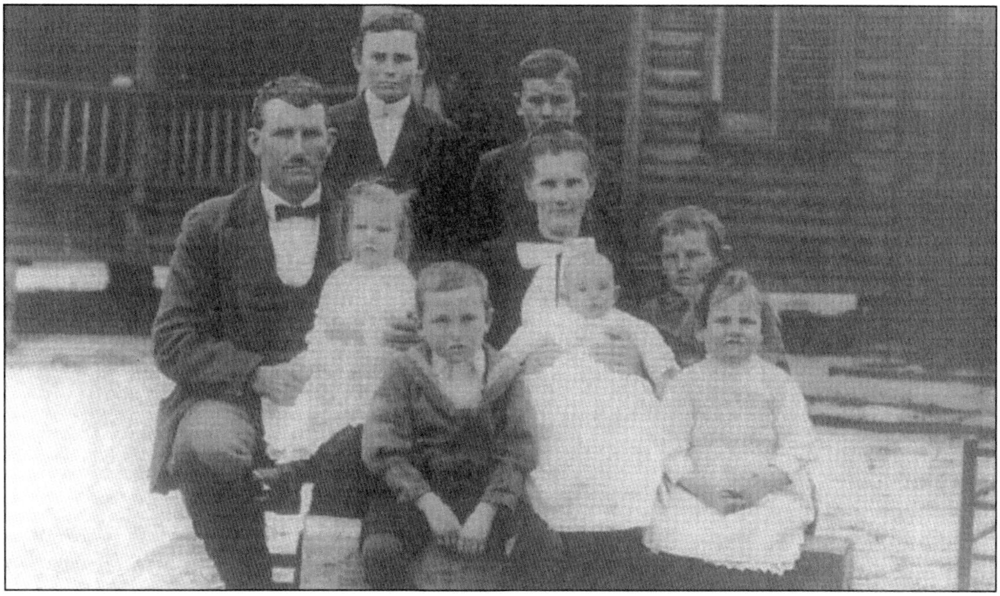

[Portrait of John Asmond Wise and His Family, *c.* 1910.] Ila Mae Wise Lucas states in the 1987 book *Sandhill Recollections* that the original home place of John Asmond Wise's (1876–1954) was located off Edmund Highway and Crystal Springs Road in the Scouter Creek area, and that he later moved to Tin City and built his home into the side of a hill. He farmed the sand hills, helped load boxcars with sand when the railroad was built, and later assisted in the construction of barracks at Camp Jackson in Columbia. Twice married and the father of 20 children, he and his first wife, Maggie Senn (1882–1922), are shown here with 7 of their 11 children. Mrs. Wise died a day after the birth of their last child. Wise and both wives are buried at Old Bethel Methodist Church on Bethel Church Road.

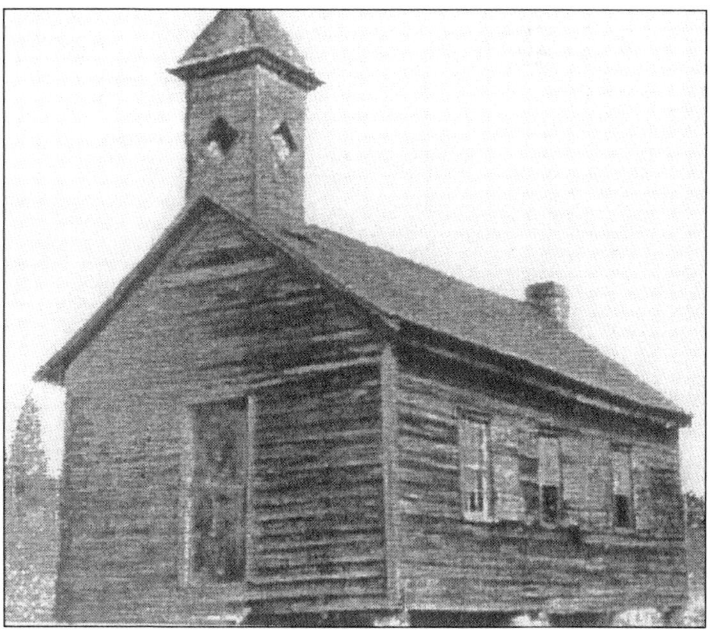

[Sand Mountain School, *c.* 1916.] The Sand Mountain School was located south of Pine Ridge near the junction of Fish Hatchery Road and Gator Road. In 1900, this was a one-room building with a teacher instructing 37 students in a 20-week session. By 1929, the principal, Miss Mincy R. Pound, had an assistant, Mrs. W.C. Gantt.

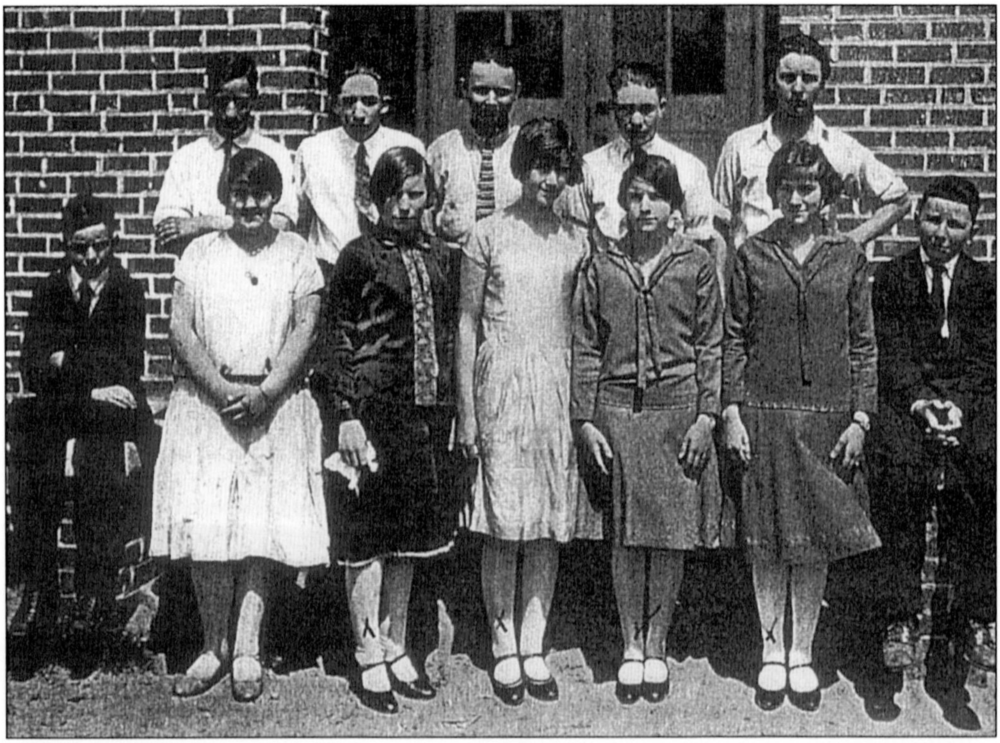

[Cayce School, Eighth Grade Class, *c.* 1927.] Included in this picture of class officers and students in 1927 were Mildred Lybrand (president), Dora Dorn (vice president), and Archie Moore (secretary-treasurer). "Consolidation of schools means a lot more than simply doing away with the one-teacher schools," J.E. Stockman wrote in 1923. "It means the putting of a good graded and high school in the reach of every boy and girl in our county."

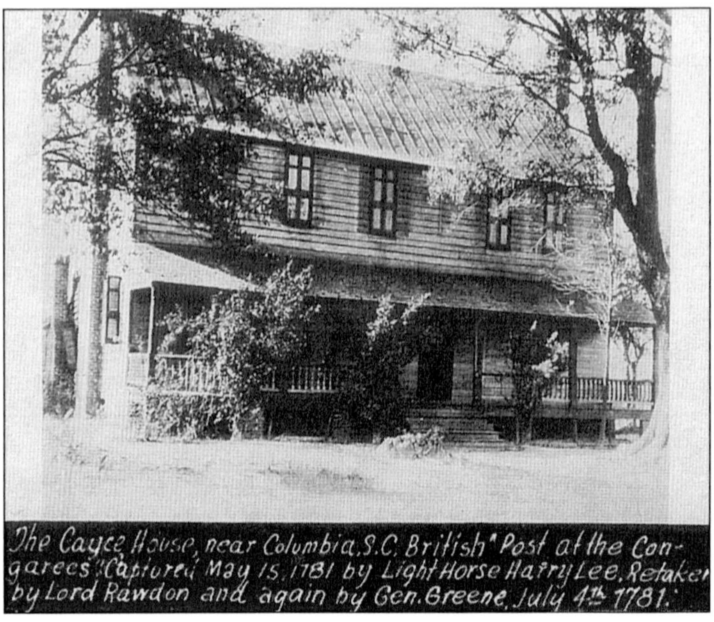

Cayce House, near Columbia, SC [*c.* 1930s]. The Cayce House was built in 1770 near the old village of Granby once located a few miles below the present town of Cayce. An important landmark during Revolutionary War days, it changed hands between the American and British forces several times. The Cayce House was demolished in 1936 and the replica built later now houses the Cayce Museum.

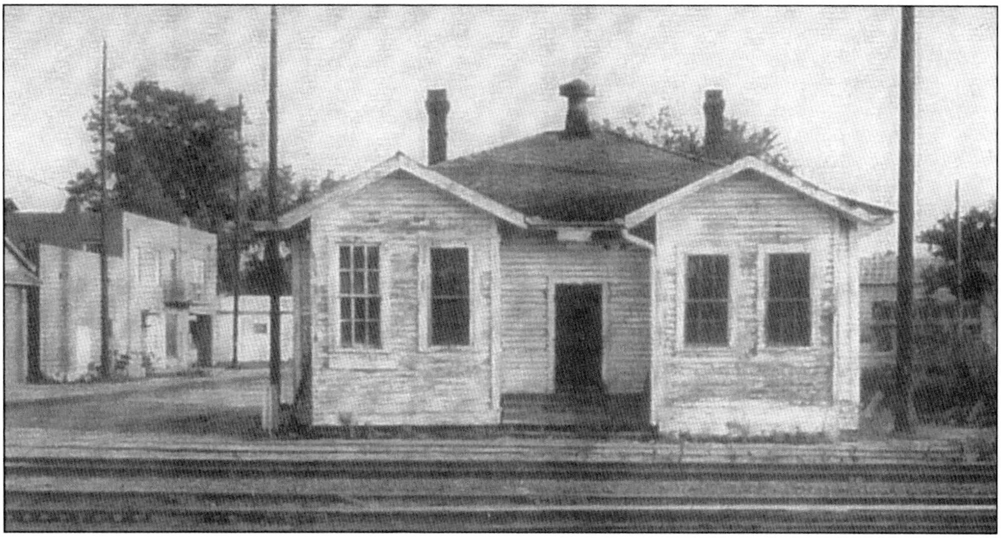

[SEABOARD YARD OFFICE, CAYCE, C. 1920.] This view looking north across the railroad tracks—where 16 passenger trains would pass each day discharging passengers and mail going to the Cayce post office—at the old Seaboard yard office also includes a short row of buildings facing State Street. The largest structure, at middle left, still stands (as does the one to its left) on the corner of Frick Street. Upstairs was a boarding house that catered largely to railroad employees; downstairs, a grocery store.

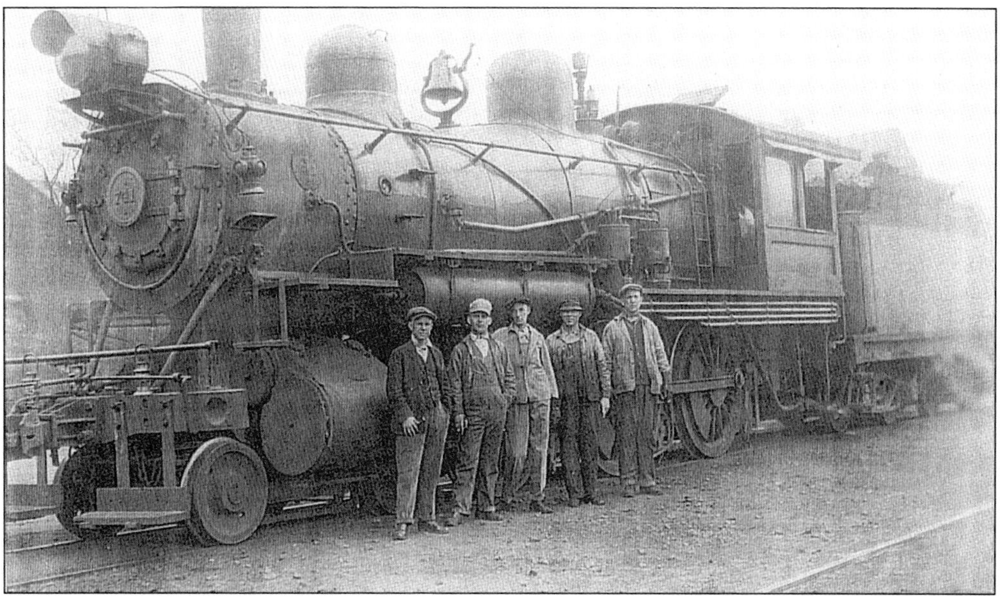

[LOCOMOTIVE #741, SEABOARD AIR LINE RAIL YARDS, CAYCE, C. 1925.] Located on the Southern and Seaboard railroads, Cayce was home to the Seaboard's repair shops. Their work consisted mainly in making repairs to locomotives and rail cars used in transportation service. The train crew portrayed here are, left to right, as follows: M.A. White, conductor; T.L. Brown, switchman; Tom Spencer, engineer; D.F. High, fireman; and Grady Smith, switchman. The payroll for the shops was large, and therefore, it was an important part of the economy of the town and its surrounding territory. Cayce's population grew from 150 in 1910 to 800 in 1923.

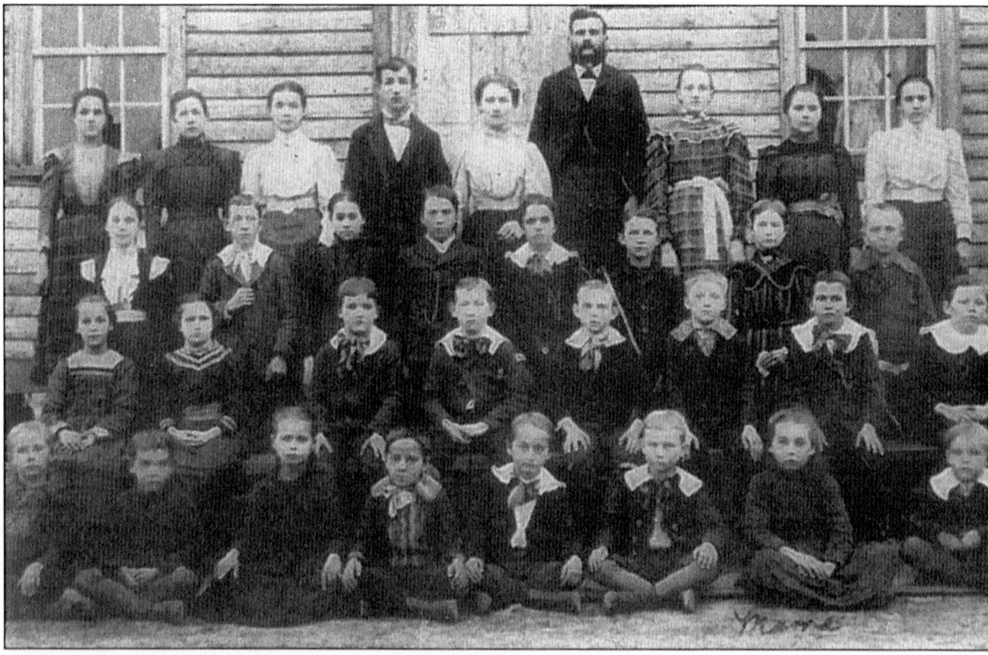

[Half Way Grounds School, c. 1905.] In 1901 the area around the county's Leaphart Road had both white and black schools. Each school had its teacher, with 13 black students in one for an 8-week session, and 45 white pupils in the other for a 16-week term. Shown here is one of these schools, with the teacher, Jim Senn, standing in the back row. The style of clothes suggests that this picture is one of the earliest in the collection. Half Way Grounds School once stood on Roof property (behind the Agape Retirement Center in 2000) at 2700 Leaphart Road on the west side of I-26 between US 1 and US 378.

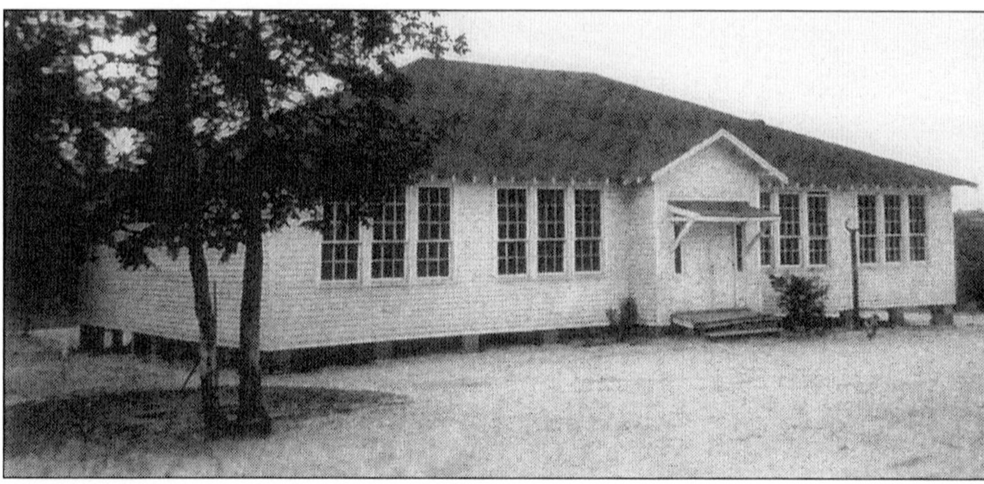

[Cayce School, c. 1930s.] This old frame grammar school for Cayce's African-American children was replaced with a complex of brick buildings in the 1940s and 1950s. Several of the larger remodeled ones remain and have been used as the westside unit of the Boy's and Girl's Clubs of the Midlands. The original schoolhouse faced Wilkinson across the street from the site of the Marion B. Wilkinson Home for Orphan Girls, founded in 1909 and lost to fire some years ago. This neighborhood is in the area behind the Cayce City Hall and museum grounds.

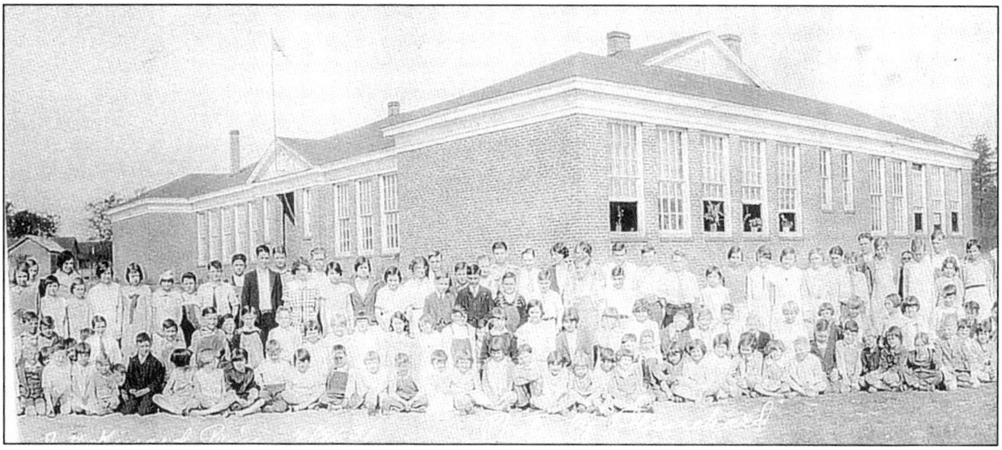

[**Cayce Grammar School, 1931.**] This six-room brick building, erected in 1925, replaced an old three-room wooden structure built in 1917. Six rooms were later added to take care of the progressively increasing enrollment. Although much altered, it can still be seen in the middle of a block bounded by Eighth, Poplar, and Third Streets and Lexington Avenue, on which it fronts. Housing a Continuing Education Center for Adults in 2000, it has continued to serve an educational function in the community. Older as well as younger pupils appear in this group picture taken on May 9, 1931, when there were 9 grades, 230 pupils, and 9 teachers including principal J.H. Kinard.

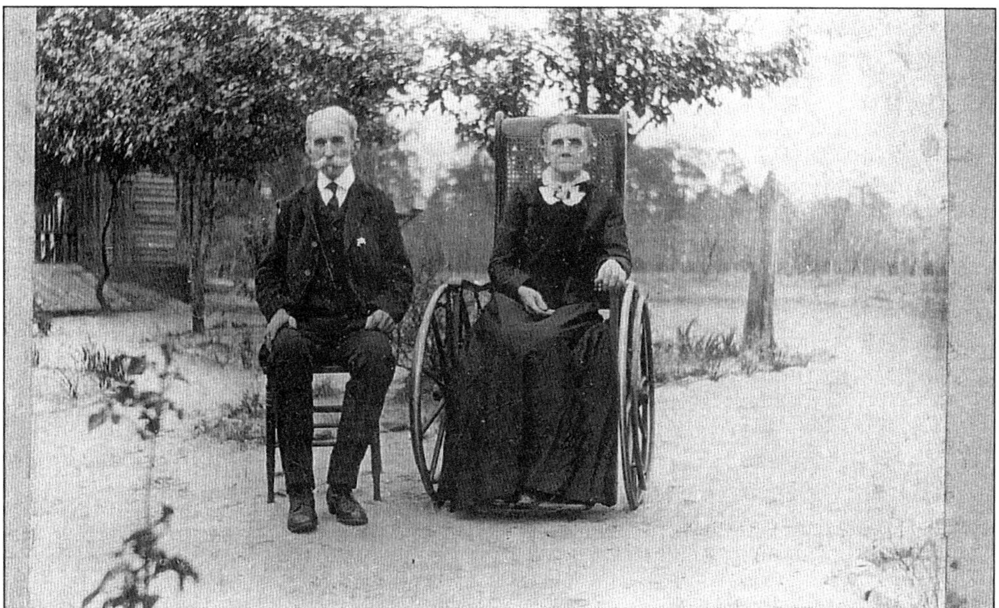

[**Portrait of Mr. and Mrs. Walter A. Leaphart, *c.* 1910.**] Walter Asbury Leaphart (1847–1934) and his wife, Elizabeth Kaigler Geiger (1850–1916), were married in 1877 and became parents of 12 children. This formal outdoor portrait was made at their Lexington County home sometime between 1910 and 1916.

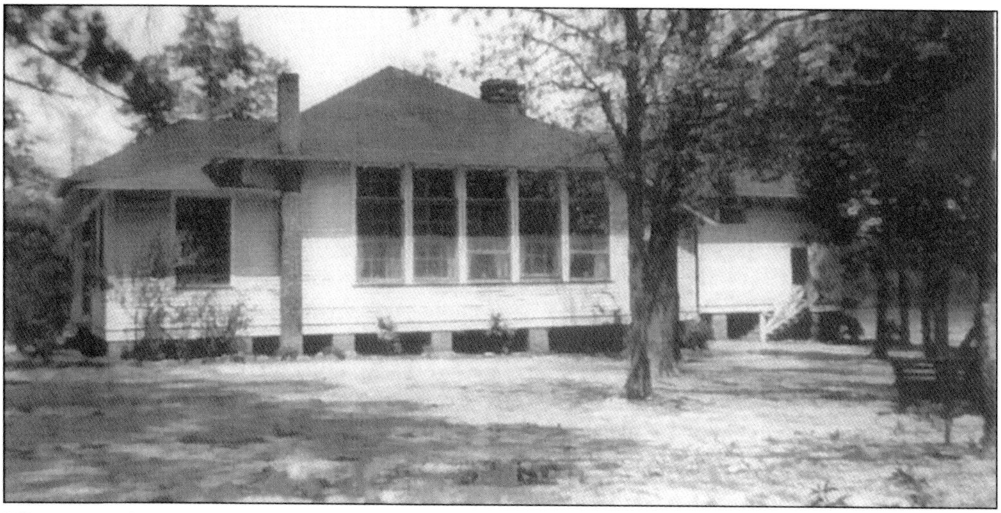

[Oakdale School, Dixiana, c. 1930s.] The Oakdale School was located south of Cayce, in the Dixiana area east of Pine Ridge and US 321 and west of I-26 near LC 129. This structure replaced an earlier one-room building of the old type, with a door in the center of one end and windows on each side. In 1916 one teacher reportedly taught seven grades here, with a student body consisting of 12 boys and 16 girls for a 120-day term.

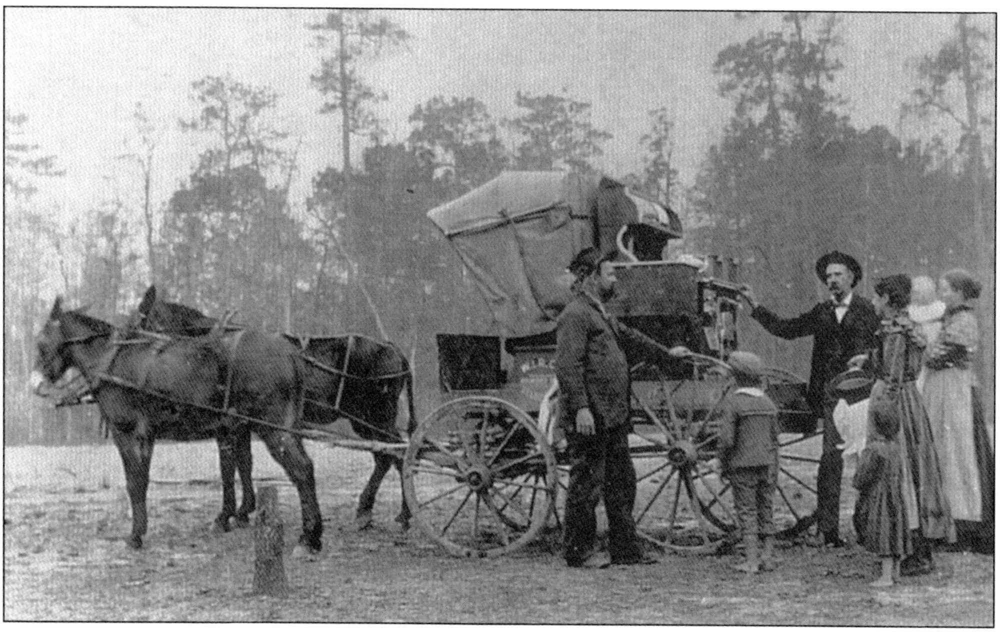

[Delivery of a Kitchen Stove, Oak Grove, c. 1900.] The delivery of a new iron wood-burning stove would have been a major domestic event in rural South Carolina during this period. Observing the unloading of this one at the Mineral Springs Road home of Ruben (1857–1926) and Sallie Buff Kleckley (1857–1931), who were married in 1881, are their children Walter, Bessie, and Ruben. The two-mule wagon has made the delivery of the stove from a store in Lexington. In 2000 the white frame home still stood on Mineral Springs Road, next to the Crooked Creek Riding Academy at 3799.

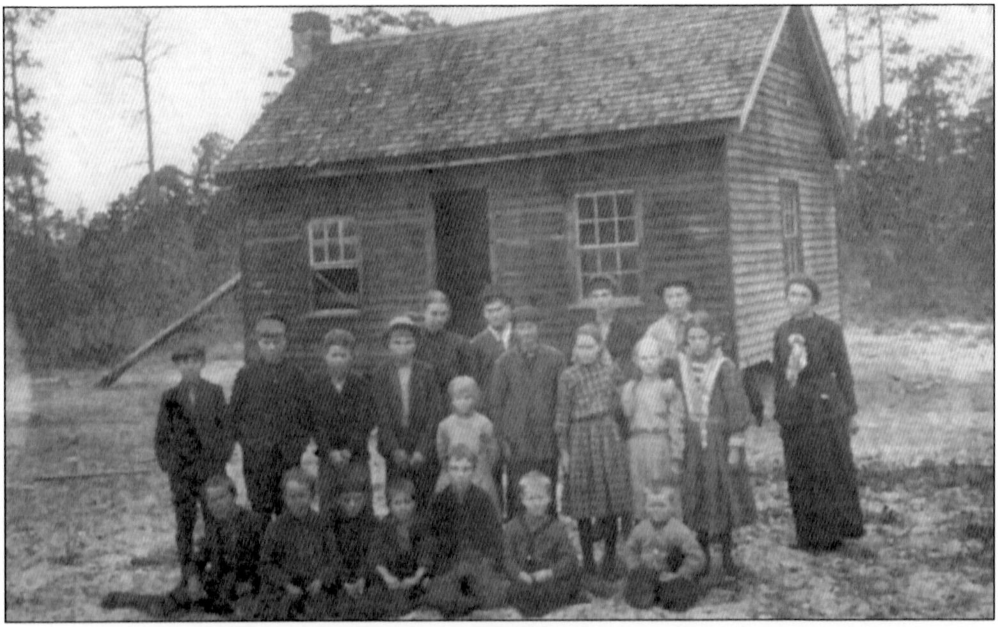

[Long Branch School, Springdale, c. 1912.] Located on Platt Springs Road, this 1900-era one-room school building—with a pole holding the brick chimney in place—served the Long Branch Community (which in 1955 became incorporated as Springdale). In 1900 one teacher taught 38 students who were distributed through seven grades for an eight-week session. The picture above shows teacher Estelle Harmon (1890–1980s) and her 20 pupils. Fire destroyed it in 1918 and the replacement was built at the same site. In 1953, the school district sold the property on which the building once stood to the Platt Springs Methodist Church for $6,500.

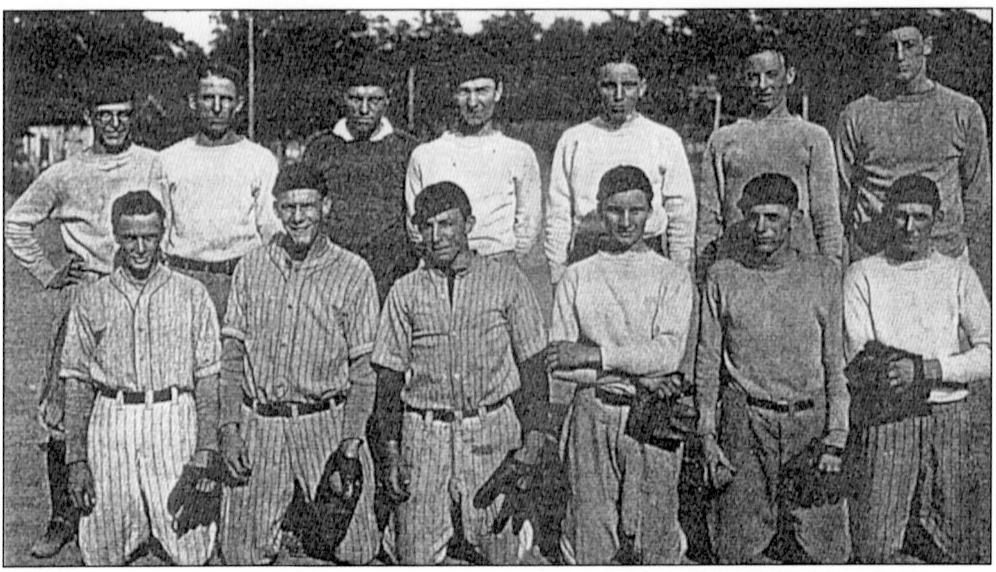

[Boys' Baseball Team, Brookland School, 1929.] This portrait of the 1929 boys' baseball team of Brookland School included Bill Oxner (captain), Wofford Ballington (manager), Scott Heise, Willie McDowell, Maylon Ware (front row, fourth player), Harry Taylor, Earl Gibson, and Mr. Robinson (coach).

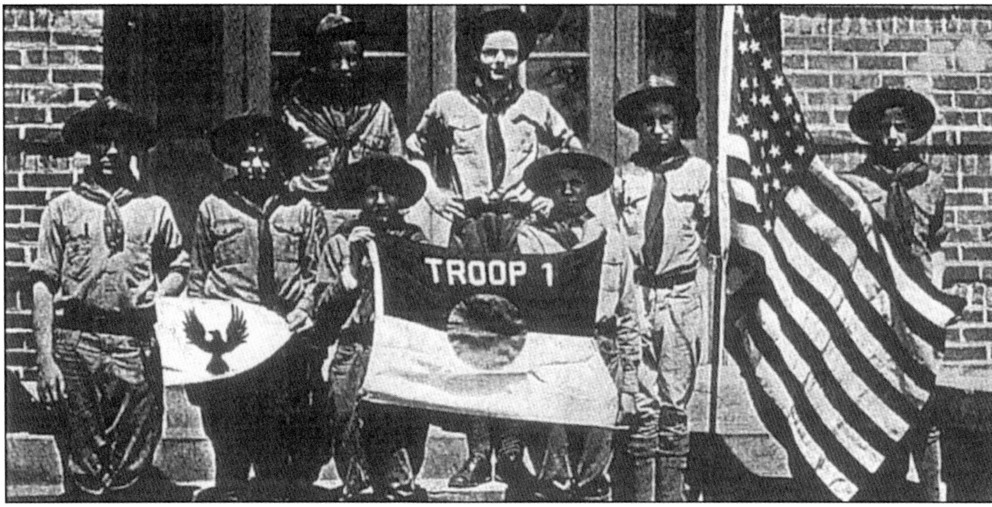

[Boy Scout Troop One, New Brookland, 1927.] This portrait of Boy Scout Troop One of New Brookland was taken at the back entrance of the Brookland School. Adult Scout leaders were E.L. Shull, scoutmaster; R. Hare and M.C. Yeargin, assistant scoutmasters; D.L. Dunlevy, chairman of the troop committee; the Reverend W.M. Owings and L. Hall, troop committeemen; J. Swygert and Ernest Charles of the Flying Eagle Patrol; and T.C. Dunlevy and Harold Hall of the Wild Cat Patrol.

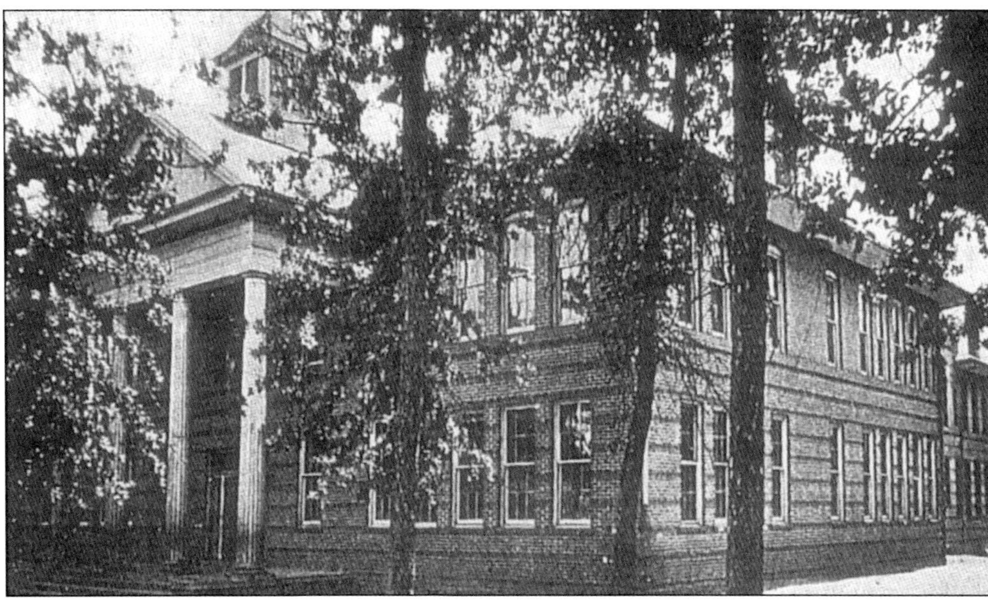

[Brookland School, *c.* 1929.] The Brookland School, built in 1911, replaced a frame one-teacher schoolhouse that in 1900 served 140 students. By 1916, it offered a three-year curriculum taught by two teachers and had already outgrown the new building. In 1919, when the town had grown to a population of 2,500, Brookland became the county's only first-grade high school. After the new high school on State Street opened in 1932, the old one continued to function as an elementary school until it was torn down in 1976. Brick gateposts on Augusta Street are all that remain on the site to indicate that a school once existed there. The Heyward Moore Fine Arts Center stood on the property in 2000.

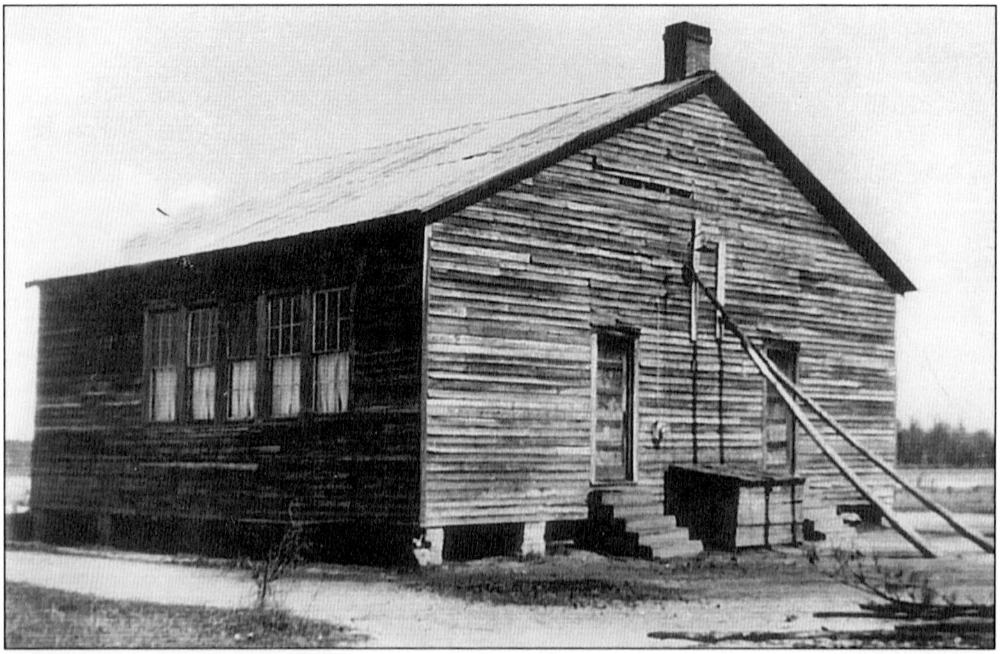

[Chalk Hill School, c. 1920.] In 1900, Chalk Hill's one-teacher school—formed from portions of Oakdale and Sand Mountain districts—had 37 students in an eight-week session. On October 20, 1928, Izah Williams and Mary Ann Gillian deeded the Chalk Hill School and a 4-acre tract to the three-member board of trustees (Wilber Sharpe, S.A. Hollyday, and H.T. Lucas) for Lexington County School District No. 41 in the Dixiana area. The African-American pupils who made up the student body of this school were part of a total of some 2,855 black students who attended the Lexington County public schools in 1931.

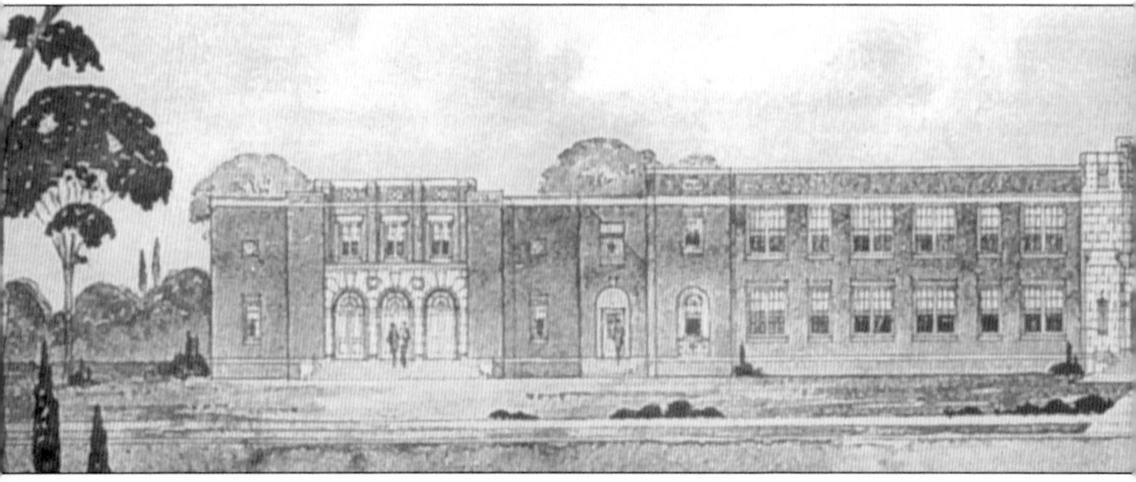

[Brookland-Cayce High School, c. 1929.] In 1930 the citizens in the Brookland-Cayce school district—with 1,135 white students and 35 teachers—voted in favor of issuing school bonds in the sum of $100,000 in the interest of erecting "a modern high school building about halfway between Cayce and New Brookland . . . which will be attended by high school pupils of both Cayce and Brookland" (*Dispatch-News*, June 25, 1930). The two-story school was designed by Columbia architects Wessinger and Stork (their architectural drawing is shown here) and was built at 1300

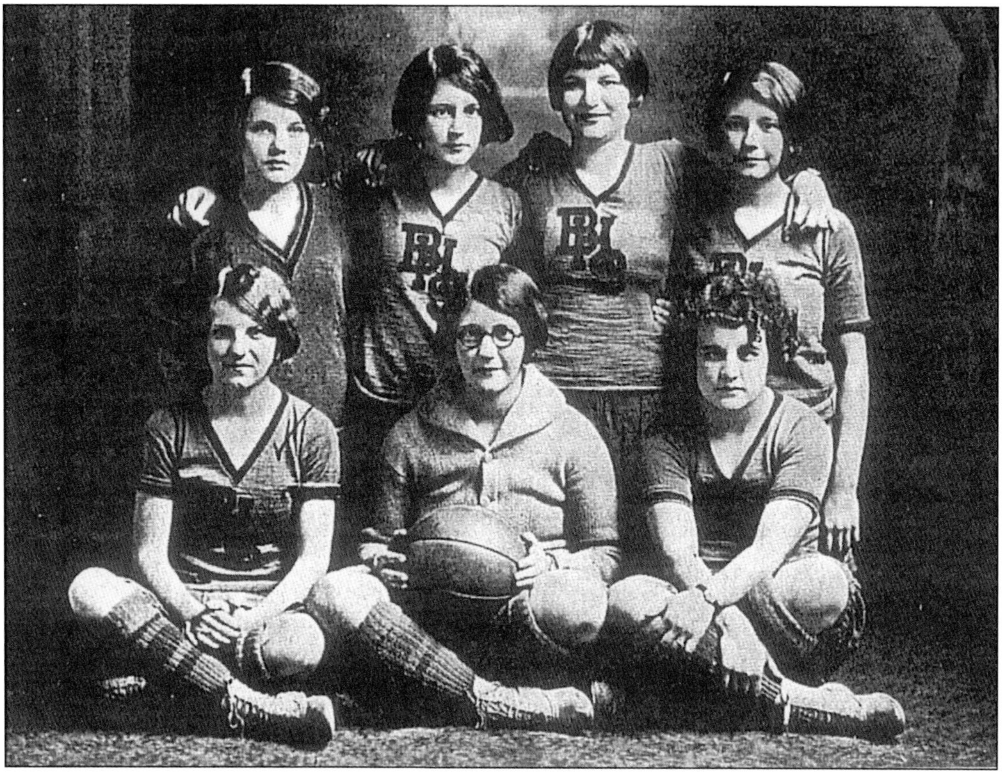

[Girls' Basketball Team, Brookland School, 1927.] This portrait of the 1927 girls' basketball team of the Brookland School included the following players: Rawl, forward; Merchant (captain), forward; Lucas, jump center; Wrenn, side center; Blume, guard; and Lybrand, guard.

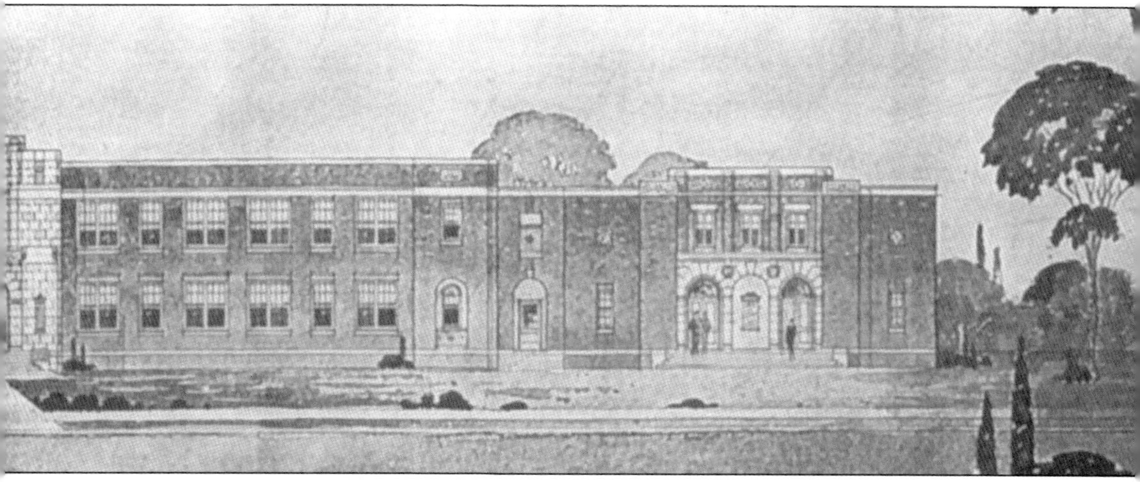

State Street for $70,997 by W.A. Crary and Sons, Columbia. The brick structure (which housed 16 to 20 teachers and about 200 students from the 8th to the 11th grades) had 16 classrooms—eight on the first floor and eight on the second—and offices and a gymnasium on one end and an auditorium on the other. It was ready for occupancy in 1932 and began with an eight-month school session. In 1933–1934 the term was expanded to a nine-month schedule.

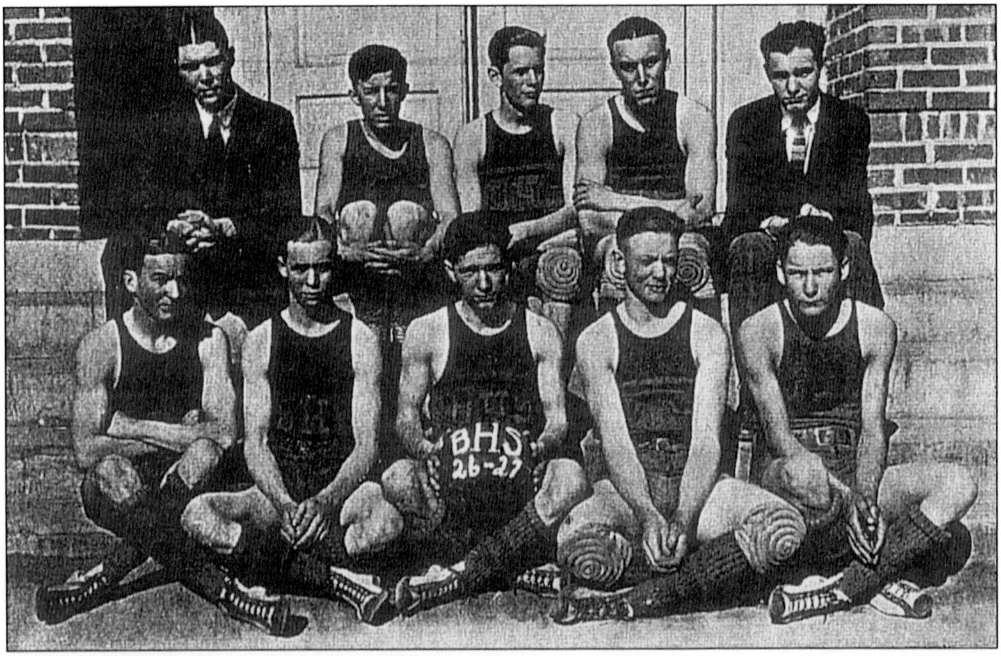

[Boys' Basketball Team, Brookland School, 1927.] This portrait of the 1927 boys' basketball team of Brookland School included R.B. Stone (back row, left), coach; W. Cromer (back row, right), business manager; and the following players: C. Kirby (captain), Bundrick (F), Shehane (F), Rikard (C), Kirby (G), and Parnell (G).

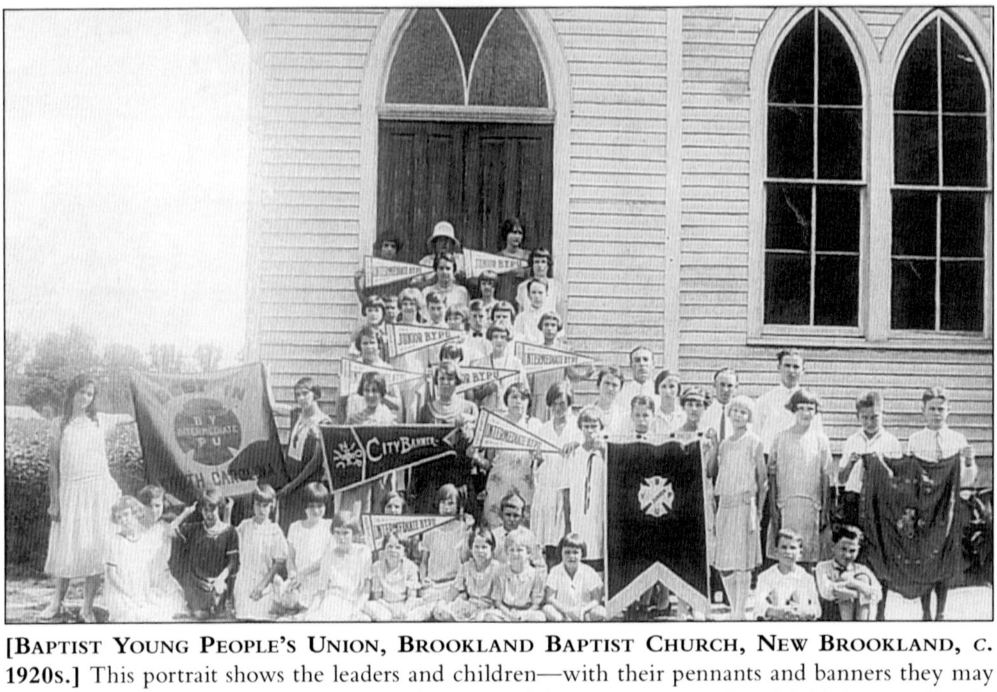

[Baptist Young People's Union, Brookland Baptist Church, New Brookland, c. 1920s.] This portrait shows the leaders and children—with their pennants and banners they may have probably won at an area church conference—of the Baptist Young People's Union standing in front of the steps and inside the doorway of the Brookland Baptist Church, New Brookland.

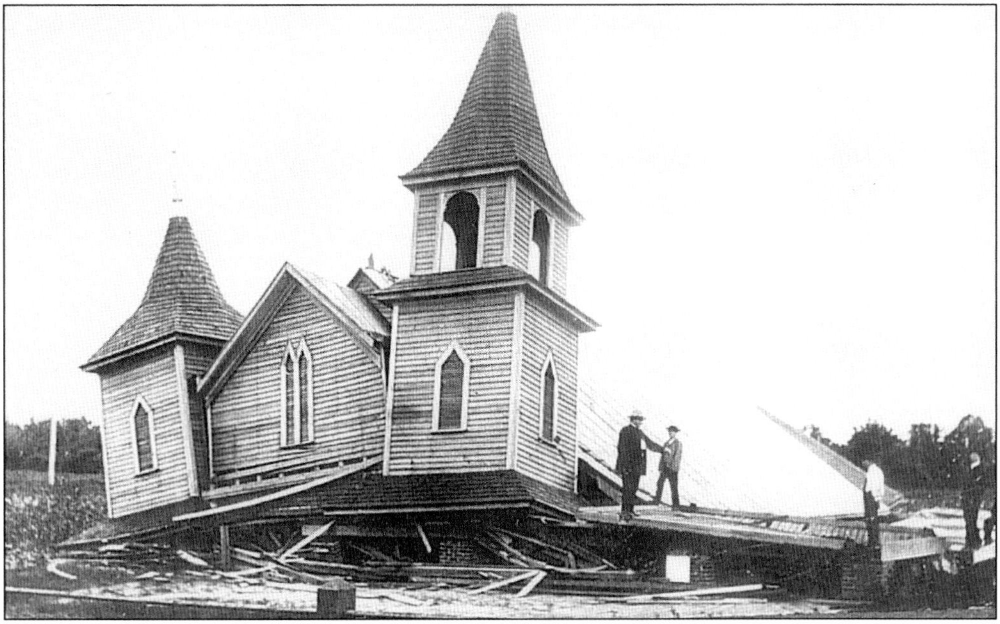

[BROOKLAND BAPTIST CHURCH IN RUINS, NEW BROOKLAND, 1906.] The Brookland Baptist Church—now the First Baptist Church of West Columbia—was organized in 1896, two years after the town was named. The timber ruins shown here are those of the church's second sanctuary on Augusta Street to be lost to catastrophe in less than two years. The first building was destroyed by fire on March 4, 1905; this almost completed second one, to a severe storm on July 1, 1906. Another one was erected by 1908. In 1942, the church built a new sanctuary, now identified as West Columbia Baptist Church and located at the corner of State Street and "B" Avenue.

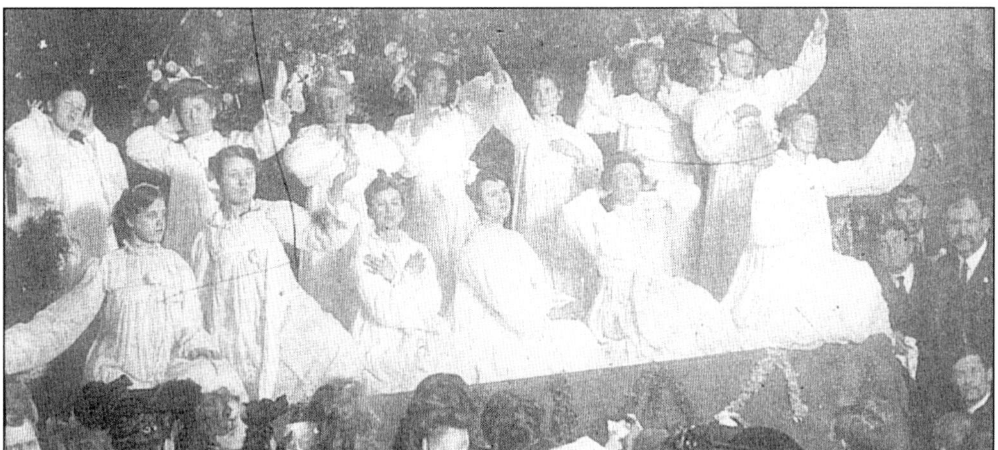

[CHRISTMAS EXERCISES, BROOKLAND METHODIST CHURCH, *c.* 1914.] This picture appears to depict a singing Christmas tree. In her book *Brookland United Methodist Church—Our First 100 Years 1892–1992*, Ruth Kleckley Hoover refers to the church's Christmas exercises and remarks that "people would come from far and near" for these special annual services. Located on the south side of the 500 block of Meeting Street, the church was established in 1892 and housed in a small frame building. In the early 1900s, a larger sanctuary with a bell tower was erected, which was expanded in 1917 and remodeled in 1930.

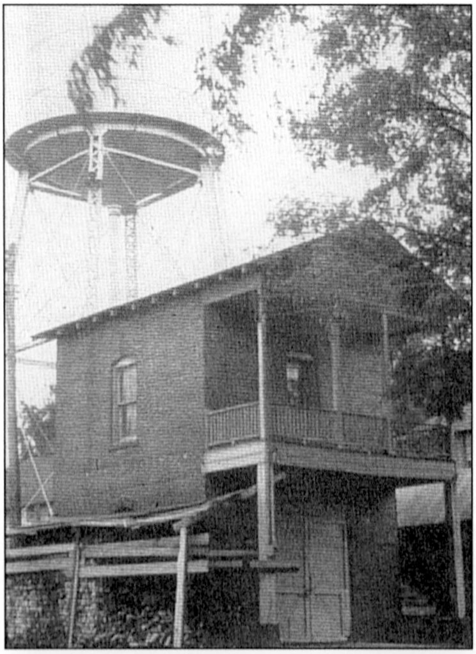

[Hook, Ladder, and Hose House with Water Tank, New Brookland Mill Village, c. 1934.] On the night of March 4, 1905, a fire in New Brookland consumed everything within a half mile radius—destroying 49 buildings, rendering 71 families homeless, and totaling $65,000 in losses. The two buildings at left were subsequently built at the southwest corner of the alley, which enters Norfolk Street in the block between Sortwell and Oliver in the mill village. Equipment was stored in the building and untreated river water was kept in the tank in case of fire.

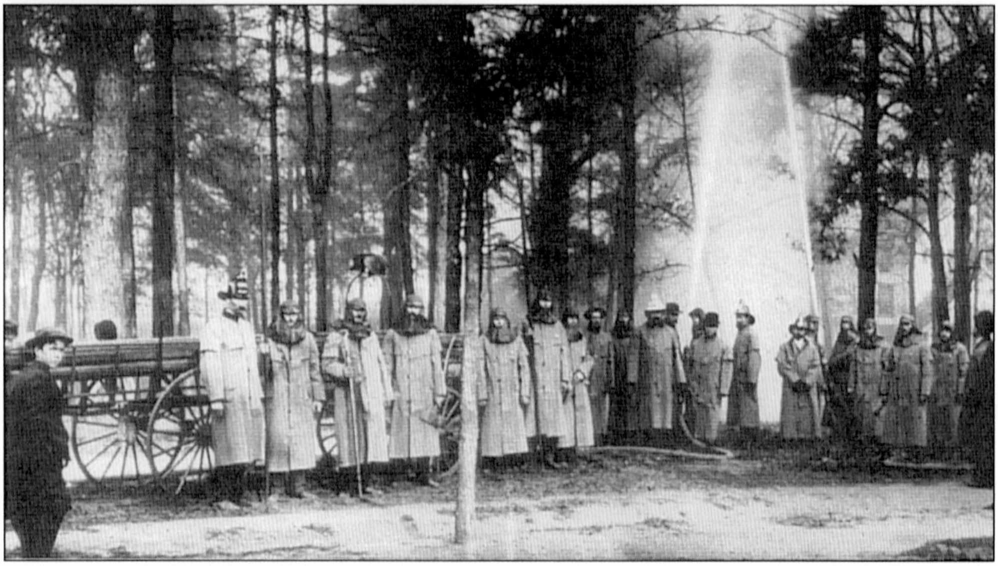

[Volunteer Fire Department, New Brookland Mill Village Park.] According to information that accompanied this picture when it was reproduced in the West Columbia *Journal* on July 29, 1970, New Brookland's fire equipment in 1906 consisted of a 1903 ladder-and-hose truck, which was used between 1903 and 1925. On special occasions, the town's volunteer firefighters would gather in the park, located between the Gervais Street Bridge and the village, and give practice demonstrations of their equipment and firefighting skills for the public. J.B. Mims (in the white helmet, center) was firechief when this picture was taken. Others who could be identified here are as follows: J.L. Gunner (far left), F.J. Grube (third from left), Willie Gunner (sixth from left), Pat Goble (eighth from right), S.K. Oliver (in derby hat behind Chief Mims), and Charlie B. Addy (eighth from left). The police officer at right was identified as Mr. Vinson.

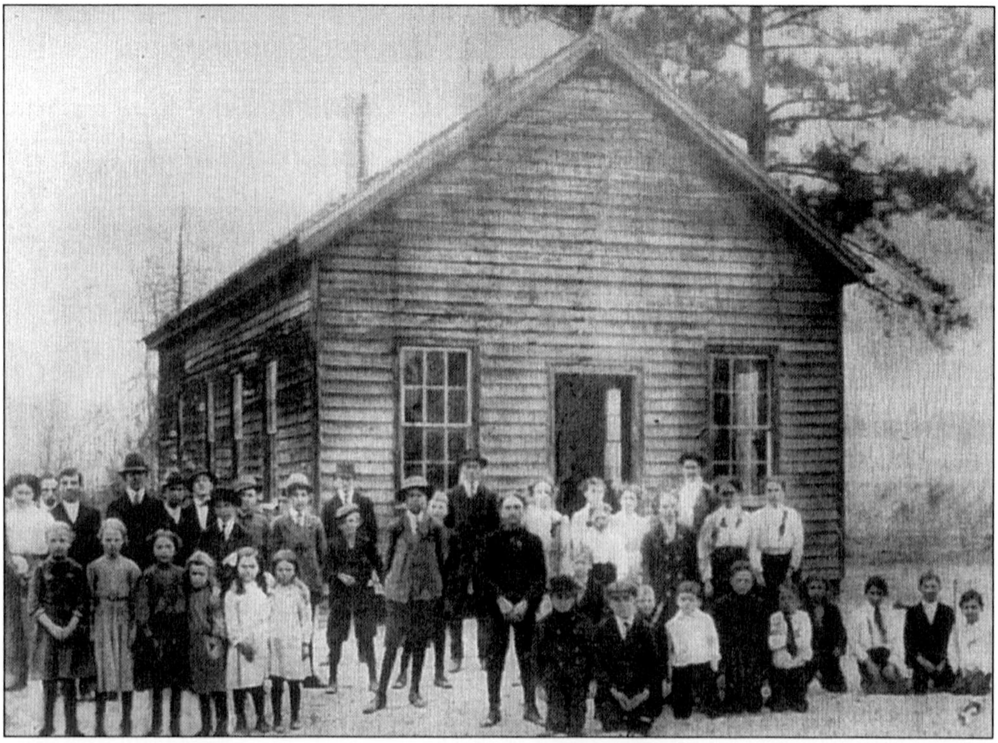

[Oak Grove School, *c.* 1903.] At the old Oak Grove School that was once located at the corner of Oak Drive and Mineral Springs Road 7 miles east of Lexington, 1 teacher taught 67 students for an 18-week session in 1900. Oak Grove graduate Bertha Kleckley [Smith], seen here behind the second row at right, later graduated from the Palmetto Collegiate Institute (1904). Lueco Gunter noted that by 1916, Oak Grove, with a modern two-story frame schoolhouse, had added a teacher for its 57 students and that the term had been extended to 120 days. In 2000 the Oak Grove Civic Club stood on the schoolhouse site.

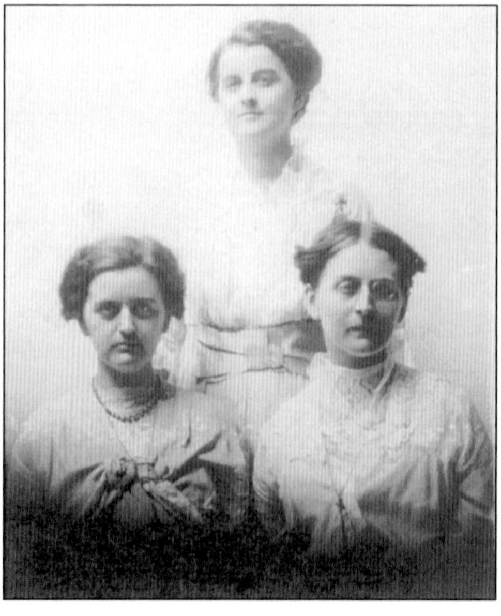

[Portrait of the Kleckley Sisters, Oak Grove, *c.* 1920.] Portrayed here are the three daughters of Ruben and Sallie Buff Kleckley, who lived on Mineral Springs Road. They are, left to right, Bertha Kleckley [Smith] (1883–1956), Ethel Kleckley [Hallman] (1891–1955), and Minnie Kleckley [Waltz] (1885–1957). All three graduated from the Oak Grove School, completed their education at the Palmetto Collegiate Institute in Lexington, and taught at Pond Branch School. Bertha taught there from 1912 to 1916.

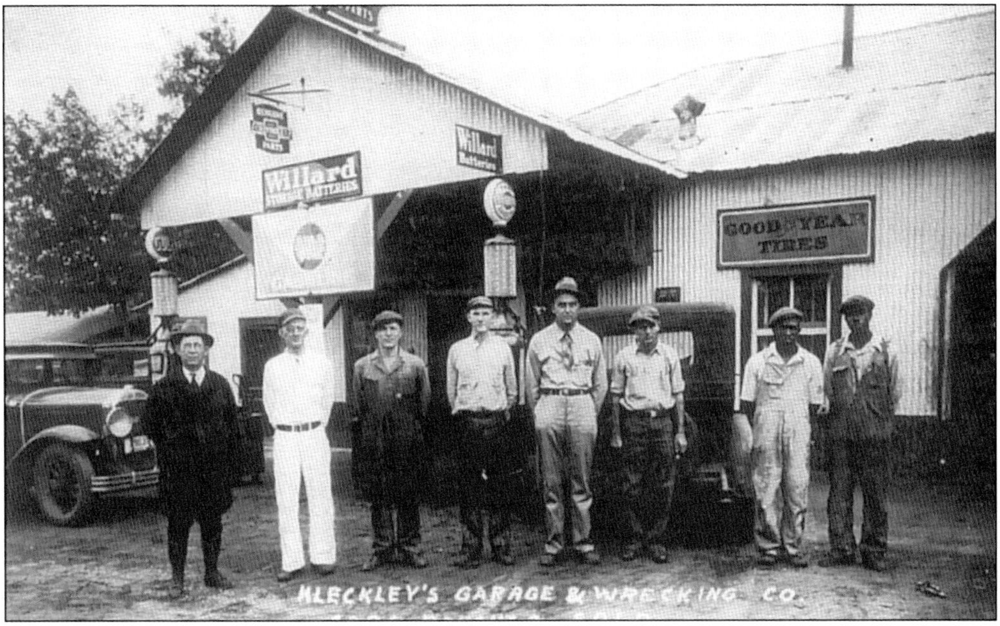

[KLECKLEY'S GARAGE AND WRECKING COMPANY, NEW BROOKLAND, *c.* 1933.] Kleckley's Garage and Wrecking Company, once located at 1015 Meeting Street (the property on which Correct Alignment Auto Repair now stands) in New Brookland [West Columbia], was opened for business in 1923. Ruben Kleckley (1899–1977)—and later his son, Jim—owned and operated it for a total of 62 years. Shown in this 1933 photograph are Kleckley and his work force of seven men (who were paid $7 a week during the Depression), as follows: Willie J. Smith (bookkeeper), Reed Addy, Thurman Metz, Enos Taylor, Kleckley, Emmett Watson, Tom Stidom, and Horace Mickens. Kleckley and his family lived in an apartment attached to the garage, visible at left.

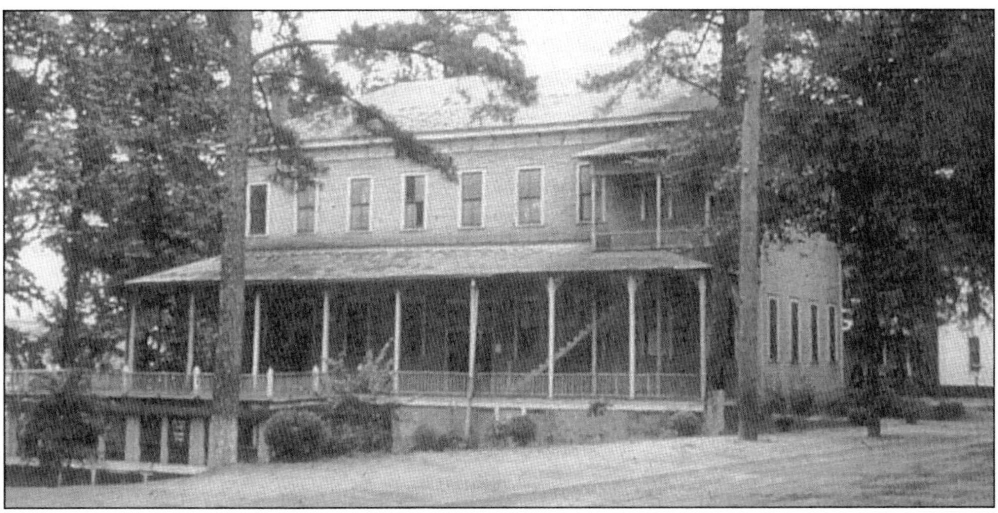

[ASSEMBLY HALL, NEW BROOKLAND, *c.* 1934.] The New Brookland Assembly Hall, owned by the Columbia Duck Mill across the river, once stood at the edge of the village park across from the intersection of Court and Oliver. It was the village's free recreational center—one of the fringe benefits for the workers. Until the Brookland School (built in 1911) could be enlarged, the first three elementary grades were taught here.

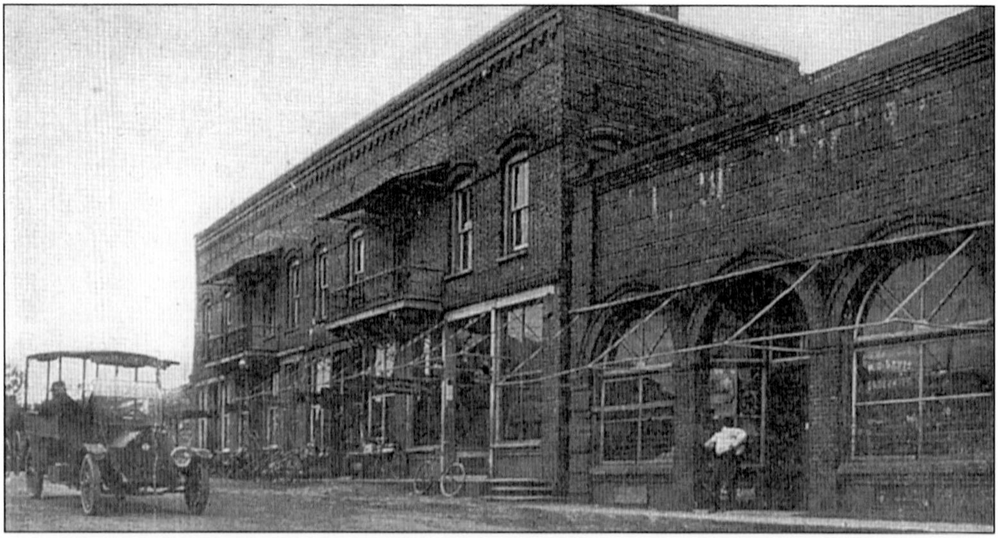

Shull Block, New Brookland, SC [*c.* 1912]. The Shull block, the large two-story brick unit that still stands as a principal commercial landmark in West Columbia (on the north side of Meeting Street at its intersection with State), was built about 1909 by Edward Walter Shull (1866–1939), who for 25 years operated a general store on the ground level (at left in the above picture) and for 15 years served as postmaster. The second floor, in addition to providing living quarters for the Shull family, contained a large assembly hall which functioned at different times as military drill quarters, a movie theatre (New Brookland's first: the Dixie Theatre), and a dance hall. Also seen in this picture, at right, is the store operated for many years by Mr. M. Gary Caughman (1860–1936).

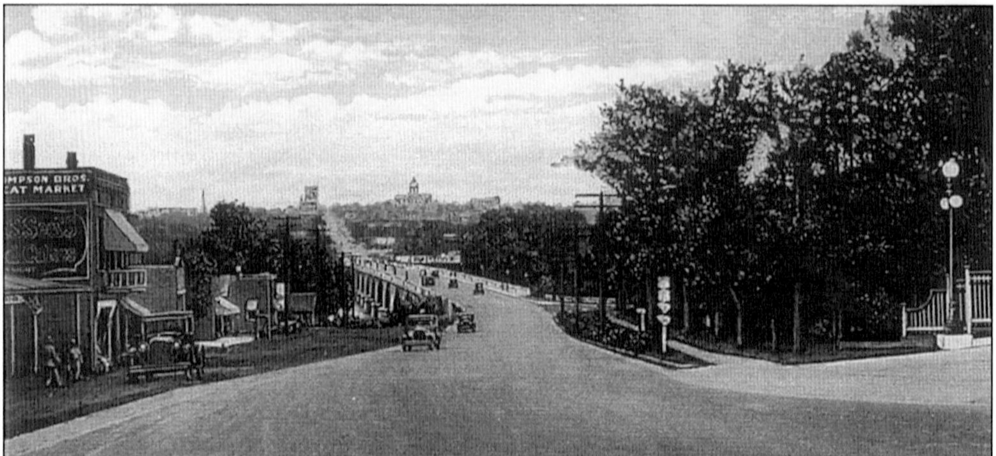

Congaree Bridge, Looking Toward State House, Columbia, SC [c. 1929]. Much of the growth and development of New Brookland [West Columbia], Cayce, and the east-central Congaree River corridor of the county resulted naturally from their proximity to the city of Columbia, to which they have been connected by bridge for almost 175 years. The first wooden bridge, completed in 1827, was burned in 1865 in order to delay the advance of Sherman's army and was rebuilt in 1870. The concrete bridge shown here was completed in 1927. At left in this picture is Thompson's Meat Market, a popular store which had its beginnings in 1912 and reportedly drew a large clientele from across the river. Al's Upstairs Restaurant has occupied the building during recent years.

Index